W9-BVN-748

CONFRONTATIONAL CITIZENSHIP

SUNY series in New Political Science

Bradley J. Macdonald, editor

CONFRONTATIONAL CITIZENSHIP

Reflections on Hatred, Rage, Revolution, and Revolt

WILLIAM W. SOKOLOFF

Published by State University of New York Press, Albany

© 2017 State University of New York

For information, contact State University of New York Press, Albany, NY
www.sunypress.edu

Production, Ryan Morris
Marketing, Michael Campochiaro

Library of Congress Cataloging-in-Publication Data

Names: Sokoloff, William W., author
Title: Confrontational citizenship : reflections on hatred, rage, revolution, and
    revolt / William W. Sokoloff.
Description: Albany : State University of New York Press, [2017] | Series:
    SUNY series in new political science | Includes bibliographical references
    and index.
Identifiers: LCCN 2017000315 (print) | LCCN 2017047298 (ebook) | ISBN
    9781438467832 (e-book) | ISBN 9781438467818 (hardcover : alk. paper)
Subjects: LCSH: Democracy—Philosophy. | Political sociology. | Political
    participation—Social aspects. | Protest movements.
Classification: LCC JC423 (ebook) | LCC JC423 .S6768 2017 (print) | DDC
    321.8—dc23
LC record available at https://lccn.loc.gov/2017000315

10 9 8 7 6 5 4 3 2 1

To Kerry

Contents

Acknowledgments

I would like to thank the following individuals who provided feedback on particular chapters of this project: Eric Anderson, David Anshen, Jocelyn Boryczka, Mary Caputi, Jennifer Disney, Basil W. R. Jenkins, Paul D. Jorgensen, Jeremy Korr, Nancy Love, Samantha Majic, Mark Mattern, Michael Moodian, Matthew Moore, Charles Noble, Myron Orleans, Cynthia Paccacerqua, Sayres Rudy, Nicholas Tampio, Owen Temby, and Adriel Trott. My colleague Clyde W. Barrow read several chapters and provided feedback that has improved this book. Finally, I thank Bradley J. Macdonald who supported this book and recommended it to SUNY press for inclusion in the New Political Science series.

While I was an undergraduate at California State University, Long Beach, Dr. John Anson Warner inspired me in the classroom and encouraged me to go to graduate school in political science. He placed me on a path that made writing this book possible. I would also like to thank Jacques Derrida who welcomed me to his seminars at University of California, Irvine and The New School. Finally, Étienne Balibar's kindness, creativity, and intellectual integrity have been a source of inspiration.

Various chapters of this study have been presented at academic conferences and research colloquia over the last number of years. I thank my former colleagues at California State University, Long Beach for feedback on "The Right of Resistance." I also thank my colleagues and students at University of Texas, Pan American and University of Texas, Rio Grande Valley for feedback on "Frederick Douglass and the Politics of Rage," "In Defense of Hatred," and "Kant on Revolution and Genius."

I would also like to thank Diane Astourian, Alexis Bay, Karina Guerrero, Amanda Iglesias, Michael Odum, and Jason Stratton for research assistance. I also thank the Dean and Provost's Offices at University of Texas, Rio Grande Valley for support to present parts of this manuscript at academic conferences and for course releases to support writing this book. Finally, I acknowledge and thank Rafael Chaiken, Ryan Morris, and Michael Rinella at SUNY Press, as well the anonymous reviewers.

I thank my partner Kerry Daly Sokoloff for her love and support while I wrote this book, as well as Frisco, Gus, and Sassy.

I acknowledge the following journals who have granted me permission to publish revised versions of the following articles as chapters in this book:

William W. Sokoloff. 2015. "In Defense of Hatred." *New Political Science* 37:2.

William W. Sokoloff. 2014. "Frederick Douglass and the Politics of Rage." *New Political Science* 36:3.

William W. Sokoloff. 2010. "Putting the Political Back into Politics: Hannah Arendt on Resistance." *Scholar and Educator* 30.

Preface

From the vantage point of anyone with a progressive orientation, we are living in something worse than a nightmare.[1] Consumerism, capitalism, privatization, deregulation, and cuts in social spending continue to create an underclass of the disposable poor.[2] A costly and permanent war in the Middle East waged under false pretense that we were told would pay for itself has killed thousands, undermined the global standing of the United States, destabilized the Middle East, created a massive refugee crisis, and spawned uncontainable radical resistance movements. Delusions of grandeur abroad mirror mental delusions at home.

The triumphant rhetoric of free market capitalism and representative democracy is broadcasted everywhere. And yet, the "Get rich quick" and "You are in charge" mottos of capitalism and democracy do not seem to fit or speak to the daily experiences and frustrations of most people who are unemployed, string several part-time jobs together to make ends meet, earn less and have to work more, have watched their wages stagnate, and confront a closed and unresponsive political system that listens to the few while ignoring the many. Just as we are told that we are living in the best of all possible worlds, Occupy and Black Lives Matter protestors took to the streets and faced militarized police forces willing to deploy shocking levels of violence against peaceful protestors. If you did not benefit from the recent government bailout of the legal looting of the banks and bonus bonanza by white-collar financial sector criminals and your economic standing is deteriorating, don't worry. You can take Florida Governor Jeb Bush's advice and work longer hours.[3]

Today, signs of the political, economic, and existential crisis are visible everywhere we look. Political and economic corruption is cynically accepted by most people as the new status quo. According to recent Gallup poll data, most individuals simply do not trust government officials to do what is right.[4] Because of this, it is not surprising that reasonable citizens have been replaced by angry and enraged ones. The legitimacy of liberal institutions is arguably in a state of peril. This crisis is dire but it also opens an opportunity to rethink core assumptions, concepts, and definitions about politics and flag openings for positive political change. *Confrontational Citizenship* is my attempt to do this.

Everyone has an interest in living in a political and economic system that prevents entrenched privilege (e.g., rule by billionaires) and changes (e.g., dialectically) in response to the demands of the people, not in one controlled by the few at the expense of the many. Americans loathe politicians and corporate executives because the rules that apply to everyone else do not apply to them. When ordinary workers lose money as a result of financial risk taking, no one is there to bail them out. When Wall Street millionaires make losing bets, politicians are tapped on the shoulder and public funds are used to bail out Wall Street millionaires and banks too big to fail. Clearly, the same set of rules do not apply to everyone. Why would anyone want to accept a social and political system rigged to benefit the few? Why would anyone want to live in a political regime that prevents real political change?

Since the state is never identical with all of the people, some of the people will always have a confrontational relationship to it. When growing numbers of people gather together, point out, and then contest this gap, the legitimacy of the state is put into question. As the gap between the people and the state widens, that is, if the state is perceived to be serving only a small percentage of the people, the authority and legitimacy of the state is undermined. And then the people take to the street.

Confrontational Citizenship is not a rejection of political order but an investigation of ways to recover the authority and legitimacy of political orders. Confrontational modes of citizenship (e.g., civil disobedience, protest, strikes, walkouts, boycotts, occupation, etc.) can reconnect political institutions to the people, provide outlets for widespread frustration, lead to positive change, and renew/transform political institutions to ensure their authority and legitimacy.

Confrontational Citizenship is also my attempt to provide a new vision of what it means to be progressive today. A few years ago popular uprisings in the Middle East toppled dictatorships. The current political and economic predicament is giving rise to a variety of confrontational countermovements, including Spanish *Indignados*, antiglobalization movements, Occupy, Black Lives Matter, and anti-Trump protests. The questions these popular explosions and movements impose on us are difficult to avoid. How might the contemporary neoliberal global political order be challenged and rebuilt in an egalitarian and humanitarian manner? What type of political agency and new political institutions are needed for this? *Confrontational Citizenship* is my attempt to answer these questions. It is important to emphasize that our answers to these questions must resist traditional ways of viewing the world and in a sense try to see the political world with new eyes. Although I shall say more about this shortly, it is necessary to include a wider range of perspectives than is normally the case to navigate the current political moment.

In this regard, *Confrontational Citizenship* is not a call for reform but is a hopeful, radical, and utopian political project. Ultimately, it is grounded on freedom of speech and the right of the people to assemble. As we shall see, confrontational and extra-institutional modes of political activity are a means to create a better political order and are ends in themselves insofar as they are the indispensable conditions for human dignity and self-rule. Confrontational citizenship thus names a wide variety of extra-institutional practices undertaken in inhospitable conditions. The meanings of confrontational citizenship unfold throughout this book. The figures who are especially important for this study are individuals on the margin of the political order who force their way into the center by opening new ways to practice citizenship, democracy, and revolt as a way of life. These figures thereby expand the meaning of the political, citizenship, and the political imagination.

The choice of *Confrontational Citizenship* as the title of this book is not accidental. This title reflects one of my core assumptions about politics, that is, the most important forms of political change are the result of confrontation, not compromise. The people are enraged about the quality and direction of public life, despise politicians, and are desperate for real political change. The obsessive preoccupation with consensus, commonality, political institutions, incremental change, and reasonable dialogue makes it difficult to grasp the current explosion of political passion.

But why do I use the word *confrontation* as opposed to nicer sounding words like *consensus, cooperation,* and *harmony*? Does not the word confrontation imply violent street protests and the unnecessary loss of life? It does not. *Confrontational Citizenship* is not a defense of violence but of the right of the people to assemble, organize, and protest in public to bring about political change. It is a call for new forms of political subjectivity essential to making the world a better place. Hence, my goal is to put the concept of confrontation at the center of the concept of the political.

But is it not the case that, historically speaking, the words *citizen* and *citizenship* are defined by the state, controlled by the state, revoked by the state, and ultimately state-centric concepts? The answer to these questions is complicated. Let me start by saying that citizenship is the subjective essence of the political since it pertains to human action. Additionally, it is important to recall that Aristotle identified two aspects of the citizen. For Aristotle, the citizen rules and is ruled in turn, thus flagging participation and obedience as the polarities of citizenship. Citizens, moreover, "know the rule of free people from both sides."[5] As the reader may have already gathered, the participatory side of citizenship is what interests me for the purposes of this study.

But what about the relationship between citizenship and the state? Is a defense of citizenship ultimately a defense of the state? Again, the answer to this question is complicated. It is true to say that political participation takes place within the polity. But political action also takes place on the edges or even outside the political sphere. Political participation is also grounded on human freedom, which makes it unpredictable. Hence, political outcomes cannot always be completely controlled by the state. Accordingly, the state and citizen often grind up against each other. Neither one is a static entity; neither one can live without the other. That is to say, there is a dialectical relationship between state and citizen, the one transforming the other, the other pushing back and forcing a renegotiation of the limits of the permissible range of action. The state may create the citizen as a legal construct but the citizen also contests its own limits and fights to expand its range of action. Even if the state defines the terms under which an individual becomes a citizen and what it means to be a citizen, the participatory component of the citizen can put into question these definitions and restrictions and in turn transform the meaning of citizenship, the state, and the public interest.

For the purposes of this study, the word *citizen* refers to the self-authorizing practices that force a redefinition of what counts as politics and force the question of who is authorized to fight for political change. In our time, citizenship generally refers to a passive legal status and momentary activity in the form of voting punctuated by years of disengagement. That is to say, the participatory dimension of citizenship has been displaced by citizenship conceived as passive political membership. Throughout this book, I hope to recover lost dimensions of citizenship that occur within but that also exceed the state form. Chris Hedges may be right to say "the citizen has become irrelevant," but only if we accept what the citizen has become as opposed to recovering and reinventing what we might call the citizen of the future.[6] Citizens of the future fight to be citizens, announce themselves as citizens, and authorize themselves as citizens, as opposed to waiting and begging to be recognized as one. I am not claiming that these aspects exhaust the meaning of the word *citizen*. I am simply arguing that without this militant aspect the meaning of citizen is nullified.

By flagging the militant aspect of the citizen my point is that there is no political life without a fight, and the word *citizen* is the locus of confrontation between the "part that has no part" and vested interests intent on subjugating, policing, and destroying the people.[7] The word *citizen* flags the utopian hope in the people's self-determination. Unfortunately, the word *citizen* has also been used as a weapon against those defined as noncitizens (e.g., wage laborers, immigrants, slaves, women, various minorities, and young people).[8] As Rogers M. Smith puts it, "lawmakers pervasively and unapologetically structured U.S. citizenship in terms of illiberal and undemocratic racial, ethnic, and gender hierarchies."[9] Citizenship is thus more than simply a legal status insofar as it names a terrain of permanent struggle between revolutionary possibility and reactionary counterrevolution. My hope is to make the word citizen relevant and grind it up against the settled and closed practices that structure our political world.

Throughout history, ruling elites have used a variety of tactics to rig the political system and reduce citizens to a state of passivity. After elites create the most optimal conditions so that the political and economic system will benefit them, the problem for elites becomes perpetuating this scam while making the majority think that they are living in a meritocracy, democracy, and a regime with unlimited opportunity for everyone. Some of the strategies for perpetuating a system rigged to benefit the few at the expense of the many include controlling the people with debt (e.g., student loans, credit cards, and home mortgages), intimidating individuals who question and challenge rule by and for the few, distracting the people with foreign wars and other entanglements abroad, manipulating people via fear of amorphous domestic and international enemies (e.g., terrorists, illegal immigrants, drug dealers), claiming the status quo is the best and only political option, manipulating the people into having an emotional attachment to the political status quo (e.g., patriotism), controlling the media to brainwash the majority into acquiescence, eliminating discussion of political and economic alternatives, creating an academic establishment that promulgates the values of the status quo, convincing people to work harder and longer hours and to blame themselves if they do not get rich, engineering unemployment so workers are forced to accept whatever terms they are offered and to keep their mouths shut about it, abolishing labor unions or rendering them illegal in 'right to work states,' cutting social spending to generalize the condition of economic insecurity, dazzling the masses with a variety of spectacles (e.g., military, sports, films) that reinforce the core values of the status quo, preventing street protests via repressive legislation against protesting and intimidation by militarized police forces, fomenting racial and ethnic hatred of immigrants and people of color, and placing strict limitations on citizenship and political participation. The war waged against the citizen as an agent of self-determination requires us to reimagine, reinvent, and reclaim the radical potential in the concept of the citizen. Why would anyone want to accept a social and political system rigged to benefit the few? Why would anyone want to live in a political regime that prevents real political change?

As these questions indicate, this book is not a history of the concept of citizenship, it is not a history of democracy's decline, nor is it an appeal for more democracy as the solution to all of our woes.[10] In what follows, I defend extra-institutional modes of political activity and new ways to conceive political institutions as a way to create political orders accountable to the people.[11] It is time to expand our political horizons and invent an alternative to the current neoliberal nightmare. For both historical and theoretical reasons, I am convinced that the only way to create a better political and economic system is through confrontation on the micro-, macro-, and global levels. As we shall see, confrontational modes of citizenship are good because they increase the accountability of a regime to the people, increase the legitimacy of regimes, lead to improvements in a political order, and serve as a means to vent frustration.

Unlike other studies that make the case for incremental change via appropriate institutional channels, stress the importance of voting, and assume the liberal state is neutral, my study is a dialectical investigation into openings for progressive political change and a transformation of what we understand as politics that result from a variety of creative and confrontational modes of citizenship. In our time, the political sphere is controlled and dominated by the agendas and interests of the few. This is not inevitable and it can be changed. The terrain of the political can be expanded and a new agenda can be set as a result of the confrontation between the excluded many and the privileged few. As Étienne Balibar puts it, "the antinomy between citizenship and democracy is a dynamic for the transformation of the political."[12]

Throughout this book, I provide counterhegemonic narratives about the resiliency of political actors fighting for social and political transformation under incredibly unfavorable conditions (e.g., Frederick Douglass, W.E.B. Du Bois, Gloria Anzaldúa, and Paulo Freire) in order to grasp the forms of agency needed for political transformation. My hope is that the reader will find something relevant in my analysis of these thinkers for the current political moment and possibly expand their political imagination beyond the terms provided by establishment politicians, the mainstream media, the growing army of conservative media pundits, and many well-intentioned but ultimately limited forms of democratic theory. *Confrontational Citizenship* is thus a critical theory of the citizen that challenges dominant ways of conceiving the citizen.

In addition to expanding the terms of political discussion, this project is also a defense of unconventional modes of popular agency that do not appear on the grids of intelligibility of dominant schools of thought in democratic theory. As we shall see, many forms of democratic theory suffer from various forms of myopia (e.g., they privilege consensus, commonality, the state, and voting and abhor conflict). But it is important to see the global political order from the standpoint of those positioned on the bottom of it and how struggles over gender, race, and class can challenge and overturn neoliberal rule by the wealthy few and expand our understanding of politics and what it means to be a citizen. Additionally, I explore the institutional forms and types of thinking about political institutions needed to perpetuate political transformation over the long term (e.g., via the writings of Machiavelli, Kant, and Arendt). Appeals to legal norms, rational argumentation, and incremental change sound great but these approaches are out of tune with the problems of our day. Anger, rage, and an explosive political situation are the new status quo. Constant political protests have become the unsurpassable horizon of our time.

But as Frances Fox Piven and Richard A. Cloward argue, "protest movements are discredited in the dominant pluralistic tradition on the ground that there is ample opportunity for the working class to pursue its interests through democratic institutional channels."[13] Because current democratic institutional channels offer little hope for substantive political change, protest is the only remaining option. The mainstream media, conservative pundits, politicians, and even some academics, however, are quick to caricature protestors as looters, extremists, and spoiled crybabies.[14] The message coming from these politicians, pundits, and academics seems to be that real freedom is simply recognizing how good the political status quo is even if it does nothing for you. Clearly, a broader mind-set is needed to frame and contextualize the domination of the political sphere by financial interests, the lack of effective channels for political change for the people, and new ways to connect political regimes to popular energy.

To this end, my book draws on a broad base of literatures and perspectives, including radical democratic theory, pedagogical theory, critical race theory, postcolonialism, Marxism, poststructuralism, feminism, critical autobiography, and African American political thought. Widening and broadening the range of perspectives enlisted to help us understand (and hopefully transform) our political world is the academic intervention that I make into the current state of democratic theory. Insurrectional perspectives are needed today as opposed to ones oriented by the project of social stabilization. My academic intervention goes hand in hand with my attempt to make this study politically relevant for social and political transformation. If a book that claims to be about politics and citizenship is not relevant to what is happening today and does not help us understand how the political status quo can be changed, I wonder why it would even be written.

In this regard, this book is designed to appeal to critically oriented scholars as well as scholar/activists. I hope to appeal to a broader audience than is normally the case for many academic books. The theme of the book—confrontational citizenship—requires this hybrid readership. It would be oxymoronic and possibly absurd for a book on confrontational citizenship in the current political context to be a solely academic exercise. However, I am a trained political theorist working in an academic environment and I value the rigor, styles of presentation, framing of issues, and writing norms in this context. In addition to a professional academic approach, however, I am also framing political problems in ways that make the work of each theorist I focus on in the book relevant to pressing political problems today. Thus, my book's hoped-for readership enacts the principle of confrontational citizenship (constituting a diverse and radical political constituency with a utopian aspiration and commitment to a humanized world) that the disillusioned and/or hypercritical Left has been unable to fashion.

Currently, there is no comparable book to this one that brings together the variety of historical and contemporary authors I engage in *Confrontational Citizenship*. Nor do any current studies bridge American, Continental, post-colonial, and critical race theory on the connections between militant activism, revolt as a way of life, and pedagogy. Jason Frank's study of "constituent moments" sets up the groundwork for a new understanding of the people as a "double inscription" who "seize the mantle of authorization," and I admire his work. As a result of Frank's focus on postrevolutionary America, though, Frank does not analyze the variety of modes of confrontation I examine here.[15]

Other attempts to grasp and transform the current political moment are limited for more substantive reasons. The "undone demos" and "American nightmare" (e.g., Wendy Brown) and "the resistance of that which has no resistance" (e.g., Simon Critchley) are interesting political interventions, but they are ultimately insufficient attempts to overcome the current political impasse and state of intellectual paralysis.[16] Wendy Brown is correct to say the citizen has been remade as "comportment with market instrumental rationality" and, as she puts it, this flags "the disappearance of freedom from the world."[17] But as a result of the theoretical choices Brown makes (e.g., a closed and static philosophy of history), she fails to provide any opening to challenge and transform neoliberalism. Moreover, Brown's reliance on a mode of theoretical inquiry inspired by Foucault (e.g., genealogical analysis and critique) arguably deepens Leftist despair. For Brown, all political positions seem to be implicated in subjection and unfreedom. For her, we are witnessing nothing less than the death of the emancipatory ideal. As I shall make clear in this book, I find Brown's work to be deeply problematic insofar as it fails to show how the neoliberal nightmare can come to an end and how the *demos* can be reconstituted as a force for positive political change.

Simon Critchley's work is also provocative but ultimately limited. Critchley offers a solid critique of how liberal regimes undermine motivation for political action, criticizes fundamentalist violence inflecting politics today, and bridges theoretical issues with practical politics in creative ways. But Critchley ultimately gets tied up in "a theory of ethical experience and subjectivity" that is grounded on "incomprehensibility" and an "infinite demand." It is not clear to me how this leads to a "motivating and empowering ethics of commitment."[18] In fact, it strikes me as potentially paralyzing. In contrast to Critchley, confrontational citizenship is grounded on an activist conception of political subjectivity, not ethical subjectivity, and thus overcomes the risk of political paralysis I detect in Critchley's work.

Other approaches for grasping the contemporary political moment are also of limited value. "Deliberative democrats" are right to point out that public deliberation legitimizes political regimes. But their fixation on achieving consensus ultimately blinds them to the persistence of the problem of power.[19] Proponents of "discourse ethics" also yearn for consensus through calm and reasonable dialogue. But this leads to a narrow concept of the political that downplays the positive role of political conflict. Discourse ethics also excludes modes of affective intensity that motivate individuals to engage in political activity in the first place. The end result is an impoverished vision of democratic citizenship.[20] Conceptions of politics grounded on or that seek consensus are ultimately predicated on and require widespread citizen passivity. For Francis Fox Piven, "the mobilization of collective defiance and the disruption it causes have always been essential to the preservation of democracy."[21]

This aspect of political disruption is precisely what makes the work of "agonistic democrats" superior to deliberative democrats. Agonistic democrats advance a politics of disturbance, contestation, and the ethos of "agonistic respect." They are correct to insist that permanent disturbance makes regimes more accountable to the people. This also prevents regimes from morphing into totalitarian nightmares. Their work thus fights against and is intended to disrupt the exclusions and injustices structured into political regimes. However, agonistic democrats ultimately rely on liberal institutions or an existing understanding of pluralism to provide the framework for this conflict, as opposed to rethinking identity claims and institutions that could perpetuate productive forms of political conflict indefinitely.[22] As Mouffe argues, "it is not enough to unsettle the dominant procedures and to disrupt the existing arrangements in order to radicalize democracy."[23]

Liberalism and rights-based modes of citizenship represent another perspective on our political situation that I find to be the most problematic in comparison to the other perspectives analyzed so far. It cannot be denied that liberal theorists have noble aspirations.[24] They argue that political institutions should be responsive to the people. Equal consideration for all, due process, limited government, the rejection of arbitrary authority, tolerance, and the rule of law are worthy goals. However, liberals have a narrow and arguably impoverished conception of citizenship and politics, and they offer limited intellectual resources for imagining how to improve the political status quo. Because of their assumption that citizens need not be actively engaged in politics, they are not particularly troubled by citizens that disengage from politics. Liberals, however, fail to understand that citizenship is much more than legal status and the guarantee of basic rights. Moreover, the liberal idealization of political life as a neutral arena of competing associations is blind to the persistence of the problems of power, oppression, and the overwhelming control of the political realm by the financial sector. Finally, as a result of their faith in the power of law as a neutral means to protect individual liberty, liberals obfuscate the ways in which law can actually position certain individuals as masters of the universe and others as a domestic colonial population.[25]

Confrontational citizens do not accept the song sung by liberals. Representative democracy, market capitalism, and the protection of individual rights seem less relevant to the lives of ordinary people than ever as a result of the increasing influence of money in politics, the fact that the economy is rigged for the few (e.g., a trillion dollar bank bailout supported by presidents George W. Bush and Barack Obama), and a criminal justice system that routinely violates procedural due process (e.g., racialized incarceration and police brutality at home; indefinite detention of prisoners in secret prisons abroad). Gallup poll data suggests that Americans are increasingly frustrated with establishment politics.[26] Persistent low voter turnout in the United States is also a sign of the widespread lack of faith in the normal political process, which is perceived to be rigged to benefit the few at the expense of the many. As former Secretary of Labor Robert B. Reich puts it, "confidence in political institutions and actions continues to wane."[27]

If the work of liberals, deliberative democrats, agonistic democrats, Left Foucaultians, and Left Levinasians is insufficient or incomplete, is there anyone out there opening more promising paths for political reflection? I believe there is. Important influences for this project come from radical democratic theorists (e.g., Étienne Balibar, Jacques Rancière, Chantal Mouffe, and Michael Hardt and Antonio Negri) who have explored a similar understanding of confrontational politics. I admire their work because, in the case of Balibar, he foregrounds the value of political struggle, recovers the lost political intensity hidden within core political concepts, and connects this intensity to current political struggles oriented to equality and emancipation. In the case of Rancière, he demonstrates that competing logics are at play in politics that pit antagonistic forces against each other, and he mobilizes the discourse of equality to polemicize the antagonism. In the case of Mouffe, she lays the groundwork for a new understanding of agonistic politics with extra-institutional and institutional components that could perpetuate an alternative to neoliberalism over the long term. Finally, Hardt and Negri's work is valuable because it is filled with hope and optimism. They think beyond the nation-state and view the crises of market capitalism and representative democracy as an opportunity for political invention.[28]

Confrontational Citizenship is influenced by this research but also attempts to improve on and move beyond it. In this book, I explore the type of citizen (e.g., radical agency) and political order (e.g., political forms that cancel themselves out as authoritarian and hierarchical modes of rule in the name of modes of nonrule) required for popular self-rule. What makes this book nontraditional is the wider range of voices I bring to the table in comparison to most democratic theorists (e.g., a former slave; an African American Harvard-educated socialist; a lesbian Spanglish-speaking Chicana feminist; a Brazilian educator of illiterate slum dwellers; a Florentine political thinker; a Prussian Enlightenment philosopher; and a neorepublican German refugee), and its commitment to utopian political change at a time when it is not fashionable to be utopian (more on this utopian aspect in the next chapter).

Since I am trained as a political theorist (but not entirely subservient to the prevailing norms and practices in this field), the choice of Niccolò Machiavelli, Immanel Kant, and Hannah Arendt's writings for careful analysis in three separate chapters may come as no surprise to the reader. My interpretations of these three thinkers, however, are designed to upset the standard interpretations of them and open new radical possibilities in their writings. The perspectives of these "canonical" thinkers are severely conditioned and limited by their core assumptions about who is qualified to enter the political sphere, what counts as political activity, and the permissible range of issues to be included in the discussion about political options.[29] However, some traditional political theorists still have a lot to offer for reflecting on the direction and quality of political life but only if these conventional authors are deconstructed to open new radical possibilities in their work. All interpretations of a text are inescapably political insofar as readers see what they believe is important to see in the text, ignore anything that complicates this, and arrive at the "correct" meaning through this process of selection. There is no original intent of the author waiting to be discovered by the reader in a text. Nor does the historical context exhaust and/or determine once and for all the meaning of texts. As I see it, there are a fairly wide range of interpretive possibilities that require reading and the courage not to be trapped by the historical context and the accepted terms of intellectual inheritance. I do not think it is a worthwhile endeavor to try to get a thinker "right" once and for all, as much as I believe it is important to hit a raw nerve in the contemporary political moment via the deployment of a particular thinker's perspectives, insights, and ways of framing problems.

If the reader does not recognize my versions of Du Bois, Douglass, Machiavelli, Kant, and Arendt as a result of my interpretations, then I have succeeded on this score. In addition to interpreting Machiavelli, Kant, and Arendt in new ways (e.g., Machiavelli as a theorist of hatred; Kant as a revolutionary anarchist; Arendt as an advocate of permanent revolution), I am convinced that conventional political theory must also be supplemented and possibly even displaced by other more relevant perspectives (e.g., critical race theory, feminist theory, and postcolonial theory) as a way to better grasp what is happening politically today, expand the boundaries of the political, rethink the concept of citizen, and chart possible openings for political change.

Confrontational Citizenship has a history but it is one that has yet to be written. Who am I to undertake this project of trying to write it? Raised in the suburbs of East Los Angeles, I am a first-generation university student from a working-class background. I obtained a state subsidized undergraduate education in political science in the California State University system. As a result of my academic record at the undergraduate level and help from a faculty member, I pursued a graduate-level education in political theory and completed writing my doctoral dissertation while on a research fellowship in Germany. After a decade of part-time, one-year, and year-to-year teaching assignments with heavy teaching and service loads, I found employment as a political theorist in Texas.

Confrontational Citizenship is the result of my experiences in educational institutions, my training as a political theorist, my commitment to intellectually engaging the contemporary political moment, my time working with nontraditional students, living abroad for three years, playing academic employment hopscotch, and my core belief that confrontation is the key to creating a better world. One of the lessons I learned from these experiences is simple: If you don't fight back, you will be crushed. And in fighting back one will inevitably run up against constraints—which are the moments for creativity and invention in the moment of struggle. Confrontational citizens will always discover new ways to resist and revolt. Practices of subversion of the disenfranchised will always evolve in response to the particular context. *Confrontational Citizenship* is the name for the creative and dynamic processes of resistance and revolt.

Introduction
Anger, Hatred, and Rage in Dark Times

Political regimes, if they are responsive to the wishes of the people, can bring tears of joy and happiness to our eyes. In the face of a swelling prison population, widespread political corruption, wage stagnation, endless war, and to top it off, the victory of Donald Trump, our tears today are not the joyful kind. Be that as it may, mounting evidence indicates we are living in an explosive political moment domestically and globally, where massive changes are not only possible but happening in front of our eyes. Who would have thought, for example, that dictatorships in the Middle East backed by the US government for decades would be toppled by protestors? Who would have thought that Donald Trump would defeat the ultimate political insider in one of the nastiest political campaigns in American history? Or that the emergence of Black Lives Matter would have occurred during the presidency of America's first multiracial president? Today, we need to rethink basic assumptions about political life that have constricted our political horizons, left us ill-equipped to understand significant political happenings of our time, and have prevented us from being able to imagine an alternative to the neoliberal status quo. The times we live in may seem dark but there are reasons to be hopeful. A powerful and unstoppable force is being unleashed and/or freeing itself today. This force is struggling against the political-economic system rigged to benefit the few.[1] I call this force confrontational citizenship, and I leverage it to engage the practices, social relations, and institutions that constitute the realm of politics.

In addition to engaging the contemporary political moment, this project is also motivated by my dissatisfaction with the current state of democratic theory. Many versions of democratic theory have a narrow conception of politics, a narrow vision of political options, and are therefore unable to adequately diagnose the signs of political sickness in the body politic as well as propose possible cures. My first claim in this regard is that intense emotions (e.g., anger, hatred, and rage) are good as sources of political empowerment, motivation, and engagement.[2] Conservatives have adroitly exploited fear (against amorphous threats [e.g., terrorists]; people of color; decaying urban centers; public schools; "radical" Islam; immigrants; criminals; drug addicts; transgender bathrooms; and sexual predators) to create a climate of paranoia and surveillance at home and enlist popular support for militarism abroad. Conservatives have also generated and tapped into popular anger against immigrants, the political "establishment," bureaucracy, regulation, taxes, and foreign governments funded by US taxpayers. Yet, many democratic theorists create ideal political scenarios predicated on the suppression or eradication of the passions and champion reason. But it is becoming increasingly clear that politics is about managing the moods of the populace and channeling this energy in various directions, not eradicating the passions. As Cheryl Hall correctly puts it, "the liberal mandate to keep passion out of politics is neither feasible nor desirable."[3] There is no way to avoid the fact that success in politics depends on the management of the moods of the populace. In our time, discontent, rage, anger, and hatred are permanent features of politics. The key question is how these intense emotions are channeled and for what political ends.

Dominant forms of democratic theory are also much less politically relevant than they could be as a result of a narrow vision of politics/citizenship, preoccupation with rational dialogue, and an overall uncritical mode of theorizing. Even the most sophisticated forms of civic republicanism and deliberative theory that value the role emotions play in political life, for example, shy away from a defense of the disruptive popular feelings of hatred and rage.[4] Hence, this work is not very helpful for grasping the explosive character of the contemporary political moment. Take, for example, Michael Morrell's *Empathy and Democracy*. Morrell embraces empathy because it is valuable for creating intersubjective dialogue. But the appeal to empathy avoids the fundamental political problems of our time that require political struggle. And political struggle is fueled by anger and hatred of corrupt political and economic elites. There is no way to avoid this fact. Of course, empathy could productively coexist with anger and could lead to solidarity. But it would be absurd to ask the demos to empathize with their oppressors. My chapters on Machiavelli and Frederick Douglass demonstrate exactly how hatred and rage are essential components of political struggle as sources of political motivation, critical reflection, and empowerment. Popular hatred of the ruling elite, as Machiavelli demonstrates, is threatening to politics as usual, and is therefore difficult to ignore.

Confrontational Citizenship makes another claim that distinguishes it from most of democratic theory. The identification of the political and economic enemy is required to clarify the terms of political struggle (e.g., *us* versus *them*) and clarify the required course of action.[5] This claim reflects my assumption that politics is about groups, not individuals. Contra liberal theorists, the human is not an isolated individual but a social and political animal. The identification of the political and class enemy simultaneously creates political identity (an *us* in contrast to *them*) and motivates people to engage in politics. The myths of overlapping consensus, open dialogue, and neutral institutions promulgated by advocates of liberal theory is an ideological masking of privilege, differential access to the political sphere, and unequal power relationships embedded into liberal democracy.

Take, for example, John Rawls, the main proponent of a contemporary version of social contract theory. The question that drives Rawls's work is simple. Given the pluralistic character of modern societies, how does one create fair and stable political institutions? The answer for Rawls is simple. Purge philosophical controversy from the political realm in order to create a basis for overlapping consensus. To get to the liberal promised-land, participants in the "original position" adorn themselves with a "veil of ignorance." The veil is a tactic of neutralization that wipes away particular aspects about the self like sexual preference, ethnic identity, religious affiliation, and so on. Not only is the veil intended to eradicate passionate disagreement about irreconcilable conceptions of the good but it cleans the historical slate of past injustice in order to create a basis for overlapping consensus.

But Rawls's idealization of the realm of politics as a sphere purged of passionate intensity, conflict, and power is a mystification. Rawls's citizen is only really a citizen in the "original position." After the conversation ends, everyone goes home and minds their own business. Revisiting foundational principles is not only unnecessary but ill-advised. Because it is not open to perpetual renewal, Rawls's social contract is at best a momentary legitimation tactic, one that over time will sever the connection between the people and the polity, which in turn brings us right back to the same problem we are staring at today, namely, unresponsive and unaccountable political regimes that serve the few and ignore the many. In contrast to Rawlsian ones, confrontational citizens constantly fight to keep political institutions connected to the people. If political accountability is our goal, active political participation must be a way a life.

Many of the disagreements I have with Rawls also apply to what is often called "deliberative democracy." The grounding idea of deliberative democracy is that "legitimate lawmaking issues from the public deliberation of citizens."[6] According to this view, public deliberation facilitates rational decision making that in turn creates stable and legitimate political regimes. For deliberative democrats, differences between opponents should be minimized in order to "find common ground."[7] On face value, this sounds great. However, it is hard to interpret the appeal for "common ground" at a historical moment of unprecedented inequality as anything other than an ideological ploy. Contra deliberative democrats, it is time to name the class enemy, challenge the false framing of political life between consensus and total chaos, and expose the empty . and depoliticizing discourse of rational deliberation and liberal universalism as ideological power plays that cloak class division with happy talk about common ground.[8]

Another claim I make that distinguishes this book from most of democratic theory is the following. Political identity (properly understood) is good and a necessary component for creating political coalitions and as a social base for political change. For theorists from a wide range of perspectives, identity claims are viewed as prepolitical, antipolitical, or politically messed up.

Arthur M. Schlesinger Jr., for example, despises what he pens the "cult of ethnicity." For him, it leads to separatism, tribalization, resegregation, and a culture of victimization.[9] John Rawls, Sheldon Wolin, Wendy Brown, William E. Connolly, and Cristina Beltrán also agree that identity claims have politically dubious value. For Rawls, identity claims prevent overlapping consensus and must be erased by the "veil of ignorance." For Wolin, identity claims undermine shared purpose, common action, and commonality. For Brown, identity claims lead to fixation on one's victim status and are depoliticizing. For Connolly, identity claims are exclusionary and based on an incontestable foundational epistemology. For Beltrán, identity claims risk becoming homogenizing and nationalist.[10] I disagree with these authors. Without a political identity (properly understood) there is no way to know where one stands, who one is, and who one is fighting against. My chapter on Gloria Anzaldúa makes the case for the value of identity as a source for productive forms of political engagement and self-affirmation.

Fourth, much of democratic theory is elitist and focuses on politics as usual and as a result is preoccupied with order, institutions, mild incremental reform, and is thereby nonthreatening to reigning power relations.[11] This is an expression of the fear of political conflict and an anti-utopian bias. Liberals, public sphere democrats, civic republicans, and social democrats are all driven by the quest for social stability. Because of this, they ultimately endorse rule by elites with a bit of the public's participation (e.g., civic republicanism) or accept the public's passive acquiescence to rule by experts (e.g., liberals, liberal pluralists). Rogers M. Smith, for example, claims that citizens "need not be constant political participants."[12] But to be a passive citizen, as Étienne Balibar argues, is a contradiction in terms.[13] Ian Shapiro states "hierarchical relations are often legitimate and when they are, they do not involve domination on my account."[14] Even if Shapiro argues that we should be suspicious about hierarchical relations, this is not enough.[15] A new and radical political vision is needed.

Michaele L. Ferguson's *Sharing Democracy* is a good exception to the rule in democratic theory because she defends active and radical modes of citizenship. Much to her credit, Ferguson accurately diagnosis appeals to order, institutions, and commonality for what they are, namely, as efforts to constrict the realm of politics.[16] The unquestioned faith in the value of commonality by most democratic theorists, Ferguson correctly argues, leads to an essentially antidemocratic view of politics, one where "the passive possession of commonality" is prioritized "over the active exercise of political freedom." As a result of the fixation on commonality, Ferguson argues, we are unable to see "those who do not engage in state-oriented politics as democratic actors." In contrast to a politics of commonality, Ferguson puts forth the dialectic of protest and counterprotest as the "paradigmatic example of democracy."[17] I agree with Ferguson but I would take this a step further.

To this end, what is needed is an anti-status quo and an explicitly utopian orientation in democratic theory. By utopian I am not referring to some sort of perfect society where all problems have been solved. Rather, I employ the word *utopian* to name the possibility of substantively better social and political arrangements, compared to the status quo, based on substantive equality and participatory democracy. A utopian orientation is good because it fuels the aspiration for a better social and political life for the 99 percent and an alternative to the neoliberal status quo. A utopian orientation is also valuable because it helps sustain the motivation for political engagement. I realize that arguing for a utopian orientation is not a fashionable position.[18] In *Why Democracy Is Oppositional*, for example, John Medearis defends a creative version of social democracy and rejects what he pens "the utopian temptation." Medearis suggests that we pursue instead a "sober view of human agency and its limits."[19] I agree with Medearis that opposition to domination must be a permanent feature of democracy, but it is unlikely that opposition can be sustained indefinitely without utopian zeal. A faith that the impossible can happen is needed to fuel and sustain widespread political engagement. Democratic theorists need to relearn how to dream and embrace utopian thinking as part of a strategy for mass political mobilization.

Anti-utopian theories of the political can also be found in approaches that embrace a tragic understanding of citizenship and public life. Stephen Johnston's *American Dionysia* is a good example of this. Johnston puts forth a defense of the type of tragic sensibility he believes is necessary for democratic societies.[20] The essence of this tragic sensibility, according to Johnston, is a "kind of wisdom and care that ensue from encounters with life's terrible quandaries" that flags the "self-subverting character of life." This tragic sensibility, moreover, contains an "appreciation for limits" and a "cheerful yet defiant resignation."[21] I agree with Johnston that these aspects can serve as a valuable check on patriotic hubris but they also risk being easily coopted by discourses that urge us to be reasonable, moderate, and realistic. A certain level of hubris, it seems to me, is needed to inspire confrontational citizens to reach for the impossible. A utopian aspiration is what is needed today to fuel political change. I fear that Johnston's tragic ethos will undermine the self-righteous indignation that can productively fuel political engagement.

But most individuals, William A. Galston argues, "are incapable of anything approaching sustained devotion to the common good." The history of utopian efforts, Galston continues, suggests that "failure is inevitable" and "efforts to avert it are bound to turn tyrannical."[22] As I shall make clear, this is a false framing of our political options based on a narrow vision of politics and a form of liberal institutional blackmail where exploring any alternative to the current political and economic status quo is cast as ill-advised because it will lead to totalitarianism. If it is true that most people are incapable of a sustained commitment to the common good, this is the result of a political system that engenders passivity, an economic system that requires selfishness as a condition of survival, underfunded educational institutions for most people that fail to stimulate the critical faculties, and a paralysis of the political imagination that results from the corporate domination of the media that deploys constant "news alerts" to shock the public into a stupor with rant and insult (which in turn makes the public despise political "discussion"). In my view, the only thing that is ill-advised is giving up on the possibility of political change and passively accepting the political status quo as the best we can hope for.

In contrast to authors (e.g., social-democratic; tragic; liberal pluralist) who reject utopian thinking, I argue that utopian theorizing is a fundamental component needed to inject a critical dimension into democratic theory. The utopian dimensions I defend include the need for institutions and counterinstitutions that sustain the tension between insurrection and constitution, access to quality education, egalitarian social and economic policy, and solidarity via gender/race/class/sexual difference. For me, utopian does not mean "no place," but something better than the neoliberal status quo. Creating something better than neoliberalism will not be an affair undertaken by a handful of individuals but will require a mass movement both domestically and globally. For decades, the Right has narrowly framed political discussion and political options as a result of corporate control of the mainstream media and has waged a war on the capacity to dream of an alternative to the political and economic status quo. Many academics have also accepted the neoconservative "end of history" hypothesis and frame the debate about political possibilities in an unnecessarily narrow manner by accepting market capitalism and representative democracy as the best we can hope for or are simply hopeless about the possibility of change. It is time to reframe the discussion in a broader and more open manner where our political horizons are not foreclosed in advance by a blind endorsement of market fundamentalism and the corrupt political status quo.[23] Utopian modes of political theorizing are needed. They are a sign that our brains are still alive, and we capable of recognizing the disastrous character of current ways of organizing our political and economic lives (e.g., market fundamentalism and rule by a corporate elite) and the disastrous practices (e.g., permanent war, prisons) for solving the problems of our time. Bringing a utopian dimension to the table is my way to contest the persistent elite rule bias, contempt for the people, fixation on social stability, and push democratic theory to be more than an ideological justification for the status quo.

In addition to the need for an explicit utopian turn in democratic theory, another core assumption of this book is that critique is not enough. As brilliant as her analyses of the contemporary political predicament may be, Wendy Brown's mode of genealogical critique is ultimately unhelpful for finding a way out of the American nightmare.[24] After Brown shows how all things that were once political have been taken over by an economistic discourse of cost-benefit analysis, discredits Marxist categories and lenses, shows how neoliberalism has undermined all forms of political agency, crosses out the possibility of resistance, shows how educational institutions have also been taken over by neoliberal assumptions and practices, and claims, finally, that humanity has entered its darkest chapter ever, she backs herself into a dead end. Very little, almost nothing, is offered by Brown as a strategy to fight our way out of this nightmare of neoliberal hell. A similar dead end can be found in the work of Giorgio Agamben.[25] Agamben's tendency to see the state of exception everywhere where the human is reduced to a state of "bare life" undercuts the possibility of political resistance. The more important question is where the signs of resistance are flaring up.

I resist the turn to apocalyptic Leftist narratives as well as narratives that make us nostalgic for a time that is past.[26] Today, more energy must be spent by democratic theorists on developing strategies of political mobilization, providing a utopian vision of a better political order, revisiting challenges of pedagogy under changed conditions, and reflecting on strategies for political change.[27]

Finally, this project departs from other studies by emphasizing the importance of political education, creativity, and pedagogy as essential components needed to make our world a better place. Education and pedagogy are long and drawn-out processes, not one-time moments for the acquisition of true consciousness from a political prophet. As I argue later in this book, democratic theory and the field of political science have given insufficient attention to questions of pedagogy and have yet to adequately recognize the interconnection between the political and the pedagogical. My chapter on pedagogy argues that democratic theorists ignore the practices of pedagogy and the work of Paulo Freire at their peril.

To give the reader a more specific sense of what is to come, I provide brief statements on the main arguments of the respective chapters of this book. Each chapter can be read as free-standing study of fundamental political problems of our time, or in succession to clarify the broader theme of confrontational citizenship. I examine historical exemplars of confrontation (e.g., Frederick Douglass, W.E.B. Du Bois, Gloria Anzaldúa, and Paulo Friere), as well as more explicit theoretical visions of confrontation/revolution (e.g., Machiavelli, Kant, and Arendt).

In chapter 1, for example, I argue that popular hatred of elites is a good accountability mechanism and increases the legitimacy of the state. I draw on Machiavelli to make this case. In order to clarify my defense of hatred, I criticize the ontological enmity of Carl Schmitt and Samuel P. Huntington. For Huntington and Schmitt, hatred is mobilized to consolidate state power at the expense of democratic accountability. My analyses of Machiavelli, Schmitt, and Huntington bring us to the following conclusion: naming the proper object of hatred is a key component in the fight against oppression. Hatred of elites emerges as the counter-institution we cannot live without. I close this chapter with an analysis of how the Occupy Wall Street movement productively mobilized hatred against the nonworking rich, bankers, and corporate-criminal elites.

In chapter 2, I read Kant against the grain, and make the case for a broader concept of revolution in his writings that results from bringing together Kant's practical philosophy, his call for independent thinking, and his work on the concept of genius. This combination shifts the meaning of revolution away from political violence and toward political creativity. I argue that this new type of non-state-centric Kantian revolution unleashes creativity and opens the possibility of political change, but requires an anarchistic moment of thinking without the constraint of rules. In this chapter, I invite the reader to reflect on the following question: How might the moment of thinking without the constraint of rules creatively inhabit political institutions, practices, and our vision of a better political order?

In chapter 3, I defend the dialectical rage of the abolitionist Frederick Douglass, because it led to good political judgment and was an effective strategy for political mobilization. The life of Douglass illustrates that rage is not always blind, counterproductive, and violent, but can be an appropriate response to injustice. In this chapter, rage emerges as an essential component of confrontational citizenship. Douglass demonstrates that confrontational citizenship is not belligerent citizenship. Indeed, his example requires us to reflect on ways to organize and deploy the fury of popular indignation to construct a better political order.

In chapter 4, I argue that revolt is an important component of democratic citizenship and collective action that restores human dignity, engenders collective solidarity, allows oppressed groups to vent their frustration, and most importantly, can create a better regime. In contrast to authors who argue that Du Bois is moderate, pragmatist, and elitist, I show that Du Bois's most important contribution to democratic theory is the idea of revolt as a way of life. All forms of revolt are not the same, though. In Du Bois's case, revolt contains a measure of thoughtfulness. This distinguishes Du Bois's version of revolt from the one Nancy L. Rosenblum criticizes as belligerent militancy.

In chapter 5, I argue that Arendt's concept of political resistance is valuable because it overcomes either/or political dichotomies, including order/anarchy, law/violence, obedience/revolt, and thereby expands the terrain of politics. For Arendt, political resistance must take the form of a double concept, as something that points in conflicting directions at the same time. Resistance as a double concept provides a way to rethink the relationship between legal orders and challenges to them that overcomes some of the limits of contemporary liberal theory (e.g., John Rawls) and the work of Michel Foucault. Even though there are some blind spots in her work, including a rigid public/private dichotomy and view that poverty is not a political issue, Arendt's work is essential for fashioning political institutions based on the dynamic between insurrection and constitution. This prevents political orders from becoming self-congratulatory and waging war against their own people.

In chapter 6, I argue that identity claims are good as sources of political motivation and can inspire collective action. Hence, I challenge Arthur M. Schlesinger Jr., Samuel P. Huntington, and Allan Bloom's critiques of multiculturalism as necessarily separatist and balkanizing. I draw on Gloria Anzaldúa's work to make this case. Her original theories of freedom, identity, and resistance are the result of the role self-craft and autobiography play in her work. Contra Cristina Beltrán, Anzaldúa does not lapse back into the conservatism of Chicano nationalism via the discourse of identity and hybridity. Reflecting on her private struggles (Anzaldúa singing the song of herself) yields a critique of violence and a new conception of freedom beyond the model of the nationalist and sovereign subject. I close this chapter with a note on the coalition building practices of Black Lives Matter.

In chapter 7, I argue that educators need to explicitly reflect on and connect teaching in the classroom to broader power relationships. Paulo Freire's work is invoked to open this new direction because he challenges the conservatism of educational institutions and expands the meaning of pedagogy, politics, and political struggle. Through dialogue, the reinvention of power, and permanent revolution in the classroom, I argue that Freire creates a nonreactionary foundation for the political sphere that cracks the iron law of oligarchy. A protracted process, political revolution starts with a revolution in the classroom that puts the teacher to rest and generates democracy without leaders in the political sphere. Freire's pedagogical-political project represents a viable alternative to Wendy Brown's "end of democracy" thesis, and also exposes how academic disciplines grounded on positivist assumptions obfuscate the most pressing political problems of our time. Through the reconceptualization of pedagogy, Freire arguably charts a path for putting the political back into political science and he provides the pedagogical groundwork for widespread confrontational citizenship.

In the conclusion, I argue that respect for a "culture of resistance" prevents the drift of democracy to something like a "culture of the riot," when the chains of political and economic oppression become so unbearable that throwing them off violently seems like the only alternative. I argue that there is a need to cultivate a culture of permanent resistance and conceive authority and political institutions in creative ways that prevent the reification of power. Political institutions must remain flexible, open, and connected to the energy that gives them their life force. Confrontational citizenship signals both the mode of agency to contest power, the value of counterinstitutions, and the utopian hope that people can open history to the song of freedom. In this regard, the work of Étienne Balibar is presented in the final chapter as a fruitful way to engage the contemporary political moment and as a supplement to confrontational citizenship.

In our political climate of paranoia, fear, the building of walls, increasing militarization/securitization both domestically and globally, confrontational citizenship risks being cast or swallowed up as unpatriotic, criminal, or unnecessarily disruptive. Even in the face of these risks, confrontational citizenship names the hope that an alternative to neoliberalism is possible. Confrontational citizenship is the product of the historical configuration of the moment, the work of people who see the cracks in the current political and economic structure, and the utopian hope that the people can create a better world.

Chapter One
In Defense of Hatred

Citizen discontent with politicians and a lack of faith in the normal channels for addressing grievances and bringing about political change seems to be at an all-time high. As liberal democracy and global capitalism are touted as the only viable programs for ordering our political and economic lives, this best of all possible worlds depends on the repressive apparatus of the state to secure access to natural resources and markets, export permanent war, squash internal dissent, terrorize poor people into submission via prolonged economic insecurity, militarize the US–Mexico border, and incarcerate a growing percentage of the US population.[1] If a total transformation of economic and political relations seems unrealistic given the lethal power that props them up, holding political and economic elites accountable to the people for their actions may be a promising first step to challenge the economic and political status quo. But how can political and economic elites be held accountable to the people?

Elections normally serve as an accountability mechanism and shut-off valve that citizens could pull when they have had enough. Unfortunately, elections today are more of a meaningless spectacle than a substantive means to control the arrogance, corruption, and criminality of the ruling class.[2] The distortions caused by the private fortunes needed to run for/stay in office and staggered reelection timelines make it nearly impossible for the people to replace/oust elected officials when they break the public's trust. Combine this with the fortress lifestyles of the ruling class (e.g., private security systems, gated communities, bodyguards), and you have astounding levels of elite nonaccountability, social prominence in the media combined with material invisibility, and political untouchability.[3] Tack on what Sheldon S. Wolin calls "the *political* demobilization of the citizenry," and we are stuck in something worse than an American nightmare.[4]

How can elites be held accountable to the people they represent? The answer is simple: via enmity/hatred. Popular hatred of corrupt elites signifies the unsurpassable rupture in political orders between rulers/ruled and rich/poor and can lead to resistance against oppression. When power is in play and regimes are only more or less legitimate in the eyes of citizens, popular discontent will drift toward extreme forms of animosity for political leaders. While hatred clearly has its dark side, hatred also represents a way to reactivate social antagonism, create collective solidarity, and increase political accountability between elites and the people.

A variety of political thinkers have emphasized the centrality of hatred as a political category. However, it is not Carl Schmitt (1888–1985) who deserves recognition as the main theorist of hatred (even though Schmitt famously reduced the concept of the political to the distinction between friend and enemy), but Niccolò Machiavelli (1469–1527). Machiavelli makes a strong case for the productive role that popular hatred can play in political regimes. Power generates hatred. Hatred, though, can be enlisted for positive political ends. For Machiavelli, an antagonistic political culture based on extra-institutional manifestations of popular hatred and violence against elites ensures the preservation of liberty and the accountability of leaders to the people. Despite the central role hatred plays in Machiavelli's work, Machiavelli has yet to be recognized as a major theorist of hatred. Hatred at a more general level has also not received the attention it deserves as a productive political force. The reasons are clear.

First, *hatred* is an ugly word and an uncomfortable topic. I hesitated defending hatred because I did not know how it would be received. Everyone is understandably squeamish when it comes to hatred, given hatred's tendency to spiral out of control, generate cycles of revenge, and lead to vigilantism.[5] Why would anyone want to defend hatred? Hatred is linked to everything that is wrong with the world today, including violence against young people at schools, genocide, white supremacists, neo-Nazis, and Oklahoma City bomber Timothy McVeigh. For these reasons, hatred is either ignored, is viewed with disgust, or is conceived of in a legalistic way (e.g., "hate crimes"), as opposed to seeing hatred as a complex political phenomenon.[6]

The reason why hatred is overlooked or downplayed in Machiavelli is related to the dominance of the civic republican interpretation of Machiavelli.[7] This view, which has come to be known as the Cambridge School, emphasizes love for *patria*, wisely designed political institutions, rule of law, and civic virtue, but arguably tames radical moments out of Machiavelli's thinking by downplaying evidence of popular agency and intense passion. Leo Strauss and interpreters influenced by Strauss are also prone to miss the central role played by hatred because their interpretations are premised on the break Machiavelli represents with the premodern and the absence of a broader theory of democratic power in Machiavelli's work.[8] Hatred, finally, has also been overlooked by radical interpretations of Machiavelli that emphasize the people as political agents of violent contestation of oppression or read Machiavelli as an advocate of a conception of freedom as nonrule.[9]

In what follows, I chart Machiavelli's view on the origin, causes, and control of hatred to address an oversight in the scholarly literature. Next, I present two examples of the appeasement of popular hatred against elites. In order to clarify my defense of political hatred, I distinguish productive political hatred for elites with hatred for the other in Carl Schmitt and Samuel P. Huntington's work. Finally, I analyze the political implications of different types of hatred. Naming the proper object of hatred emerges as a key component in the fight against oppression and is a central aspect of confrontational citizenship.

Hatred

Machiavelli accords hatred a central role in political life in his most advanced reflections on politics in the *Prince* and the *Discourses*. Hatred as a defining feature of politics is also apparent in many of Machiavelli's other writings too, including "The History of Florence" and his poems.[10] Unlike a tradition of political thought predicated on replacing hatred with reason, Machiavelli argues that hatred cannot be eliminated and, more importantly, hatred can play a positive role in politics. For Machiavelli, hatred serves a variety of productive roles, especially in terms of policing the behavior of arrogant elites and punishing them.[11]

Hatred tends to be interpreted as an irrational and apolitical force. This is an oversimplification grounded on a bias against hatred. For Machiavelli, hatred possesses, as Louis Althusser correctly puts it, "a class signification."[12] The poor have good reason to hate the rich. The ruled have good reason to despise rulers. For Machiavelli, hatred is not a private emotion but is an essentially political feeling. Nor is hatred more of a problem in one type of regime than in others. Hatred is an issue in both principalities and republics.[13]

Machiavelli does not define hatred. The closest Machiavelli comes to defining or providing a genealogy of hatred can be found in "Tercets on Ambition." There, Machiavelli states,

A hidden power which sustains itself in the heaven . . . sent two Furies to dwell on the earth. . . . Each one of them has four faces along with eight hands; and these allow them to grip you and to see in whatever direction they turn. . . . Envy, Sloth, and *Hatred* are their companions, and with their pestilence they fill the world, and with them go Cruelty, Pride, and Deceit. . . . These drive Concord to the depths. To show their limitless desire, they bear in their hands a bottomless urn.[14]

A mysterious power sent Furies to the earth to "deprive us of peace and to set us at war." Envy, sloth, and hatred have otherworldly origins, and are Ambition's companions who fill the world with their pestilence, to "take away from us all quiet and good." One human climbs up on the back of another: "To this our natural instinct draws us." Ambition, if unchecked, will burn down towns and farmsteads if "grace or better government does not bring her to nought."[15] The management of hatred was not explored in "Tercets on Ambition," but was treated systematically in Machiavelli's political writings.

Throughout these writings, hatred is posited as an explosive and unpredictable feeling.[16] Leaders find out that they are hated too late, or simply presume they are hated and take the necessary security precautions. Even though Machiavelli states that "men do you harm either because they fear you or because they hate you," hate is more problematic than fear. Fear may trigger a response to something threatening, but fear can also paralyze and stupefy. In contrast to fear, hatred empowers.[17] When someone is filled with hate, their energy is directed back at the despised object. As we shall see, Machiavelli's presentation of how to hold onto power receives its contours from Machiavelli's advice on how to avoid being hated.

In his discussion of the methods used to acquire and retain principalities, Machiavelli advises leaders as to how they can avoid being hated. This is an important subject because the downfall of a leader is caused by "hatred or scorn."[18] Although eliminating hatred is impossible, prestige can protect you from hatred.[19] Prestige is wrought by "great campaigns and striking demonstrations."[20] Princes must also work to retain "the friendship of the people" and "avoid being hated by the people."[21] Grounding one's rule on the favor of the people makes princes powerful and secure. Princes who are not hated by the people are more difficult to attack. The lack of hatred of the ruler is the index of the internal strength of a principality. If you are hated, fortresses will be needed for protection but will become your prison: "The best fortress that exists is to avoid being hated by the people."[22] The best safeguard against conspiracies is "to avoid being hated by the populace."[23] For Machiavelli, "a prince can never make himself safe against a hostile people: there are too many of them."[24]

What causes hatred? Laying "excessive burdens on the people," being "unarmed," "severity," and "extraordinary vices" cause the people to hate leaders.[25] The prince should also avoid "ferocity and cruelty."[26] Being from "the lowest origins" can make the prince hated, while being old leads to "scorn."[27] Disarming your subjects will cause them to hate you because your actions communicate that you distrust them.[28] No definite rule, though, can be given as to how a prince can win the people over.[29] Buying people will not work. Generosity practiced over the long term will make you despised and hated since you will be compelled to take back what you have given.[30]

In chapter XIX of the *Prince*, Machiavelli yet again advises leaders to avoid the hatred of the people. As Machiavelli states, "princes cannot help arousing hatred in some quarters."[31] Even good deeds can lead to being despised: "One can be hated just as much for good deeds as for evil ones."[32] The prince must nonetheless endeavor "to avoid anything which will make him hated and despised."[33] For this reason, sometimes it is necessary to "delegate to others the enactment of unpopular measures."[34]

Hatred of a leader can also be the result of the character of political leaders, as well as how they are perceived. For Machiavelli, the prince will be despised "if he has a reputation for being fickle, frivolous, effeminate, cowardly, irresolute; a prince should avoid this like the plague and strive to demonstrate in his actions grandeur, courage, sobriety, strength."[35] The leader will be hated above all if "he is rapacious and aggressive with regard to the property and the women of his subjects."[36] The ruler lives in constant fear of secret conspiracies, and for good reason: "Princes cannot escape death if the attempt is made by a fanatic."[37] Even if a ruler plays his harp perfectly and appeases the populace with rhetorical melodies, there will always be malcontents but they are much more likely to come from the nobility who are easier to contain. If the malcontent comes from the people, an outlet must be provided: "Every city should provide ways and means whereby the ambitions of the populace may find an outlet."[38]

For Machiavelli, the management of hate is the essence of politics conceived of as an essentially volatile practice in the realm of mirrors, shadows, and echoes. Since elite political accountability to the people is always a problem, leaders begin their first day in office despised by those who opposed them, despised by those whom they injured to obtain office, and despised by those who stand to lose from their reign. When the coercive apparatus of the state is deployed against political enemies, this exacerbates the hatred. As time goes on and politicians are perceived as corrupt, popular hatred will grow and trigger a revolt.[39] For Machiavelli, hatred is the main political problem linked to holding onto power but, as we shall see in the following examples, it can also serve as a way to hold elites accountable to the people.

Hatred and Accountability: Two Examples

Two examples of extra-institutional violence as accountability measures are instructive for understanding Machiavelli's view on the political value of hatred. The first indicates the dark side of extra-institutional appeasement of popular hatred. The violence in this example is used to justify the rejection of extra-institutional appeasement of popular hatred.[40] The second example illustrates how the humiliation of an authority figure can reestablish the public's trust in leaders. The second example also demonstrates that the populace needs to be reassured that arrogant and scheming elites will get what they deserve if they violate the public's trust.

Spectacular Violence

The political agent must be human but also an animal as the situation requires. The priest's garb should be worn by political leaders to pacify the people and project an image of gentleness and priestly asceticism. But this is only a costume, that is, a form of deception that masks the violence of political life. In the *Discourses*, for example, Machiavelli recounts an instance where Clearchus did not dismember one person but "he cut to pieces all the nobles to the immense satisfaction of the popular party and satisfied the demand for vengeance."[41] Even if a political actor dutifully and effectively serves their political superior, they can still be annihilated as the need to appease popular hatred dictates. In the *Prince*, Machiavelli discusses the case of the successful but ill-fated ruler Remirro de Orco.

As this point deserves close study and *imitation by others,* I will not leave it out. Now, the duke [Cesare Borgia] won control of the Romagna and found that it had previously been ruled by weak overlords, quicker to *despoil their subjects* than to govern them well. They had given them cause for anarchy rather than union, to such an extent that the province was rife with brigandage, factions, and every sort of abuse. He decided therefore that it needed good government to pacify it and *make it obedient* to the sovereign authority. So he placed there messer Remirro de Orco, a cruel, efficient man, to whom he entrusted the fullest powers. In a short time this Remirro pacified and unified the Romagna, winning great credit for himself. Then the duke decided that there was no need for this *excessive authority,* which *might* grow intolerable, and he established in the centre of the province a civil tribunal, under an eminent president, on which every city had its own representative. Knowing also that the *severities of the past* had earned him a certain amount of *hatred,* to *purge the minds of the people* and to win them over completely he determined to show that if cruelties had been inflicted they were not his doing but prompted by the harsh nature of his minister. This gave Cesare a pretext; then, one morning, Remirro's body was found cut in two pieces on the piazza at Cesena, with a block of wood and a bloody knife beside it. The *brutality of this spectacle* kept the people of the Romagna at once appeased and stupefied.[42]

As the citation makes clear, Remirro de Orco was a hated man, and this was used as a justification to eliminate him. Since Remirro de Orco was hated, eliminating him appeased the people of the Romagna. In order to intensify the impact of the violence, the deed was not done in front of the people but was orchestrated so that Remirro de Orco's dismembered body would be found in public. Hence, the people were spectators of the violence after the fact as opposed to being perpetrators of the violent act. The shock value of the act was also intensified by the absence of the agents of the violence so that the violence itself would be center stage. Even though it satisfied the people, this violence could support the case for institutional protections against intra-elite conflict. For John P. McCormick, the temptation to forsake institutions for controlling elites should be resisted.[43]

But this overlooks the effectiveness, at least from Machiavelli's perspective, of the extralegal dismembering of Remirro de Orco.

The image of a politician chopped in half is horrifying.[44] Clearly, the dismemberment of Remirro de Orco or any politician is not the ideal path for satisfying popular hatred. Machiavelli implies, though, that some politicians may deserve to be treated in this manner given Machiavelli's unconditional endorsement of Cesare Borgia who orchestrated the violence: "I know no better precepts to give a new prince than ones derived from Cesare's actions."[45] I will comment on this in greater detail shortly. Let's move on to the second example.

"An Excellent Example"

Machiavelli's view on violence and politics is believed to be encapsulated in his statements about *fortuna*, who as a woman, it is necessary to "beat and coerce."[46] As Hanna Fenichel Pitkin puts it, "Machiavelli's image of fortune embodies his central teachings about the human condition."[47] Based on Machiavelli's advice, the leader asserts his will and gives form to raw matter. Since *fortuna* is a female goddess, Machiavelli is arguably promoting an understanding of politics as sexual conquest. As does the violence against Remirro de Orco, Machiavelli's feminization of *fortuna* and advice about dominating her makes readers of Machiavelli justifiably uneasy. In these instances, Machiavelli is seen as too violent and possibly as a psychopath. Although there may be grounds for interpreting Machiavelli in this manner, I hope to complicate the picture. An important, albeit overlooked, example pertaining to the relationship between violence and politics is contained in a story about the beating of a schoolmaster. In the following example, I suggest that *fortuna*, in addition to being a woman, is also a schoolmaster.[48]

The second example of extra-institutional violence as an accountability measure is from the *Discourses*. The subtitle of the section is "A SINGLE ACT OF COMMON HUMANITY MADE A GREATER IMPRESSION ON THE FALISCI THAN DID ALL THE FORCES OF ROME."[49] This example is significant because it demonstrates how extra-institutional punishment of elites appeases popular hatred, but this violence does not necessarily spiral out of control. Indeed, public humiliation of elites can play a significant role in ensuring accountability to the people. Moreover, this example displays, in the words of Machiavelli, "common humanity and kindness, continence or generosity."[50] Violence was not only lesser violence in this case but ironically a form of humanity and kindness.

A schoolmaster claimed to be leading his students to the countryside for physical exercise. The schoolmaster actually intended to hand over the students to Camillus, who was invading the city. The schoolmaster's offer was refused by the powerful general:

> When Camillus and his army lay before the Faliscan city, which he was besieging, a schoolmaster who taught the most noble youths in the city, thinking to *ingratiate himself with Camillus and the Roman people*, went with his pupils outside the town ostensibly to give them exercise, led them to where Camillus was encamped, and offered to hand them over, saying that, if they were used as a lever, the town would place itself in his hands. Camillus not only rejected the offer, but had the teacher stripped, his *hands tied behind his back*, and to each of the boys gave a rod with which to beat him *often and hard* on his way back to the town. When the citizens saw this, they were so pleased with the *humanity and integrity* of Camillus that they no longer wanted to go on with the defense, but decided to hand over the town. This authentic incident affords us an *excellent example* of how a *humane and kindly act* sometimes makes a much greater impression than an act of ferocity or violence.[51]

The schoolmaster was stripped, his hands were tied behind his back, and then he was surrounded by the students who beat him with rods.[52] Clearly, the schoolmaster's *fortuna* had run out. Machiavelli regarded the public beating of the stripped teacher as a humane and kindly act because Machiavelli was able to see it from the vantage point of the students and the Roman people. A reversal of expectation adds to the humor and power of this example. The schoolmaster was expecting to be rewarded by Camillus and the Roman people for betraying the students. As opposed to rewarding the schoolmaster, Camillus sided with the betrayed students, arguably the popular element, and punished the schoolmaster.

In contrast to the dismemberment of Remirro de Orco where the assassin was not observed during the murder, the schoolmaster's punishment was a participatory symbolic act staged in front of the people on the long walk back to town. Participatory in the sense that the students' agency is called upon to beat the schoolmaster, but symbolic because it is only through Camillus's refusal of the schoolmaster's offer that the students are empowered to punish the teacher. The students did not contest the power of the teacher from a sense of collective agency that they acquired on their own but as a result of the direction of Camillus.[53] Even so, the student's inclusion in the punishment of the schoolmaster gave them a taste of redemption insofar as the students were able to avenge being betrayed by the schoolmaster.

The schoolmaster incident is not as spectacular and violent as chopping a public leader in half but it nevertheless sends a powerful message to leaders who abuse their power. For Machiavelli, the public staging of violence against elites is a necessary component of effective governance. To generalize from the example of the schoolmaster's beating to the larger political context is precisely what Machiavelli has in mind. Arrogant elites should be publically humiliated by the people when they violate the public's trust. If an authority figure is hated, once the hatred passes a critical limit, this hatred should be appeased. The leader must keep the people satisfied or he will suffer their wrath. As we saw with the beating of the schoolmaster, localized popular violence did not turn into a bloodbath and spiral out of control but contained comedic aspects apparent in the reversal of relations of power between students and teacher, the rods used by the students to beat the teacher, the nakedness of the teacher, and the staging of the beating in front of the entire population of the city.[54] More importantly, humor in this example emerges as a means to build collective solidarity against oppression. This renders it superior to the violence imposed on Remirro de Orco by Cesare Borgia that was arguably too extreme and had the effect of stupefying the people, which has dubious political value.[55] The violence against the schoolmaster, in contrast, created a sense of collective solidarity against a corrupt member of the elite because it settled the score, it was effectively staged in front of the Roman population, and the beating of the schoolmaster by the students contained humor.[56]

It could be objected that elite in-fighting in the Remirro de Orco and schoolmaster examples are only a source of distraction to the real project at hand, namely, the consolidation of state power. I disagree. In the Remirro de Orco example, one elite massacred another. In the second example, the punishment of the teacher is mainly about public humiliation. Including the students in the teacher's punishment opens the possibility of the liberation of the *demos* from their exclusion from state power. That is to say, it lays the groundwork for future resistance to oppression.

We might call it a pedagogical moment in the fight against oppression. Camillus, not the schoolmaster, was the real teacher of the students.

Popular violence against elites is often depicted as irrational and of limited value, especially by interpreters who adhere to the civic republican interpretation of Machiavelli.[57] The fear is that hatred of elites could easily morph into a popular dictatorship. Class enemies could be massacred. This fear is unfounded. Machiavelli has a much more nuanced understanding of popular violence. As Yves Winter puts it in his article on the Ciompi uprising, "violence functions not merely as an instrument of coercion but also as a way to mobilize popular support in a manner that appeals directly to popular demands for redress against oppression."[58] Machiavelli adds an important qualification to his endorsement of popular violence against elites, though. Popular violence should be used to mend, not to spoil.[59] The violence against the schoolmaster mended the public's trust. Nothing was spoiled.[60]

Against Carl Schmitt and Samuel P. Huntington

As we have seen, Machiavelli's interpretation of the political significance of hatred is connected to the problems of elite accountability to the people, violence, preventing oppression, and avenging injustice. In order to illuminate the role that hatred plays in Machiavelli's thinking and to develop further my defense of hatred, I compare Machiavelli's view on hatred with two other theorists of hatred, namely, Carl Schmitt and Samuel P. Huntington.

Hatred emerged in twentieth-century politics as an ideological weapon to consolidate state power and ward off a series of crises in political legitimacy. Through propaganda techniques and mass rallies, the *demos* were enlisted via hatred to support the political projects of an arguably criminal political class. Both Schmitt and Huntington can be situated within this context because they advised the managerial-political class on the most effective practices to ward off the crisis of political legitimacy and consolidate the power of the state. The former for Weimar Germany and the Third Reich, the latter for the American imperial empire in the face of a crisis of authority stemming from rising expectations and, what Huntington notoriously penned, an "excess of democracy."[61] For Schmitt and Huntington, the answer to the crisis of the state was found in the politics of hate.

To be more specific, Schmitt and Huntington mobilize, manipulate, and redirect hatred to obfuscate social and economic antagonism between elites and the people as a way to manufacture consent and increase the power of the state. Fused with an increasingly sophisticated propaganda apparatus that incorporated communication technology (e.g., loudspeakers, megaphones, radio, and television) for explicitly political means, hatred for Schmitt and Huntington serves as an ideological tool to build national (Schmitt) and civilizational (Huntington) collective identity. Political rallies and mass sporting events also serve as means to mobilize the masses into a unit where national symbols (e.g., flags, the national anthem) and displays of military strength (e.g., bombers flying overhead) produce patriotic outpourings of support. For both Schmitt and Huntington, the target of mass hatred was shifted away from the problem of elite political accountability to the *demos* and redirected to the formation of political identity.

This move to construct a homogeneous political identity simultaneously constitutes the new body politic as well as the political enemy. In a Hobbesian manner, hatred as a tactic to form political identity defines the collective "we" and gives birth to "them," the political enemy. As Schmitt states in *The Concept of the Political*, "the political enemy is the other, the stranger." Schmitt continues: "He is existentially something different and *alien*."[62] With a definition of the enemy as vague and broad as this, anyone could qualify as an enemy.

Like Schmitt, Huntington also deploys a politics of hate. In *The Clash of Civilizations and the Remaking of World Order* (1996/2011), Huntington quotes and agrees with Michael Didbin who states that "unless we hate what we are not, we cannot love what we are."[63] Huntington then goes on to state: "For peoples seeking identity . . . enemies are essential."[64] And, finally, Huntington states "we know who we are only when we know who we are not and often only when we know whom we are against."[65] For Huntington, hatred and an oppositional stance to the other emerge as the epistemological conditions for stable self-identity insofar as it purifies the self of foreign contamination: "America cannot become the world and still be America. Other peoples cannot become American and still be themselves."[66] As opposed to directing a critical eye toward rulers who only serve a limited segment of the population with favorable legislation at the expense of the majority, hatred of the enemy/other is used as a tool by Huntington to distract the *demos* and keep the ruling class in power.

There is an important difference between Schmitt and Huntington, on the one hand, and Machiavelli, on the other. Machiavelli argues that hatred is caused by an oppressive ruling class. Hence, the proper object for political hatred is the political-managerial class. In contrast to Machiavelli, Schmitt and Huntington depoliticize hatred of the enemy/other. That is, they divorce the target of hatred from social and economic divisions perpetuated by the ruling class.[67] By creating new targets for hatred, Schmitt and Huntington arrest the crisis of the state originally identified by Machiavelli and enlist popular hatred in the project of building state power, while simultaneously excluding the *demos* from real political participation. Clearly, the legacy of Schmitt and Huntington lives on today. It is no wonder that we are constantly directing our attention to new enemies to hate, whether it is terrorists, drug addicts, welfare recipients, homeless people, or illegal immigrants.[68] The existence of an infinite number of internal and external enemies justifies expanding military spending and an increase in executive prerogative. Cast in this light, US domestic and foreign policy emerges as an ideological weapon against the home population insofar as it forces the *demos* to fixate their gaze on the wrong objects of hate.[69]

Schmitt's ties to National-Socialism are well known. Huntington also risks going in a troubling direction. If one combines Huntington's view of hatred in *The Clash of Civilizations and the Remaking of the World Order* (1996/2011) with his book *Who Are We? The Challenges to America's National Identity* (2004), where he argues that Mexican immigrants are unassimilable, the danger to Huntington's thinking and use of hatred as a way to obfuscate class antagonism and build white national identity against brown Mexican immigrants is clear.[70] Since Huntington believes the language of class no longer fits the contemporary situation (despite staggering evidence suggesting otherwise), Huntington turns to *culture* as the marker for new forms of political conflict.[71] This move deflects attention away from the current corrupt ruling class and to the amorphous Islamic and/or unassimilable Mexican cultural other. Huntington's appeal to culture as an access point and justification for increased security against external and internal enemies leads to, as Michael Shapiro has put it, the "ontological grounding of the political."[72] At the end of the day, Huntington's appeal to *culture* is only a ruse to enlist the *demos* in the project of consolidating state power at their own expense. Identity politics grounded in hatred is a tool used by Huntington to deflect attention away from the real object of hatred, namely, the ruling class and the crisis in political legitimacy caused by excluding the *demos* from real political participation.

Machiavellian hatred is superior to the ontological hatred of Schmitt and Huntington because Machiavellian hatred is essentially political, that is to say, it is the people's response to political oppression. For Machiavelli, political hatred is a result of the material conditions of political life. Hatred is not a weapon used against the people to shore up state power. As a result of its connection with identity formation, hatred as Schmitt and Huntington conceive of it risks transforming anyone into a domestic foreigner, especially for those others who are cast as unassimilable and become permanent scapegoats and targets for white resentment.

When the political order is grounded in a static ontological foundation, political life becomes a stage of sacrifice for the internal others who are unable to make themselves act, look, and think like the true American peddled by authors like Huntington.[73] These internal foreigners become targets of state violence in the form of racial-profiling, police harassment, confinement in ghettos, disproportionate incarceration, preferential unemployment, and criminalization. The failures of these internal scapegoats are then linked to "their" culture of poverty, "their" culture of criminality, and "their" lack of initiative and motivation, which, in turn, confirms "their" genetic degeneracy and need for added police and state surveillance.[74] Huntington's message is both horrifying and hypnotizing. So hypnotizing, in fact, that Huntington can advance these arguments and still state that he attempts to engage in "as detached and thorough an analysis of the evidence as I can."[75]

Apparently, keeping a watchful eye on these internal enemies and cultural others is satisfying for a dwindling, resentful, and economically deracinated white working and middle-class, precisely the audience Huntington targets as most receptive to his message which he whispers into the ears of the ruling class who can then appeal to this conditioned population for political support. The oppression of marginalized and powerless groups becomes the fundamental condition of this angry electorate's freedom, identity, and values. If a net or cage needs to be dropped on internal enemies, so be it. After all, "they" deserve it. The marginalization and punishment of scapegoats reaffirms the correct and pure form of national and civilizational identity. Ironically, identity empowerment corresponds to economic and political impotence. Through the persecution of dehumanized scapegoats, they get the satisfaction that someone else is lower on the food chain.[76] A pyrrhic victory is still a victory, I suppose.

It could be objected that I have overstated the difference between Machiavelli, on the one hand, and Schmitt and Huntington, on the other, given that all three wrote for the ruling class and see the management of hatred as a fruitful way to consolidate state power. I disagree. Unlike Schmitt and Huntington, Machiavelli exposes the original dilemma of elite accountability to the *demos* and thereby names the proper object of hatred. Machiavelli destroys the illusion that leaders serve the common good. By naming this rupture, Machiavelli foregrounds the problem of elite accountability to the *demos* as a fundamental political problem. Machiavelli's *Prince*, then, is a dangerous book in the hands of the *demos*. Machiavelli's message is simple. Do not be duped by leaders directing your attention to enemies. Your leaders are the real problem. Schmitt and Huntington, in contrast, tell us to look away from the ruling class and toward a never-ending list of powerless enemies to hate, who the state will then pound into oblivion which, in turn, serves the function of creating political identity and simultaneously strengthens state power at the expense of democratic accountability. The real target of ontological hatred for Schmitt and Huntington is the home population, because the intent is to disempower the *demos* while giving them the illusion that the state is on their side. The target of hatred for Machiavelli, in contrast, is the ruling class.

Conclusion

As the first part of this chapter demonstrates, hatred occupies a central place in Machiavelli's thinking. The second part illustrates that hatred can play a productive role in the political realm. In the case of Schmitt and Huntington, hatred can also pave the way to a living hell. In contrast to Schmitt and Huntington, Machiavelli's fundamental goal is to increase elite accountability to the *demos* and generate collective solidarity against oppression via a radical populist politics (but without forgetting or abandoning the rule of law), based on the humiliation of arrogant and corrupt elites.[77] For Machiavelli, antagonism between antithetically positioned groups ensures the preservation of freedom: "The nobility vomit forth against the plebs the poison hid in their hearts."[78] The plebeians strike back through the popular hatred of elites.[79] Extra-institutional means to secure elite accountability are not advanced by Machiavelli as a panacea, but Machiavelli argues that they are effective for venting popular hatred, building collective solidarity, and rebuilding public trust in shared governance.[80] When Leo Strauss claims that "noble rhetoric" should be wielded against the multitude to bridge the gulf between the masses and elites, this conclusion seems to be precisely what Machiavelli is arguing against.[81] When the people find out that they have been duped, the people will avenge the wrong.

As long as political hatred is directed at its proper target (the ruling class), Machiavelli shows that hatred can provide a valuable political check on the arrogance and criminality of elites and lead to social transformation. But political hatred can do more. It can be a permanent force of insurrection and condition of a mass popular movement against a corrupt political order. Hatred can also prevent leaders from oppressing the people and abusing power. In the words of the Florentine political sage: "For all do wrong to the same extent when there is nothing to prevent them doing wrong."[82] And, the people only wish "not to be oppressed."[83]

In these final quotes, resistance to oppression is cast as the necessary counterweight to political domination. Political hatred, and the collective solidarity it can trigger, names the beginning and the end of the fight against oppression. Given that hatred is both a problem linked to the formation of political identity and simultaneously a possible solution to political oppression, the repudiation of hatred as a topic worthy of investigation in favor of empathy, hope, and recognition might just turn out to be a symptom of the depth and hold that the reigning ideology has on us. Like it or not, hatred is here to stay. The question is whether hatred will continue to be used as a means to provide the empty solace of petty identity superiority to the masses at the price of real democratic accountability or whether hatred against the proper enemy (e.g., the ruling class) will be mobilized for greater political accountability and progressive political ends. Cast in this light, the Occupy Wall Street movement is a positive example of the deployment of political hatred via the identification of the 1 percent as the political enemy. The language of the 1 percent has fundamentally changed our political discourse and understanding of the role of the financial sector and corporate power play in determining the outcomes of political elections, policy choices, and the imposition of starvation on the people via debt, unemployment, and low wages. As the Occupy movement consolidated popular hatred against corporate elites and their puppet politicians, it also created relations within the movement that contested the hierarchical and increasingly unequal ones in the society via transparency, community, participatory democracy, and equality.

Chapter Two
Immanuel Kant on Thinking
without the Constraint of Rules

Introduction

No political category poses more of a problem for contemporary political theory than the concept of revolution because of its historical variety (e.g., British, American, French, Russian, Haitian, Mexican, Chinese, Cuban, Iranian, Tunisian, Egyptian) and theoretical complexity (e.g., justification, legitimacy, legality). Initially an astronomical term that referred to planetary circulation around a central point, the French and socialist revolutions became the index of revolutionary movement. Led by a political vanguard, the French revolution promised a radical break from the past ushering in an entirely new egalitarian political order. At their high point, the revolutionaries pursued their ideals through discrediting practices of the ancient regime, destroying the power of the aristocracy, suppressing internal dissent, and eliminating political opposition.[1] The Russian socialist revolution broke the stranglehold on power of the Romanov monarchy and eliminated private property as the sole determinant of political power but relied on a series of never-ending purges to protect revolutionary purity. Ironically, our capacity to envision a new form of revolution is constricted by the dominating influence of the French and socialist revolutions, which construe revolution as the violent takeover of power and the re-creation of the political order from the ground up.

Even if we ask, what other political possibilities exist beyond the horizon of today's oligarchic-corporate dominated polity? The problem remains: How can political transformation be conceived outside of the French and socialist models of revolution, models that continue to determine our core political categories (e.g., Left, Right), and political vocabulary (e.g., democracy, equality) that seem to have significantly less meaning today than they did in 1789 and 1917?

I turn to Immanuel Kant (1724-1804) to explore the possibility of political creativity and a new kind of revolution and read Kant against himself to open wider parameters for political thought. I also hope to challenge conservative readings of Kant that cast him as a precursor to "justice as fairness" and an antirevolutionary thinker. Kant's seeming condemnation of state-centric revolution in his philosophy of right does not rule out the existence of other revolutionary undercurrents in his thinking. Exploring these revolutionary undercurrents requires linking the idea of revolution in Kant's thought to his concept of genius. Kant's concept of the creative genius is crucial for reassessing his status as a radical political thinker. As we shall see, the Kantian moral agent is not only similar to the artistic genius but can easily be a revolutionary genius too. I argue that this hybrid figure—the "free genius"—overcomes the limits of Kant's conservative philosophy of right and can lead to, borrowing the words from Kant, a "true reform in ways of thinking," and by extension, new modes of action.[2] My interpretation radicalizes Kant beyond the conservative appropriation of him by contemporary liberal theory and brings the pedagogical significance of his critical project into focus via the concept of genius.[3]

There are three crucial moments of revolution in Kant that go far beyond his rejection of revolution in his philosophy of right. These revolutionary moments can be found in Kant's ethical thinking (e.g., autonomy), in his plea for enlightened thinking (e.g., dare to think for yourself), and, most importantly, in his presentation of the concept of genius (e.g., imperative of creativity and originality). In this sense, Kant is not an enemy of revolution but provides an outline of how to expand and broaden the concept of revolution and link it to creativity. In doing so, one could say that Kant civilizes revolution insofar he tries to overcome the violent legacy of the French revolution, but without giving up on the creative moment of revolutionary anarchy.[4] In this regard, Kant reconceives revolution as a never-ending practice of political creativity.

In terms of the outline of my argument, I present Kant's view on revolution in *Metaphysics of Morals* and complicate the interpretation that he is an antirevolutionary thinker. Then, I connect Kant's ideas about enlightenment and moral agency with revolution. After that, I turn to the concept of genius and show how it unites revolutionary undercurrents in Kant's thinking in the expression "freedom from the constraint of rules." I draw out the connection between Kant's non-state-centric theory of revolution and genius. Revolution emerges as a question of *padaeia*: "man can only become a man by education."[5] These themes—revolution, creativity—connect to the broader idea of confrontational citizenship explored in this book.

Revolution

To properly understand Kant's work on revolution, it is important to take into account his views on revolution throughout his writings, not just in *Metaphysics of Morals*. It is well-known that Kant discusses revolution in *Metaphysics of Morals*, specifically, in "The Doctrine of Right."[6] In this book, he seems to categorically condemn revolution. Indeed, Kant was horrified by the fate of Louis XVI during the French Revolution, which was, in a rare moment of Kantian exaggeration, "worse than murder." Kant continues: "The execution of a monarch seems to be a crime from which the people cannot be absolved, for it is as if the state commits suicide."[7] Such an act, Kant claims, "makes it impossible to generate again a state that has been overthrown."[8] In *Perpetual Peace*, he continues this line of thought: "Everyone who violently or covertly participated in the revolution would rightly have been subject to the punishment due rebels."[9] In reference to the French revolution, though, Kant seems to hesitate to condemn it: "This revolution has aroused in the hearts and desires of all spectators who are not themselves caught up in it a sympathy which borders almost on enthusiasm."[10] Even so, Kant is usually interpreted as an enemy of revolution.

Indeed, Kant is interpreted as someone who sees revolution as a logical contradiction because it annihilates the order of right, upsets the stability of the social order, leads to secrecy (secrecy violates principle of publicity without which enlightened thinking could not occur), and as an act of unjustifiable violence.[11] As Hans Reiss puts it, those advocating rebellion would be acting on a maxim that would defeat its own purpose. Rebellion, Reiss continues, "renders the existence of the state impossible."[12] Revolution would, as Kant states, "nullify the basis of the order of right."[13]

It is important to note, though, that in "Answer to the Question: What Is Enlightenment?" (1784), Kant claimed a revolution could put an end to oppression but the revolution Kant had in mind was not one that involved overturning political forms. This other type of revolution was inside humans and emerged into the public via the rational faculties.

Only the public use of reason, Kant states, "can bring about enlightenment among men."[14] Political and social upheaval could actually make
life worse. In contrast to this mental or cognitive revolution, a strictly
political revolution is conceived by Kant as an upheaval with short-term
bang but long-term bust. Although a revolution may end oppression
in the short term, a revolution can lead to new forms of oppression and
prejudices. Something much more radical than a political revolution
is needed. Kant states:

> A *revolution* may well put an end to autocratic despotism and
> to rapacious or power-seeking oppression, but it will never
> produce a true reform in ways of thinking. Instead, new preju-
> dices, like the ones they replaced, will serve as a leash to control
> the great unthinking mass.[15]

This citation is important because Kant believed only a revolution
in thinking could lead to improvement, although this revolution in
thinking was admittedly a "protracted process."[16]

Even though Kant seems to unequivocally condemn political revolution, not all commentators on Kant are convinced. For example, Hannah
Arendt claims Kant was equivocal on the question of revolution.[17] For
Arendt, Kant never wrote a complete political philosophy, which makes
pinning him down on certain political positions difficult.[18] But, Arendt
contends, "Kant's sympathies in the matter of revolution were clearly
with revolution."[19] As we shall see, the word *revolution* occurs in a variety
of contexts in Kant, not just in his philosophy of right. Hence, it would
be a mistake to interpret Kant as a counterrevolutionary thinker, or as
the *Urvater* (e.g., primordial father) for contemporary liberal theory,
with its praise of institutions and cold shoulder for protest and political
resistance. Rather, Kant should be seen as a thinker who explored the philosophical conditions of revolutionary activity and thinking and sought
creative ways to reconceive revolution in the broadest possible terms.

Enlightened Thinking

My first point is simple. Kant's emphasis on intellectual independence
is arguably revolutionary. Kant viewed the reliance on the guidance
of others as an obstacle to intellectual enlightenment and political

change. As Romand Coles states, Kant had an awareness of the "widespread laziness, cowardice, socially engendered stupidity, and fear" that plague most humans.[20] Even so, Kant had faith in the eventual widespread public use of reason. The heroic tone in "Answer to the Question: What Is Enlightenment?" is unmistakable and a plea to the reading public to wake up and think for itself. Kant argues that using one's own understanding without the guidance of others, a latent possibility in everyone, opens the path to enlightenment and liberation.[21] Enlightened thinking, or thinking for oneself, required courage because it was considered "highly dangerous." Enlightened thinking, moreover, threatens power relations because certain institutions depend for their survival on ignorance and fear, and even engender ignorance in order to profit off of it.[22] With their hands held by their guardians, most people rely on "dogmas and formulas," which Kant viewed as the "ball and chain of permanent immaturity."[23] The only thing needed for the type of enlightenment Kant had in mind was freedom; freedom to make public use of one's reason "in all matters."[24] Thinking was not a solitary affair but required interlocutors and testing of ideas to work. The immediate political consequences of the public use of reason might not be measurable, but the long-term consequences of freedom of thought, Kant argued, were revolutionary.

In addition to the potentially revolutionary consequences of intellectual independence and the public use of reason, Kant's work on the concept of genius is consistent with his plea for the public use of reason in "Answer to the Question: What Is Enlightenment?" Although genius might be rare, it might not be as rare as one might assume if one takes Kant at face value in terms of the possibility of the widespread use of the free exercise of reason and the need for everyone to be minimally original in the sense of using their own understanding without relying on others. As we shall see, thinking for oneself is similar to the imperative of originality that is central to Kant's conception of genius. Both are predicated on free action as opposed to imitating others.[25] Thinking for oneself is also necessary for autonomous moral practice.[26]

Introducing Genius

Kant's reflections on genius are essential for understanding his view on revolution and how it connects to other core aspects of his critical project. Indeed, Kant's political views can be improved by importing concepts from other parts of the critical project, especially his aesthetic theory. In this sense, I agree with Hannah Arendt that Kant's *Critique of Judgment* comprises his most advanced reflections on the political.[27] My argument is that aesthetic creativity as exemplified in the work of the genius can revolutionize the Kantian revolution. Although the importance of Kant's ideas on genius have been defended (or at least explored) by a few contemporary scholars, including Hannah Arendt, Romand Coles, Jacques Derrida, Julia Kristeva, Jean-François Lyotard, and Linda Zerilli, the relationship between genius and politics remains largely unexplored.[28] This oversight has foreclosed an aspect of Kant's thought that is particularly relevant to the contemporary political moment, which requires creative forms of political engagement.[29]

As we shall see, genius is a good revolutionary force because the genius creates new rules, promotes freedom and independent thought, and allows thinking from another person's vantage point. As a result of the multiple ways in which the concept of genius can be conceived in Kant's thinking, it can lead to a reevaluation of Kant's contemporary relevance and a renewal of the idea of revolution. Multiple forms of revolution were possible for the critical philosopher. For Kant, some revolutions occur in the empirical world but there are also revolutions that may not be immediately visible. Kant states: "The mightiest revolution coming from the inside of man is his departure from his self-incurred tutelage."[30] But for a philosopher who dedicated his life to restraining the pretentions of reason via critique, what could be more pretentious than deeming oneself a genius? Also, would not the genius be yet another enunciation of the vanguard revolutionary politics bequeathed to us by the French and Russian revolutions? As we shall see, the answer is no.

The Kantian concept of genius discussed in the *Critique of Judgment* (1790) appears in the context of Kant's discussion of art and this is, generally speaking, where it remains. Because genius is, as Paul Guyer puts it, "a genuine gift of nature" as opposed to the result of learning, the concept of genius tends to be regarded as an anomaly in Kant's thinking, or as an elitist fetish.[31] To complicate matters further, genius is difficult to grasp because it cannot be taught and originality is difficult to recognize.[32] Even among contemporary thinkers sympathetic to Kant, genius is skipped as a topic worthy of investigation or one states, as in the case of Jacques Derrida, that "this noun 'genius' makes us squirm."[33]

Nevertheless, the concept of genius is one of the most important concepts in Kant's massive body of work.[34] By definition, genius eludes categorization and frustrates efforts to understand its origin and end. According to Giorgio Tonelli, "most of the discussions about genius originated in the field of aesthetics."[35] Indeed, Kant's work on genius was influenced by Alexander Gerard's 1774 *An Essay on Genius*, where he defined genius as the "faculty of invention."[36] Genius leads, according to Gerard, "to new discoveries in science, or for producing original works of art." These formulations about invention and originality were carried over into Kant's Third Critique, and can be found in Book Two, specifically in the section called "The Analytic of the Sublime." Although Kant explores the idea of genius in the context of fine art, "Fine Art Is the Art of Genius," Kant's work on genius goes beyond art and the aesthetic dimension insofar as his discussion of genius is an explication of how not to be a slave to the opinions and views of others, exactly the same theme discussed in Kant's "Answer to the Question: What Is Enlightenment?"[37] As we shall see, moral independence, the answer to the question of how not to be a slave to the actions of others (explored in *Groundwork of the Metaphysics of Morals*), and intellectual independence, the answer to the question how not to be a slave to the mental habits of others, is also similar to Kant's conception of genius.

What, then, is genius? According to Kant, genius is a "power of the mind."[38] Spirit, Kant continues, is the "animating principle of the mind," and gives the mind "purposive momentum" and imparts "play."[39] Genius, moreover, is an "innate mental predisposition."[40] Hence, genius "cannot be taught" or learned.[41] Genius is also a "rare phenomenon."[42] For Kant, originality is an essential component of genius. To be a genius, though, one has to be more than original. Kant states "genius is the exemplary originality of a subject's natural endowment in the free use of his cognitive powers."[43] Exemplary originality means the genius is not an imitator. Even though the genius is not an imitator, she is not a solitary lord of nature. Indeed, the emerging genius has a special relation to the product of other geniuses. Kant states: "The other genius, who follows the example, is aroused by it to a feeling of his own originality, which allows him to exercise in art his *freedom from the constraint of rules* [*Zwangsfreiheit von Regeln*], and to do so in such a way that art itself acquires a new rule by this."[44] Through following an example, the genius is aroused to a feeling of his own originality and then departs and breaks from the example and the constraint of rules. The genius starts with a rule by following an example, but the break with rules (e.g., the opening, the leap) in the moment of creativity is the decisive moment.

Since there is a lot at stake in this expression, it is worth repeating. The defining characteristic of genius is "freedom from the constraint of rules" and "some deviation from the common rule."[45] Just as in Kant's practical philosophy, the servile attachment to rules negates the possibility of moral conduct and also snuffs out the creativity of the genius. For Kant, rule-following becomes a form of moral imitation where people relieve themselves of the burden of thinking through their maxims for action. In the aesthetic sphere, rule following would mean an artist would imitate the art of a recognized master. Academically, rule following would mean the student would be a disciple/imitator of the professor. Verbal plagiarism or speaking in clichés also relieves individuals of having to articulate themselves freely because they submit to and repeat the stock phrases used by others. Politically, rule following would mean the obedient citizen would thoughtlessly obey the law as opposed to being a law unto herself. For Kant, the genius is free because she thinks and acts without the constraint of rules.

The implications of thinking without the constraint of rules are clear. Thinking without the constraint of rules implies cognitive flexibility and a "broadened way of thinking."[46] When freed from the constraint of rules, one can think from any particular perspective, even perspectives that have no name. One can also think from the vantage point of another person, combine concepts that are not normally thought together, think in a contradictory fashion, criticize and question aspects of life that are regarded as off-limits for critical interrogation, invent a new language, recover and reflect on the strange aspects of life hidden right in front of us, reread something that is old in a new and creative way, defend something that is universally despised, or criticize something that everyone worships. When you think like a genius and think without the constraint of rules, there are no logical impossibilities, absurdities, and silly thoughts. These designations are arguably cognitive power plays that shut down experimentation and police the boundaries of acceptable thinking defined as rational analysis and arranging or judging particulars under general categories.

Kant's freedom from the constraint of rules has other components as well that pertain to fundamental aspects of the human condition. For example, freedom from the constraint of rules strikes me as a minimal condition of intellectual independence in both moral and aesthetic practice, which in turn facilitates creativity, innovation, and new discoveries. In light of these aspects, thinking without the constraint of rules strikes me as the essence of thinking if not of life. Thinking without the constraint of rules, how the genius thinks, also complicates the perception of Kant as a cold and rigid rationalist because thinking without the constraint of rules requires one to be playful, innocent, and naive. When we think without the constraint of rules, we are able to see the world, Kant suggests, "as poets do," that is, "in terms of what manifests itself to the eye."[47] Thinking without the constraint of rules also allows one to be open and nondogmatic.

True, thinking under the constraint of rules may serve as a helpful way to discipline the rational faculties and prevent flights of the imagination. Additionally, it might not be necessary or even possible to reflect on every aspect of human existence, rule, and practice at every moment. It might be a waste of time, for example, to deconstruct or analytically obliterate the food options available at fast-food restaurants while traveling in the US. One could simply shop for healthier food options elsewhere or bring one's own lunch. And, some conformity to linguistic rules and common sayings might be necessary to ensure mutual understanding. However, a broadened way of thinking that strategically departs from given arrangements and rules is necessary for intellectual growth and creative transformation. For Romand Coles, "Kant views the idea that thinking is wholly continuous with given rules as erroneous and constitutive of the shackles of permanent immaturity."[48] I agree. The point Kant was trying to make in terms of the genius having freedom from the constraint of rules was simple. Thinking in accordance with given rules can become a defensive mechanism to prevent creativity and contain the "new" in a category or concept. Kant viewed the mental activity of the genius as revolutionary because it was an act that liberated something from the weight of the past. It is not difficult to see how thinking like a genius challenges rigid attachment to rules in the legal sphere and disrupts herd mentality in the social and political realms.[49]

But does the radical originality of the Kantian genius bring us right back to the same problem I posed at the beginning of this chapter in reference to the French and socialist revolutions, namely, the danger of a self-appointed vanguard or political elite speaking and acting for the people, a vanguard that enforces conformity to a political program, and one that uses violence both against internal dissent and external enemies to annihilate the past and build a new political order from the ground up, a vanguard, finally, that announces itself as a tribe of geniuses? The answer is no. First, I read Kant against the grain and see genius as a latent possibility in everyone, not as something inborn, something unable to be learned, or something monopolized by the few. I would even go so far as to say everyone is a potential genius.[50] Too often creative individuals are punished for exhibiting freedom from the constraint of rules. There may be more cases of creative genius than we realize but fail to see them as a result inequality of condition, differentials in privilege, and unequal educational access.[51] Second, the Kantian genius is original but has an important relation to the work of past geniuses. There is no radical break condemning all aspects of the past as was the case with radical Jacobins who were rewriting history from day one (e.g., a new revolutionary calendar) with the French revolution as the starting point. For Jacobins, the past was to be washed away and the world begun anew. For Kant, freedom from the constraint of rules is not freedom from all rules. The genius does not leap out of time. How, then, does Kant's concept of genius connect to the concept of revolution?

Revolution and Genius

Kant called for a revolution on multiple levels that go beyond his critique of revolution in his philosophy of right. Kant saw the possibility that all humans might one day use their critical faculties and dare to think for themselves. The consequences of this would be nothing less than revolutionary. Kant's prohibition on using yourself or another person as a means was a check on abusive forms of power and has revolutionary consequences.[52] To become morally good, Kant argued in *Religion within the Boundaries of Mere Reason* that a "revolution in the disposition of the human being" was needed.[53] Self-legislating, what Kant calls the "Supreme Principle of Morality," was yet another moment when the individual needed to become political, if not revolutionary, and lay down a new law for human conduct not by force but by example.[54] Additionally, Kant argued that "the mightiest revolution coming from the inside of man is his departure from his self-incurred tutelage."[55] Kant's use of the word *revolution* in these passages is not accidental, but demonstrates a broader concept of revolution operating in his work that can be easily missed if one focuses only on his critique of state-centric revolution in his philosophy of right. It would be a mistake to insist that Kant's use of the word *revolution* in *Metaphysics of Morals* exhausts his views on it.

The concept of genius is yet another moment of Kant's revolutionary thinking where he explores the possibility of creativity that could free humans from being trapped by the values of the present, but without the destructive violence of the Jacobin model of revolutionary activity. Kant's concept of genius holds promise for rethinking what it is we do when we try to think about the concept of revolution, and exactly what we need to do when we think politically. It is important to emphasize the "double movement" in the activity of the genius. The genius thinks without the constraint of rules and also creates a new rule. The anarchistic moment of departure from the constraint of rules also involves the creation of a new rule. Just because the genius creates a new rule, this rule is not fixed for all eternity but can be challenged by another rule that is also susceptible to being challenged.

As a revolutionary figure, the genius creates new rules, promotes freedom and independent thought, and allows thinking from another person's vantage point. Ethically, he is a law unto himself. Intellectually, he never rests but is permanently creative and fights against the constraint of rules. Socially, he refuses to imitate others and challenges everyone to rise above the comfort of rituals and conformity. Aesthetically, he shatters past aesthetic forms. All of these aspects lead us to the following questions: What rules have constrained us when we try to think about the concept of revolution? Has our failed investment in a particular model of revolutionary politics deepened our resistance to exploring other revolutionary options?

Response to Objections

It could be objected that it is not enough to say that genius is akin to the project of thinking for oneself and the project of revolution. But why not? All three threaten authority. Indeed, genius, self-legislating, and thinking for oneself strike me as the metapolitical conditions of possibility for revolutionary action. I disagree with the assertion that there is only a surface connection between thinking for oneself, the activity of the genius, and revolution. It could also be objected that Kant's concept of genius is twice removed from Kant's philosophy of right, which negates its political relevance. I disagree again. Even if it is twice removed, the point of this chapter is to show how aspects of Kant's Third Critique can productively supplement and broaden Kant's political philosophy in order to underscore a revolutionary, anarchistic, and creative moment in Kant's thinking. It could also be objected that the spontaneous creativity of the genius may not always be appropriate in the political realm;

that analytic thinking may be more productive at times. This is a reasonable objection. However, it seems to me that it would be a mistake to ban creative thinking from politics just as it would be a mistake to completely ban analytic rule-bound thinking. However, if we are always realistic in the political realm, nothing will ever change.

But how does the Kantian genius challenge the conservative nature of his revolutionary theory? "Be no man's lackey," Kant says.[56] And yet, "argue as much as you like and about whatever you like, but obey."[57] How do we reconcile these statements? To say that the latter statement about obedience sums up Kant's position on politics and enlightenment would obscure the revolutionary aspect of his work. Kant does not advance a model of citizenship as total submission to the state. Nor is he a radical Jacobin. Kantian obedience operates alongside the possibility of freedom, creativity, and a departure from the constraint of rules. Kant is not conservative if one factors in the broader revolutionary components to his defense of intellectual enlightenment, moral autonomy, and thinking without the constraint of rules.

As I have already suggested, Kant's views on revolution are not exhausted by his *Metaphysics of Morals*. As Hans Reiss argues, "the revolutionary aspect to Kant is obscured by his [Kant's] denial of the right to rebellion."[58] For Reiss, though, Kant is still a revolutionary thinker. The point of this chapter has been to show the presence of broader revolutionary currents in Kant's thinking. Kant was never an advocate of slavish submission to authority. This would go against even a minimal defense of human dignity. Throughout all of his work, Kant called for a "revolution in the disposition of the human being."[59] But what type of revolutionary was he? Kant was a unique theorist of revolutionary politics conceived as practices of creative resistance to the devaluation of human dignity in all its forms based on the defense of human freedom, thinking for oneself, self-legislating, and the exercise of creative genius outside of the suffocating constraint of rules. These connections have been for the most part overlooked or entirely missed by the liberal appropriation of Kant's legacy.[60]

Finally, even if we accept this broader revolutionary aspect in Kant's thinking that links together critical thinking, autonomy, and genius, what good is it? It does not take a genius to notice that something is horribly wrong with our political options today, with our politicians, with our political vocabulary, with our political institutions, and with the limited range of our political imagination. It is not that we need to renounce or reject the state, as Sheldon Wolin suggests, but we need a new concept of the state, new modes of action, new politicians, a new vision, and it is going to take a free and creative mind (e.g., the genius that is latent in all of us) to envision these radically new political alternatives and possibilities.[61] Challenging rules is not enough. One must strategically break with the constraint of rules and lay down a new law. As I have already stated, the Kantian revolutionary is a revolutionary in the broad sense of thinking for oneself, being a moral law-giving example to others, productively challenging and breaking with past aesthetic and political forms, laying down new laws, which in turn, can be challenged and re-created. Kant thus contributes a valuable component to confrontational citizenship in the sense that he prioritizes the moment of creativity and spontaneity on which everything depends.

Conclusion

The individual genius who ventures to think without the constraint of rules is not taking an easy path. She may be persecuted by those who mistake thinking for following rules. He may be ridiculed, ostracized, branded an intellectual terrorist, and labeled irresponsible. But without a minimal and momentary departure from the constraint of rules, human existence will be trapped in the presumptuous cage of the values of the present. Overcoming self-imposed tutelage in thinking and acting requires courage, creativity, and boldness, if not a certain level of recklessness. The renewal of revolutionary political thought hinges on the capacity to perpetually renew the revolutionary model of politics that starts with a new way of thinking, that is, thinking like a genius, thinking without the constraint of rules. There is always the risk of falling back on known concepts, and this is precisely what the activity of the genius attempts to arrest. Thinking need not always mean positioning the particular under a general category. It might be necessary in certain situations but it would be catastrophic to mandate deductive reasoning as the only permissible form of cognition.

The link between Kant's practical philosophy and his concept of genius hinges on human freedom, being original, and the will to permanent creativity. The militant commitment to genius and freedom helps preserve a space for a political future and keeps a place open for dissent. Even if Kant only provides a rough outline of a new type a revolutionary possibility and fails to articulate how it might take an institutional form, and even if Kant has a rather broad notion of revolution as the widespread public use of reason and autonomous human agency, when one adds Kant's reflections on genius into the equation it is one that is worth exploring as an alternative to the Jacobin and socialist models that demand conformity to a model of revolution and enforces, if not demands, this model's supremacy. Even if the universality that Kant defended was context bound and reflected Kant's own male, Eurocentric, and at times racist assumptions, thinking without the constraint of rules can be wielded against Kant in this regard and push and shatter Kantian categories beyond their problematic dimensions.[62]

In light of all of this, the fact that Kant has been reduced to a conservative philosopher of right turns out to be a distortion of his legacy and puzzling given the radical character of Kant's broader philosophical agenda.[63] In human affairs considered in the widest sense, Kant believed, "nearly everything is paradoxical."[64] The questions for us today are whether Kant's mantra "freedom from the constraint of rules" can free us to dream of a political horizon beyond neoliberalism. The second one is how to lodge and constantly renew radical creativity in the heart of the confrontational citizen.

Chapter Three
Frederick Douglass and the Politics of Rage

Introduction

Throughout the world, protest movements driven by rage are over-throwing oppressive regimes and corrupt rulers. From the main square in Cairo, Egypt, to the streets of Caracas, Venezuela, enraged individuals have taken to the streets and have given up on normal channels to voice political grievances. Ignoring contemporary manifestations of rage could prevent us from understanding a new form of radical citizenship.

Mainstream and liberal traditions in political theory view rage as anathema to democratic citizenship, and as a result have a narrow conception of democratic agency.[1] For them, rage is a remnant of the Hobbesian state of nature—irrational, apolitical, and counterproductive. Rage undermines reason and leads to violence. Historically, anger and rage have been thought as incompatible with participation in political life because anger/rage interrupt the harmony of the soul, lead to unpredictable action, and threaten political order.[2] Among prominent members of the African American intelligentsia, a similar skepticism about rage is present.[3]

The way rage has been defined is also part of the problem. The *Oxford English Dictionary* (*OED*) defines rage as a form of "madness, insanity, and rashness"; it is "manifested in looks, words, or action." It is "vehement and violent" and leads to "extravagant, riotous or wanton behavior."[4] Etymologically, rage is connected to the Latin word *rabid* and to *rabies*. It implies ferocity, fervor, enthusiasm, and excitement. Given these associations, it is not surprising that rage is reduced to "road rage," criminalized, and dismissed as apolitical or as a psychological pathology.[5] A better understanding of rage is needed that politicizes rage and views the larger political context within which rage occurs. Once this contextual turn is taken, rage emerges as an essential component of confrontational citizenship.

Over last few decades, the tide against rage seems to be turning. Radical women of color, for example, have defended rage as an important political emotion. For bell hooks, rage is "an appropriate response to injustice."[6] She encourages us to see black rage not as pathological, but as "a potentially healthy, potentially healing response to oppression and exploitation." For hooks, rage can "inspire courageous action" and be a "catalyst to develop critical consciousness." Rage, finally, can provide a "vision of militancy that is necessary for transformative revolutionary action."[7] Audre Lorde also flags the creative potential of anger: "Anger is a source of empowerment we must not fear to tap for energy rather than guilt." Lorde continues: "Focused with precision it can become a powerful source of energy serving progress and change."[8] My research builds on this innovative work but tries to take our understanding of rage further.

As we shall see in the case of Frederick Douglass, rage is a dialectical political emotion that emerges from abuse, triggers reflection, and leads to creative responses to political oppression.[9] In this sense, rage leads to an oppositional relationship to a particular political order. All forms of rage, though, are not the same. Rage becomes dialectical when one controls one's rage through self-reflection and then acts to change the circumstances that caused it. Hence, dialectical rage produces a delayed and possibly more intelligent and strategic response than blind and impulsive rage. In this regard, the rage of the slave is a fundamental but insufficient condition for overthrowing slavery. The dialectical deployment of rage is the missing piece of the puzzle.

Frederick Douglass

In order to delve deeper into the dynamics of rage, I turn to the writings of former slave Frederick Douglass (1818-95).[10] Rage led to creative forms of political resistance in Douglass and gave him a political life, but this has been missed by multiple commentators. Douglass is cast as a moral suasion abolitionist or as an activist who was not militant enough.[11] Leonard Harris, for example, argues that there is an unbridgeable gulf separating the observer from the activist, "like the difference between Douglass and Brown."[12] Harris also argues that Douglass could support radical militant slaves as a literary gesture in the "Heroic Slave," but Douglass did not have any beliefs that required him to be an insurrectionist. Similarly, Angela Davis acknowledges that Douglass was the "premier black intellectual of his time," but argues that his faith in the principles of the Enlightenment, his tendency to define freedom as access to political rights, his belief in the inevitable future progress for former slaves, and his confidence in law "blinded him to the ways in which black people were constructed, precisely through law, as only fit for slavery."[13] Charles W. Mills argues that Douglass represents the assimilationist view of African American political thought. According to Mills, Douglass "stood up for all of us," but Mills argues that Douglass's "wrath was misdirected." For Mills, Douglass's political significance was crippled by his naive faith in "official institutions" and his "myopia arising from his own identification with the White West." Douglass, moreover, took the polity to be "essentially non-racial." For Mills, "everything Douglass said was wrong."[14] Finally, Leslie Friedman Goldstein argues that Douglass embraces "all the political weapons available," but Goldstein emphasizes Douglass's "more mature views on the need for compromise in politics."[15]

Harris, as well as Davis, Goldstein, and Mills, unnecessarily back Douglass into an either/or political position (observer or insurrectionist) that does not do justice to his political life. Douglass was a fugitive and was prepared to fight. Although he backed him financially, Douglass turned down John Brown's offer to help trigger a slave insurrection because he knew it would have disastrous consequences and it did, even though Brown became a hero in the process. But Douglass was not pacifist. Pacifism could "appear to be complicit with the institution of slavery's continuation and expansion."[16] As Robert Gooding-Williams puts it, "more than one mind, more than one voice, animate Douglass's intellectual career."[17]

Indeed, Douglass's rage allowed him to engage the political world on multiple levels: organizer, leader, revolutionary, intellectual, militant, agitator, and statesman. Douglass carved out a position between pacifism and insurrection that exceeds natural rights and liberal notions of the political. Rage gave Douglass the flexibility to strategically move between the poles of the pacifism/insurrection opposition as the specific political situation required.

Douglass and Rage

For his entire life, rage was an important component of Douglass's political sensibility. Douglass's rage is visible in the intense sarcasm, irony, mockery, invective, and mimicry in his speeches and autobiographical writings, in his selective defense of violent resistance to slavery, in his fight with the slave breaker Edward Covey, and in his response to the Taney court decision in *Dred Scott*. Douglass's rage is also visible in his defense of John Brown, his defense of the killing of a deputy US marshal in Boston, and his defense of the right of slaves to kill slaveholders.[18] But let's not conclude from all of this that Douglass was a raging lunatic. Douglass's rage was not reactive but complex in how it was deployed. Douglass was aware of and experienced the double-sided character of rage as a political force. For example, Douglass was beaten unconscious by a raging mob in Pendleton, Indiana in 1843, where he lost the use of his right hand. He was again beaten by a crowd of white men in New York in 1850. Douglass's home in Rochester, New York was burned down (he suspected arson), which destroyed the only complete archives of his work in periodicals, including *North Star, Frederick Douglass's Paper*, and *Douglass's Monthly*. He was also aware of the ways in which law was a mask for white Southern rage.[19] Douglass, finally, wrote about white rage manifest in spectacular extralegal lynch mob violence.[20]

Even in the face of the dark side of rage, Douglass was dialectically propelled by rage until his death. This is evident in how Douglass performed his rage, tapped into rage to fight Covey, and in his reflections on the need for an economy of rage. Rage also gave Douglass the acumen for a political-philosophical critique of slave-plantation politics. The reflective and dialectical character of Douglass's rage never morphed into impulse-driven violent rage.

Rage on Stage

Douglass's first visit to an abolitionist meeting with William Lloyd Garrison afforded Douglass the opportunity to describe his life as a slave or stage his rage, even though Douglass ultimately broke with Garrison because Douglass wanted to have a more independent and intellectual role in the political movement and he disagreed with Garrison's interpretation of the US Constitution as an eternal slave document. At this early point in Douglass's initiation into abolitionist political associations, rage and outrage were used by abolitionists to build a sensus communis, a mass of popular support for the abolitionist cause via affective intensity. At these meetings, Douglass stepped onto the stage and described his life as a slave. As Robert Gooding-Williams claims, "Douglass's rhetorical performance of his degradation serves both aesthetic and moral ends."[21] Performing rage outraged the audience and overcame the ineffectual character of rational approaches to challenging racist common sense. Of course, abolitionists were willing to argue. African Americans could argue against slavery as much as they wanted but no one was there to listen. The ocular dimension intensified affect and worked to transform racist common sense.

Rage was an essential component of Douglass's self-presentation as someone who once lived a life as a slave but who had escaped and was in a position to tell his story to others. Focusing on how Douglass stages his rage opens up new ways to understand what it means to be an engaged (non)citizen living in dark times. In particular, Douglass insisted that his various audiences try to see the world from the vantage point of the slave in order to challenge injustice and for them to become human. Whipped, beaten, exploited, and repeatedly dehumanized, Douglass was justifiably enraged and sought to share these aspects of his life with his audiences. But Douglass was called a fraud as a result of his refined articulation and comportment during public gatherings. In response, Douglass "rhetorically invoked his own scarred back," while on stage to shock the audience into self-reflection and authenticate his experiences.[22] This is one of the ways Douglass performed or staged his rage.

There was another stage of rage but it was a sinister one. As I have already stated, Douglass knew that rage and outrage also worked in counterproductive ways. Douglass realized that white defenders of America's racial dictatorship were enraged by the abolitionists' challenge to their privilege and denunciation of America's mendacious commitment to abstract universalism. In his pamphlet called "Why Is the Negro Lynched? The Lesson of the Hour" (1894), Douglass claimed the Southern mob "in its *rage*, feeds its vengeance by shooting, stabbing, and burning their victims, when they are dead."[23] In its "*frantic rage* and savage extravagance," an African American is killed by a mob and then repeatedly desecrated to transform the murder into a spectacular public act that serves to reinforce the racial borders of citizenship through terror.[24] This was the other stage of rage, the one on which African Americans were sacrificed.[25]

If black rage was a potential time-bomb waiting to be detonated, white rage ground down tobacco-stained teeth, then triggered violence against African Americans.[26] When white passions spiraled out of control, the slave was an easy and ever-present target: "Slave-holders are so imperious when their passions are excited, as to construe every word of the slave into insolence."[27] Hence, Douglass's deployment of rage should not be mistaken for an open-ended endorsement of "passions running wild."[28] Douglass saw the rage that accompanied the beating of the slave Esther by her master for keeping company with Edward, and feared it. This hesitation about the value of rage is also clear in Douglass's article "Capt. Brown Not Insane" (1859), where he praises John Brown's "cool self-possession."[29] Brown, Douglass goes on to explain, "was neither insane or actuated by vengeful passion."[30] The fictional character Madison Washington in Douglass's "The Heroic Slave" also had the discipline and foresight to "smother his rage" and then lead a mutiny when the time was right.[31] Oppression may generate rage, but rage does not have to release itself in immediate action. Rage, with Douglass, was a dialectical force because it took an inward turn, lead to self-reflection, and then found external expression in action at opportune moments. If Douglass's rage was released in immediate action like the noble class discussed by Friedrich Nietzsche, Douglass knew he would be a dead man.[32] The temporary suppression of rage does not necessarily embitter, but can become "an investigation of whatever has caused it."[33] In this sense, rage sets reason into motion.

Narrating Rage

Rage was something more than an emotion that was staged in Douglass's life. The slave narrative was another way Douglass deployed and communicated his rage. Indeed, the slave narrative was an outlet for Douglass's rage and a rage-inducing practice. Through the narration of his life story in his writings, Douglass hoped to change the reader's perspective on slavery and broaden the sense of who qualified as a member of humanity. From his early days, Douglass tapped into his own rage, which was generated by his experience of oppression, and channeled it through the written word.

As a child, Douglass taught himself to read from a combination of street-level cleverness, interactions with Daniel Lloyd, and instruction from the wife of his owner, Sophia Auld. Ms. Auld gave Douglass a few reading lessons but discontinued them as a result of her husband's angry decree that a literate slave would be ungovernable. Douglass, though, had acquired enough of the groundwork needed to read, developed it further, and slowly acquired political consciousness and "opened his eyes."[34] Through dialectical analysis of his owner's reasons for prohibiting him from reading, Douglass realized that "education and slavery are incompatible."[35] With his newly acquired skill, Douglass read Caleb Bingham's *Columbian Orator* (1797), the Bible, documents pertaining to the American founding, and the writings of William Lloyd Garrison. Even though Douglass wanted to, he could not stop thinking. Rage started to bubble into his consciousness. Douglass slowly came to understand his wretched condition, and there were times when he "wished himself dead"[36] or wished that he had "never been born."[37]

Douglass's newly won literacy was both an exit from psychological bondage but also lead to an intensification of his rage. Douglass recounts a moment when his "blood boiled."[38] Following his conversion to Christianity, Douglass sought to teach other slaves how to read the Bible.[39] After the first meeting, his second Sunday school class for slaves was violently broken up by his master Thomas Auld and a small mob armed with rocks and sticks. The white-Christian world's moral hypocrisy intensified Douglass's awareness of the illogical nature of his status as a sentient and intellectual being trapped in the body of a politically construed nonentity. The intellectual independence that accompanied literacy in the context of slavery turned Douglass into a hybrid formation, a free man and a slave in the same body.

As time went on, the impossible duality Douglass embodied, similar to what W.E.B. Du Bois describes as the "double self" of the Negro, became unbearable. The warring affects within Douglass made him suffer, but also attracted him to the abolitionists who could become sympathetic compatriots. The abolitionist's meetings served as a place where the political struggle against slavery could be waged. Douglass was drawn to the meetings for another reason too. He was increasingly aware of his own rage and also detected the rage of the abolitionists: "I saw there was *fear*, as well as *rage*, in the manner of speaking of the abolitionists."[40]

In addition to his autobiographical writings where Douglass's rage is a ladder the reader slowly climbs, and Douglass's attraction to the rage of abolitionists, Douglass's speech given in Rochester on July 5, 1852 is infused with rage as a rhetorical device. The essence of the speech "The Meaning of July Fourth for the Negro" concerns the problem of perspective or vantage point from which one views America's political sacraments. Douglass's earlier narration of rage in his autobiographies is transformed into rage as a public incendiary device. As stated in "Capt. John Brown Not Insane," "moral considerations have long since been exhausted upon slaveholders. It is in vain to reason with them."[41] In the Fourth of July speech, the time for verbal warfare had come. Douglass's point was simple: July Fourth does not mean the same thing to everyone.

In this speech, rage is no longer an individual but a collective emotion. Douglass announces that he will speak "in the name of humanity which is outraged." Rage fuels his global appeal for emancipation. Douglass informs his audience that he will use "the severest language I can command." He condemns American political and religious institutions and targets the hypocrisy of a nation blind to its own oppressive practices. As George Shulman claims, "Douglass is arguing even as he denies the value of argument."[42] As Douglass puts it, "scorching irony, not convincing argument, is needed. . . . For it is not light that is needed, but fire; it is not the gentle shower, but thunder. . . . Your celebration is a sham. . . . For revolting barbarity and shameless hypocrisy, America reigns without a rival."[43] Douglass goes on in this speech to attack churches as participating in empty ceremony and "siding with the oppressors." American Christianity is a religion for "oppressors, tyrants, man-stealers, and thugs"; one "that favors the rich against the poor"; it says "to the man in chains, *stay there*; and to the oppressor, *oppress on*." Douglass continues: "Your republicanism is a sham, your humanity a base pretense, and your Christianity is a lie."[44] Douglass's rage took a narrative form in his autobiographies and an incendiary/rhetorical form in the Fourth of July speech. In these instances, his rage was not a psychological imbalance but a political response to America's racial dictatorship.

Tactical Rage

Rage was more than a narrative and rhetorical practice, though. Douglass's fight with Edward Covey reveals the precise ways that rage motivated Douglass and led to strategic violence. Once Douglass's owner realized the literate Douglass was becoming ungovernable and posed a threat to the slave order, he sent him to Covey, the slave breaker, who nearly worked Douglass to death and whipped him into submission every week. While under Covey's tutelage, Douglass witnessed and endured ritual brutalization as a tactic of terror used to enforce submission.

Whipping, for example, was an unquestioned component of the culture of the South: "Everybody in the South wants the privilege of whipping someone else."[45] According to Douglass, slave masters whipped those who were "most easily whipped." "He is whipped oftenest," Douglass continues, "who is whipped easiest."[46] Whipping served a dual purpose: "To be *kept* good and to be *made* good."[47] Whipping was also a public spectacle, another form of rage on stage. It was intended to produce "docile subjects."[48] Not so with Douglass; his docility while enslaved by Covey was a ruse.

After months of abuse, Douglass had had enough under Covey. Douglass decided he would no longer submit to being whipped, even if this meant his death, but Douglass bet it wouldn't, since Covey had a reputation to uphold as a successful slave-breaker not as a slave killer. In the chapter of his second autobiography called "The Last Flogging," Douglass writes about the feeling that he had "no friend on earth, and doubting if I had one in heaven,"[49] but the "embers of freedom"[50] were smoldering within him.[51] After enduring countless beatings, Douglass decided to cast aside the religious imperative not to resist his master, for "the fighting madness had come upon me."[52] One bright day Douglass was attacked by Covey. Douglass responded:

> *I was resolved to fight.* . . . My resistance was entirely unexpected, and Covey was taken all aback by it, for he trembled in every limb. . . . *"Are you going to resist,* you scoundrel?, said he. To which, I returned a polite, *"yes sir".* . . .[53]

The context described above gives the words—*yes sir*—special significance. Douglass's statement *"yes sir"* performs the two faces of his existence. On the one hand, Douglass's polite articulation of it implies acceptance of his life as an obedient slave and racial Southern etiquette. On the other hand, *"yes sir"* answers Covey's question in the affirmative as to whether Douglass would resist. Hence, it flags Douglass's subordination and simultaneously subverts it. *"Yes sir"* is a dialectical manifestation of rage because it is an utterance filled with both rage and self-control.

During the fight, Covey's assistant Hughes came to help, but Douglass gave him a blow that sent him off "bending over with pain."[54] Covey also called on slaves for assistance, but they refused and simply observed Douglass in combat: "We were all in open rebellion, that morning."[55] Covey was frightened and finally gave up after two hours of battle with the sixteen-year-old Douglass. Douglass recounts his victory:

> This battle with Mr. Covey . . . was the turning point in my *"life as a slave."* It rekindled in my breast the smoldering embers

of liberty; it brought up my Baltimore dreams, and revived a sense of my own manhood. I was a changed man after that fight. I was *nothing* before; I WAS A MAN NOW. It recalled to life my crushed self-respect and my self-confidence, and inspired me with a renewed determination to be a FREEMAN. A man, without force, is without the essential dignity of humanity.[56]

This rage, or fighting madness, "made me a freeman in fact, while I remained a slave in form." Douglass's capacity to fight back was, as Margaret Kohn states, the "key to his personhood."[57] Freedom was not the goal of the fight. Freedom was the fight. Through struggle, Douglass became individually visible to himself as a human with dignity. Indeed, force and violence constituted Douglass's dignity and lead to his "glorious resurrection."[58] If Covey attempted to try to brutalize him again, Douglass resolved to "do him serious damage."[59]

Booker T. Washington argues that Douglass was "utterly reckless of consequences" while fighting Covey.[60] I disagree. Douglass knew he had to fight Covey at the right time. Douglass also knew that his fellow slaves would not come to Covey's assistance. Additionally, Douglass knew Covey's reputation as a slave breaker would in all likelihood prevent Covey from killing him. Through the sublimation of his rage, Douglass reflected on the consequences before the fight and bet it was to his advantage to fight Covey at that precise moment. Rage and the smoldering "embers of freedom" worked with Douglass's knowledge of slave plantation politics. Rage did not blind Douglass to the consequences of resisting Covey. Yes, the "fighting madness" had come upon Douglass, but he deployed this surge of energy strategically to mitigate the potentially lethal consequences of his insubordination.

In addition to the theatrical and rhetorical dimensions of rage, Douglass's fight with Covey demonstrates how dialectical rage can lead to tactical resistance. Douglass's rage was not blinding but a dialectical force that conditioned Douglass's response to his oppression, intellectually and practically.

Rage as Critique

As I have already demonstrated, rage is not always good. Among oppressed groups, rage may lead to dangerous boomerang effects where suppressed emotions poison the human agent regardless of how hard one tries to shake them off. As long as rage had to be sublimated as a condition of survival, rage's thwarted expression in action might lead to lifelong sickness. Rage could be sublimated and expressed in political-philosophical form but the same risk of self-poisoning was in play. Douglass's rage could be "too extreme to articulate yet too amorphous to act upon."[61] He nonetheless managed to articulate his rage and act on it. The final component of Douglass's rage that I discuss is how rage fueled his political-philosophical critique of slave plantation politics.

On the slave plantation, a variety of means were used to instill and cement subjugation. To be more specific, Douglass learned that slavery depended on external or empirical manifestations of terror (e.g., the spectacle of black death), as well as interior ideological tactics to habituate the oppressed to domination, turn slaves against themselves and each other, get the subjected to participate in their domination, instill the presence of the master everywhere, abolish interiority through mind-numbing gregariousness, and enforce conceptual inversions (e.g., freedom is slavery) that snuff out the possibility of insurrection. Deception, surveillance, the illusion of omnipotence, and other mystifications were weapons used against slaves. As Douglass puts it, "Mr. Covey's *forte* consisted in his power to deceive. His life was devoted to planning and perpetuating the grossest deceptions. Everything he possessed in the shape of learning or religion, he made conform to his disposition to deceive."[62] Covey's farm was also a complex system of surveillance. Covey was everywhere, "under every tree."[63] Covey had the "faculty of making us feel that he was always present" via "adroitly managed surprises."[64] In addition to these surprises, slave owners needed to give slaves a sense that there was not an alternative to slave existence and resignation to total power. Slave owners "impressed the slave with the boundlessness of slave territory and his own illimitable power."[65]

Nevertheless, explosive divisions on the slave plantation could ignite at any moment. Hence, there was a need for the slave owners to habituate slaves to accept slavery. To accomplish this, slaves were separated from their families as children in order to make them totally dependent on their masters and to deprive them of the nurturing necessary to develop their self-confidence. Slave owners also needed to convince slaves that they were naturally inferior and hold them in their place through law, violence, terror, and divine sanction.[66] As Douglass describes in his second autobiography, moments of illusory freedom, or "holidays" were also used on the slave plantation to perpetuate the slave system and to squash the spirit of insurrection. These holidays provided a momentary release for slaves that slave owners used to perpetuate bondage. Freedom was not defined as a Kantian moment of self-legislation but as license for slaves to engage in those "wild and low sports, peculiar to semi-civilized people."[67] Excessive alcohol consumption was also encouraged during these holidays:

> I have known slaveholders resort to cunning tricks, with a view of getting their slaves deplorably drunk. A usual plan is, to make bets on a slave, that he can drink more whiskey than any other; and so to induce rivalry among them, for the mastery in this degradation. The scenes, brought about in this way, were often scandalous and loathsome in the extreme. Whole multitudes might be stretched out in brutal drunkenness, at once helpless and disgusting. Thus, when the slave asks for a few hours of virtuous freedom, his cunning master takes advantage of his ignorance, and cheers him with a dose of vicious and revolting dissipation, artfully labeled with the name of LIBERTY. . . . It was about as well to be a slave to *master*, as to be a slave to *rum* and *whiskey*.[68]

Drinking "fostered coarseness, vulgarity, and an indolent disregard for the social improvement of the place."[69] A self-undermining and slavery-perpetuating conception of freedom thrived on slave plantations that reinforced racial power relations.[70] The goal was to make slaves content, meaning thoughtless, and "darken their moral and mental vision and annihilate the power of reason."[71] In addition to sports, alcohol, fake holidays, and annihilating the capacity to imagine an alternative to the status quo, slave-owners encouraged talkative slaves. The more slaves talked, the better; a "silent slave"[72] was dangerous; silence communicated interiority.[73] Like gesticulating puppets, slaves were also trained to state how content they were and acknowledge the kindness of their masters who "take care of them."[74] Douglass was not looking for a release from slavery via a fake holiday, alcohol binge, and through mindless chatter but he sought to intensify the explosive divisions in slave society.

In sum, Douglass's exposes three strategies used on the slave plantation to perpetuate oppression. First, convince a population that there is no alternative to the present and then eliminate the capacity to envision an alternative future through enforced illiteracy and an education in submission. Second, distract the oppressed with barbaric sporting events, stupefy them with alcohol drinking games, train them to engage in mindless chatter, trick them into mistaking subjection for freedom via conceptual inversions, and erase the idea of slavery having a border. Third, keep the oppressed under constant surveillance, promote self-hatred, get slaves to worship their oppressors, darken their moral and mental vision, and summon the ideological force of religion and the legal order to naturalize and put a stamp of approval on it.

Douglass dissected these ruses of power and fought them with unflinching intensity: "Slavery is a system of brute force. It shields itself behind *might*, rather than right. It must be met with its own weapons."[75] As Douglass learned, playing by the rules can be a futile exercise that perpetuates powerlessness. Through the sublimation of his rage, Douglass articulated a political-philosophical critique of slave plantation politics, and he exposed the material and psychic modes of domination so that it could be challenged and overthrown.

As we have seen, Douglass staged or performed his rage, employed rage in narrative form in his autobiographical writings and rhetorically in his speeches, tapped into his rage during his fight with Covey, and used rage to articulate a political-philosophical critique of slave plantation politics. Douglass's life indicates that rage is not incompatible with mental clarity and productive participation in politics. Indeed, rage gave Douglass a political life. Douglass became visible to himself and others as a human with dignity and honor, exposed the horrors of the slave plantation, and targeted American hypocrisy through rage understood as a dialectical force that controlled the outward expression of anger through a process of self-reflection.

Defending Rage

Based on my analysis of rage in the life of Douglass, rage emerges as a valid source of political motivation and a fundamental component of confrontational citizenship. Hence, I oppose mainstream and liberal traditions in political theory that see rage as anathema to productive participation in public life. As I see it, rage is a basic condition of human dignity. If properly deployed, rage can contribute to meaningful and truthful public discussion, an antagonistic political culture, and can ensure the accountability of political institutions or lead to the creation of new ones if they are beyond repair. As we have seen in the case of Douglass, rage does not necessarily lead to road rage, mute and self-destructive action, and political withdrawal. If rage is deployed dialectically, it can lead to strategic militancy situated between pacifism and insurrection. Rage transformed Douglass from a victim of oppression into a threatening democratic individual who would not go away. Booker T. Washington claimed there was always "something so mysterious, as well as commanding in the manner of the young Douglass."[76] Washington arguably noticed Douglass's unique combination of reflectiveness and affective intensity. Douglass inaugurated a tradition of political resistance and rage that can inform critical political consciousness today. But Douglass did not endorse all forms of rage.

The rage of the slave-master and the racial political order he inhabits warrants critique because it is based on the lie that the ruling elite speaks for and is the entire body politic. The rage of slave owners appeared as a scowl on their faces, led to revenge against slaves to perpetuate domination, and was used to shock other slaves into submission via displays of ritualistic and spectacular violence. In contrast to the rage of the master, Douglass's rage led to actions that sought to improve the status quo for all through political engagement broadly conceived. Without the rage of the slave, no political change was possible. Rage is political when it is effectively sublimated and seeks, via action, to eradicate unequal power relations. Rage is annihilating when it seeks revenge out of a sense of injury for lost privilege and perpetuates political domination.

It could be argued that the abuses Douglass suffered are no longer in play, and so Douglass's rage and relevance are limited to the confines of his historical context or as uplifting stories for schoolchildren visiting a Smithsonian museum in Washington, DC., who can thus be thankful that we do not live in that unfortunate historical moment that permitted slavery and that rage is no longer necessary today. I disagree. Douglass believed the past is "useful to the present and to the future," which undermines this first objection because, as Michelle Alexander demonstrates, the legacy of slavery lives on today.[77]

It could also be objected that my interpretation of Douglass overstates the role of rage in Douglass's life and work and that Douglass could be more accurately regarded as a cautious militant, one who avoided the extremes of radical abolitionists like William Lloyd Garrison and John Brown. This is a legitimate point but one that misses important aspects of Douglass's life. Douglass changed and evolved as an intellectual and political activist but he never lost his militant core. Rage never blinded Douglass in the way that it did Garrison and Brown, even though Douglass respected both men. Douglass knew he might die for resisting Covey but he did it anyway. Douglass also knew it would be smart for him to travel abroad when a warrant was issued for his arrest due to his association with John Brown. Douglass was propelled by rage but never dominated by it. Living a life of rage does not rule out flexibility, although it would be too far of a stretch to call Douglass a pragmatist.[78]

Finally, it could be objected that rage is a double-edged sword and that it might not always lead to good judgment. This is a legitimate objection. As we have seen, Douglass deployed his rage strategically. Douglass was flexible when he needed to be, but he was also willing to fight when compromise was out of the question. Douglass's commitment to literacy, an ideal of freedom rooted in autonomy, as well as his awareness that passions running wild were dangerous, prevented his rage from subverting his intellect. Douglass knew that slaveholders were also enraged by the threat he posed to their existence that triggered gruesome violence, which is why Douglass does not cast rage as a panacea and neither do I. However, political change is impossible without some level of rage.

Conclusion

Douglass embraced many ways of resisting slavery politically: Tactical naïveté (following directions so literally that successful completion of a task was subverted); criminal acts; self-defense; civil disobedience; rejecting the Supreme Court's monopoly on the interpretation of the law; international travel; verbal denunciations; political organizing; agitating; sabotage; public speaking; lifelong learning; publishing. Rage is the unifying force underlying these forms of political engagement. Through rage, Douglass inserted himself as a new force in history. Douglass did not try to reach freedom as an abstract goal, but practiced freedom on a daily basis.

From the perspective of those who have no part in a political order, rage is the political emotion par excellence. But we need to be careful.

Rage is the vehicle for political change and the path to a better political future only if it is dialectically deployed and leads to self-reflection. As Joel Olson puts it, the abolitionists urged citizens to become "*more* zealous, more fanatical, and more extreme."[79] This may be true, but Douglass was a cautious and reflective person. With Douglass, the tactical deployment of rage was not a thoughtless plunge·into the abyss of violence, but generated strategic responses to oppressive political conditions.

Chapter Four
W. E. B. Du Bois on Revolt as a Way of Life

All regimes generally allow a process for excruciatingly slow change to take place because it does not threaten established power and interests. From the vantage point of the victims of American democracy, slow change means no change.[1] When no other alternative makes sense, when so-called justice seems to be yet another way a regime that was initially a racial dictatorship continues the legacy of racial oppression, marginalized groups are pushed to the breaking point.[2] As events in Chicago, Baltimore, Ferguson, Missouri, and elsewhere illustrate (as a result of video images of police brutality), all politics, but especially black politics, faces a dichotomy between the yearning for peaceful incremental change and protest for immediate redress of grievance/revolutionary transformation of the status quo. The pursuit of incremental reform, however, risks leading nowhere. Playing by the rules can perpetuate powerlessness. How can racist structures of power be challenged and transformed to achieve progressive change and prevent a conservative retreat? How can the pursuit of a new utopia avoid becoming a horrendous nightmare? W.E.B. Du Bois has a compelling answer to these questions, which is contained in the expression "revolt as a way of life."

Du Bois provides a new conceptualization of revolt that overcomes the opposition between incrementalism and the radical overturning of the regime.[3] For his entire life, Du Bois placed himself on the fault lines, hit raw nerves, and in the process he became America's bad conscience who simply would not go away. An indicted criminal, denied a passport, called a dangerous person by Theodore Roosevelt, prevented for a time from leaving the United States, shunned by the academic establishment, forced to retire from Atlanta University, ultimately relocating to Ghana before his death shortly thereafter, Du Bois practiced revolt as a way of life.[4] For Du Bois, fighting for political change was not a one-time moment of conflict but a lifelong battle. As Du Bois states in "Methods of Attack," the "real battle is a matter of study and thought; of the building up of loyalties; of the long training of men; of the growth of institutions; of the inculcation of racial and national ideals. It is not a publicity stunt. *It is a life.*"[5] Du Bois is thus an intellectual committed to politically relevant academic work and the struggle to make the world a better place. He is a thinker who practiced revolt as a way of life and helps us think beyond the dichotomy between reform and revolution. Revolt as a way of life, Du Bois shows us, is one of the forms confrontational citizenship can take.

At different moments, revolt for Du Bois was psycho-spiritual, existential, and Marxist, or a mix of all three, evolving dialectically in response to the particular historical moment. This makes it difficult to pin down the exact meaning of revolt in Du Bois's work or posit one trans-historical concept of revolt that captures Du Bois's entire life.[6] Hence, my intent here is not to force a static definition on the concept of revolt in Du Bois but to show how the concept of revolt unfolds throughout Du Bois's work and to make the case for a broader understanding of revolt in Du Bois. This sets the stage for a critique and confrontation with how the militant is cast by liberal theorists.

Nancy L. Rosenblum, for example, characterizes the militant as an unproductive and infantile extremist, as intolerant, reactive, and lacking judgment, a person who, in the name of moral purity, willfully refuses to compromise.[7] For Rosenblum, the militant wages a personal war against the world but it is a war driven by impotence and powerlessness.[8] By rejecting Rosenblum's negative caricature of the militant, and the opposition between the ideal liberal subject and extremist/militant that frames it, I build the case for a thoughtful mode of militancy that disrupts the binary created by Rosenblum (and the one between reform and revolution). Hence, I seek to broaden the permissible range of political action beyond the institutional and incremental parameters set by Rosenblum's form of status quo liberal theory.[9] As we shall see in the case of Du Bois, it is a mistake to put moderation and tolerance on one end of the binary and uncompromising militancy at the other. Thoughtful revolt (as a way of life) is an option missed by Rosenblum and may turn out to be the only wise form of political action, especially for individuals and groups whose voices have been historically excluded from the political institutions claimed to be open to everyone.[10]

Indeed, revolt as a way of life is good because it leads to positive change, it allows pent up anger resulting from past and present oppression to be vented, it builds collective solidarity against oppression, and creates a better foundation for a political regime. Even though Du Bois seems to prefer moderate approaches to correcting the race problem in America, Du Bois as time went on gravitated to revolt as a way of life as a call to explore all available options for social, political, and economic transformation to improve race relations.[11]

W. E. B. Du Bois

Born in Great Barrington, Massachusetts, on February 23, 1868, William Edward Burghardt "W.E.B." Du Bois was an academic, activist, historian, poet, sociologist, and pan-Africanist who dedicated his life to fighting for people of color. Du Bois attained a classical liberal arts education at Fisk University, continued his education at Harvard University, where he was mentored by William James, and then Du Bois studied in Berlin at Humbolt University. For his entire life Du Bois continued to study, write, and fight for people of color positioned at the bottom of the social order.

Du Bois had a long and distinguished teaching career, and he was also constantly engaged with progressive political movements. He taught at Wilberforce University, Atlanta University, and joined the Niagra Movement. In 1910, Du Bois joined the NAACP and became editor of its magazine, *The Crisis*. Du Bois received the International Peace Prize and Lenin Peace Prize. Since Du Bois was denied a passport by the US government (1952–58), he could not travel abroad for speaking engagements during this time. Du Bois's intellectual accomplishments and productivity as an author were massive and reflected his evolving understanding of the role of value commitments in research, the global significance of racial problems, and opportunities for progressive social and political transformation. On August 29, 1963, Du Bois died in Accra, Ghana. Du Bois lived through the failure of Reconstruction, World War I, the Red Scare, World War II, the Depression, and McCarthyism, but never surrendered his critical voice. Du Bois practiced revolt as a way of life which is the most important aspect of his legacy and contribution to contemporary political thought.

Black Revolt: Historical Context

The word *revolt* had a special meaning and value for Du Bois and is invoked throughout his work. *Revolt*, unlike the word *revenge*, captures the political act of resistance, withholding allegiance, as well as the affective state of being revolted and disgusted.[12] Revolt is active; revenge is born of reactive weakness.[13] Revolt as a way of life does not refer to the call for "war, force, and revolution," but should be understood as a tactical political stance involving a permanent and protracted dissent against the concentration of wealth, the legacies of imperialism/colonialism, and rejection of political oppression and racism.[14] As we shall see in the case of Du Bois, *revolt* is a word that is never exhausted by conventional understandings and practices but assumes new forms when it runs up against walls. This creative dimension to revolt is evident in the rich traditions of African American revolt in the United States. Because of the centrality of revolt as a defining aspect of the African American experience, they have been and remain one of the most strategic groups for bringing about progressive political change.[15] For Du Bois, revolt was not a one-time moment of resistance but a way of life.

Historically speaking, the most important changes in the legally marginalized status of black people in the United States resulted from radical action, not from patience and restraint.[16] The US Constitution was a weapon of mass destruction used against African Americans to institutionalize their subordinate status. A legal racial caste system was not an afterthought or oversight but was the essence of the US Constitution and determined legal representation (e.g., Three-Fifths Compromise), the protection of all forms of property including human property (e.g., Fifth Amendment), and set up the federal government to suppress all forms of rebellion, especially slave rebellions. African Americans, as a result of this, were an internally colonized population set up for unlimited economic exploitation, denied political voice, and were considered to be expendable subhumans. If African Americans wanted political change, they had to challenge the legitimacy of the entire social and political order that was grounded on the protection of property. As human property, slaves embodied an impossible contradiction.[17] Their freedom required the negation of the regime grounded on the protection of property rights; it would not come in any other way.

Backed into a political corner by the US Constitution as a result of their legally codified subhuman status, African Americans had no choice but to fight every aspect of the political status quo. Hence, revolt, broadly understood, is a defining feature of black life and politics.[18] And Du Bois makes it clear that *revolt* means more than one thing: "The Negro revolted by armed rebellion, by sullen refusal to work, by poison and murder, by running away to the North and Canada, by giving point and powerful examples to the agitation of the abolitionists and by furnishing 200,000 soldiers and many times as civilian helpers in the Civil War."[19] From insurrections aboard slave ships led by kidnapped Africans, to revolts on forced labor camps and plantations, to secret networks of escape, to acts of desertion and running away, to abolitionist agitation, to armed insurrection, to exposés on lynching, the creation of independent periodicals dedicated to correcting academic mendacity against African Americans, and nonviolent civil disobedience, the idea of revolt has been and remains essential to black political action as a way to force recognition of grievance and as a strategy for political change.[20]

For African Americans, revolt was also a matter of basic survival and injected life and power into pleas for equal treatment and the acquisition of political voice. As Lawrie Balfour puts it, "African Americans have historically had no public language to make their suffering audible to white ears."[21] African American invisibility and denial of voice was institutionally and politically sanctioned and produced cold indifference to their plight among whites, especially poor whites who competed with African Americans for employment. Even though this fundamentally contradicted the language of universality in the Declaration of Independence and US Constitution, it was simply easier to live a lie than it was to acknowledge the presence of African Americans as human. This is what Du Bois calls the "American Blind Spot" for the Negro and his problems, a mode of being premised on rendering the black population invisible, expendable, and irrelevant, which in turn makes logical argument about race relations impossible.[22] In addition to omission by willful blindness, collective mendacity, and fake universality, black agency has been excluded from the historical record to perpetuate the ideology of racial dictatorship masquerading as freedom, which impoverishes discussions about race relations.[23]

Du Bois: Political Moderate or Theorist of Revolt?

Most commentators on Du Bois emphasize the moderate, pragmatist, and reformist character to his political views. These aspects are definitely present in Du Bois's work. However, there are also radical currents.

Du Bois was a subtle thinker and never articulated his political positions in a simplistic and straightforward manner. Du Bois's apparent ambivalence about revolt and revolution conceals a deep commitment to radical political change. True, Du Bois argues for a "union of intelligence and sympathy across the color-line" and that a better understanding of the contributions of black folk to America will crack through prejudice and allow whites to see them as human.[24] Du Bois also claims that a spirit of "calm, patient persistence" in their attitude toward fellow citizens will bring about change, and that revolution represents a "lowering of ideals."[25] Also, consider Du Bois's pacifism, his glorification of liberal European culture and education, his aristocratic comportment, his defense of self-realization, his philosophy of the talented tenth, his renunciation of violence to bring about political change, and his words on the ineffectiveness of "sudden assault."[26] These aspects suggest that the commentators who argue Du Bois is moderate, pragmatist, and reformist are right.

However, it is also important to remember that Du Bois's writings span more than seven decades and that he frequently altered his viewpoints. At one time, for example, Du Bois defended the knowledge generated by social science because he thought this knowledge would convince white America that African Americans were human. However, he gave up on the power of social science to change minds as a result of the horrific torture and execution of Sam Hose in Newman, Georgia while Du Bois was teaching at Atlanta University. Du Bois states: "One could not be a calm, cool, and detached scientist while Negroes were lynched, murdered and starved; and secondly, there was no such definite demand for scientific work of the sort that I was doing."[27] Additionally, given how long Du Bois lived and how closely he was watched, it was often necessary to craft his arguments in ways that implied his political position by intimation, negative presentation, or via the process of elimination, as opposed to the direct proclamation of his political positions.[28] Finally, Du Bois's subtle theoretical style has been arguably clouded by scholars who are quick to classify him within conventional political categories (e.g., pragmatism; elitism), which does not do justice to the complex and evolving character of his work.[29]

Much of the scholarly research on Du Bois has brought him into the forefront as the most important African American intellectual in the twentieth century.[30] Nevertheless, Du Bois's politics, according to most of these commentators, is punctuated by a deep pragmatism, as opposed to a philosophy of revolt.[31] I challenge this position and contest interpretations of Du Bois that claim he is politically moderate. I build the outline of Du Bois's theory of revolt through close analysis of his political writings. Given the frequent references to revolt, insurrection, Haiti, and uprisings throughout Du Bois's work, and the fact that he wrote a book-length manuscript that was sympathetic to John Brown, and the enormous energy Du Bois dedicated to triggering black radical agency, there is sufficient reason to explore the idea of revolt as a way of life in Du Bois.[32]

Revolt

Du Bois created a new language for understanding the connections between race, class, citizenship, and revolt in the global context. For Du Bois, the African American experience is a "record of attempts at revolt."[33] In order to see the importance the concept of revolt plays in Du Bois's work, one has to take a comprehensive view of him. This is only possible if one gives relatively equal value to Du Bois's major and minor writings, as opposed to *Souls* serving as the primary text and center of gravity for understanding his work.[34] According to Rampersad, "the idea of revolt among the darker races of the world against the power of Europe and America had long intrigued Du Bois."[35]

Du Bois has a complex understanding of revolt, and it is explicitly and indirectly present in all of his writings. At times, revolt is a haunting shadow of violent insurrection; at other moments, revolt takes the form of retelling the history of black agency in America. Du Bois's earliest academic work contested the dominant narratives of American political history that minimize the importance of slavery. Du Bois demonstrates that slavery was not an accidental or minor departure from US ideals, but the defining feature of American democracy. In *Black Reconstruction*, he analyzes the role of black agency played in the transformation of American democracy. By providing an alternative narrative of the relationship between democracy and slavery at the origin of the American regime, on the one hand, and highlighting the role played by slaves during the Civil War, on the other, Du Bois set the stage for a completely new understanding of American democracy. It was an understanding of American democracy that hinged on seeing the centrality of black agency as a force for political transformation.

Democracy as Revolt or, Look! A "Free" Negro

For Du Bois, capitalism and slavery were interconnected systems of oppression.[36] Slave owners worked slaves to death, since it was cheaper to replace a physically broken slave with a new one than it was to nurse one back to life. The tradition of unlimited exploitation of slaves continued as the unlimited exploitation of newly "freed slaves" after the Civil War. For African Americans, freedom was an empty word. Juridical freedom, Du Bois indicates in the following quote, is essentially worthless if it is viewed as an end in itself and lacks a material dimension: "Not a cent of money, not an inch of land, not a mouthful of victuals,—not even ownership of the rags on his back. Free!"[37] The word *freedom* was spoken with a forked tongue when it came to former slaves, insofar as "freedom" signified new forms of oppression for black people after the end of slavery. As Du Bois put it, "a free Negro was a contradiction, a threat and a menace. As a thief and vagabond, he threatened society; but as an educated property holder, a successful mechanic or even professional man, he more than threatened slavery. He contradicted and undermined it."[38] "Freedom" was simultaneously a whip, a rhetorical power play, as well as a lure to keep blacks chasing something they would never reach while whites stood by with their arms akimbo and said "Keep running after it. You are almost there."

For Du Bois, it was necessary to view the story of American democracy and freedom from the vantage point of those who "have had their faces ground in the mud."[39] If your face was pounded into the mud, the meaning of freedom was inseparable from combat against a narrowly defined juridical notion of freedom that still permitted economic exploitation of the freed people and mobilized a reign of terror to enforce it. Interpreting democracy and freedom from the perspective of slaves was essential for Du Bois for expanding intellectual and historical horizons. The collision between slavery and democracy, according to Du Bois, set the stage for a distinctly American version of democracy: "It was the rise and growth among the slaves of a determination to be free and an active part of American democracy," he asserts, "that forced American democracy continually to look into the depths."[40] Du Bois continues: "The motive force of democracy has nearly always been the push from below rather than the aristocratic pull from above."[41] Yet again, he goes on to declare that "the Negro in the US has emancipated democracy, reconstructed the threatened edifice of freedom and been a sort of eternal test of the sincerity of our democratic ideals."[42] In the first two quotes, freedom and force work together. The determination to be free for those who have been excluded, Du Bois suggests, forced Americans to analyze the foundation of the regime. In the final quote, he claims, the Negro's presence served as a reminder of the extent and depth of the hypocrisy of the American state, flagged the need to free democracy from itself, and rebuild freedom. For African Americans, democracy was not a static institution but a continuous practice of revolt against official definitions and practices.

Critique and Truth Telling as Modes of Revolt

From his earliest writings to his final more autobiographical ones, Du Bois was a fierce critic of the United States. The assumption of African American inferiority was embedded in the American psyche and passed down to new generations by centuries of social conditioning. Hence, relying on the goodwill of the white majority to improve the plight of African Americans was a dead end. American democracy needed intelligent critics to save it. Indeed, Du Bois maintained that "criticism is the soul of democracy."[43] Action was needed to materialize it in the political sphere. In the economic sphere, the strike, or the threat of the strike, was for Du Bois the only way to inject democracy into the workplace.[44]

Critique for Du Bois was needed and employed to make African Americans aware of themselves as political agents. Du Bois had to chip away at the personality type African Americans acquired under the social, political, and economic conditions of American racial apartheid. In a similar way that it was diagnosed by Frantz Fanon in *The Wretched of the Earth* for colonized African populations, Du Bois showed that African Americans had internalized a debilitating inferiority complex and were alienated from themselves.[45] African Americans viewed themselves from the standpoint of their dominators and had a double self. For Du Bois, "such a double life, with double thoughts, double duties, and double social classes, must give rise to double words and double ideals, and tempt the mind to *pretense or revolt*, to hypocrisy or to radicalism."[46] Because African Americans saw themselves through the eyes of white Americans, they developed a psychological complex consisting of self-hatred and mental distress that inhibited the development of positive self-consciousness and also turned them into ticking time-bombs. The former psychological state negated African American agency; the latter explosive personality risked pushing African Americans into the hands of lynch mobs. Chipping away at the personality sickness acquired by African Americans living in the United States was a key component of Du Bois's academic work.

A critique of establishment narratives of American history was also central to Du Bois. The chapter in *Black Reconstruction* called "The Propaganda of History" makes this clear. Du Bois was forced to retell the history of the presence of African Americans on American soil to widen the discussion of available political options, so blacks could see themselves outside of the subhuman identity imposed on them by their white oppressors. Through writing an unwritten history about the slave trade, civil war, and the daily lives of African Americans in Philadelphia, Du Bois gave African Americans examples of heroic greatness, perseverance, and resilience. He shattered the myths perpetuated by racist historiography that African Americans had accomplished nothing, were incapable of accomplishing anything, were without culture/history, and were in need of the perpetual benevolent guidance of the white world.[47] Indeed, Du Bois philosophized with a hammer: "My stinging hammer blows made Negroes aware of themselves, confident in their possibilities and determined in self-assertion."[48] Democratic regimes, if they were to have a future, must be willing to strike themselves with the same hammer. For Du Bois, democracy named a form of energy kept alive by critique and truth telling: "We must complain. Yes, plain, blunt complaint, ceaseless agitation, unfailing exposure of dishonesty and wrong—this is the ancient, unerring way to liberty, and we must follow it."[49] African Americans, if they were to change their life conditions, had to become aware of their own "strategic global significance."[50] A historical understanding of their accomplishments gave African Americans a different perspective that led to their own self-affirmation. The weapons of critique and truth telling were deployed by Du Bois to lay the groundwork for his defense of revolt as a way of life.

Revolt and Pedagogy

In addition to his interrogation and condemnation of the limited character of juridical freedom and his attempt to rebuild black agency through the hammer blows of his pen via critique and truth telling, pedagogy is also an important unifying thread throughout all of the works of Du Bois pertinent to the concept of revolt. As Du Bois states, "all human problems center in the Immortal Child and his education is the problem of problems."[51] Moreover, Du Bois's disagreement and debate with Booker T. Washington was the result of incompatible visions of the educational needs of African Americans.[52] For Du Bois, education had to be reconceived as a democratic and truthful practice that interpreted the world from the vantage point of the oppressed and was grounded in the needs of particular communities.[53] This would give marginalized groups the intellectual resources and confidence to contest their oppression. Education for life, in contrast to an education in training, prepared an individual for self-actualization and militant citizenship. An education in training was ultimately an education in submission to reigning societal prejudices, since one would lack the intellectual resources to think independently. One would be unable to contest practices that were viewed as neutral and prepolitical by whites but were designed to perpetuate white racial privilege. As Herbert Aptheker puts it, "Du Bois saw education (to be truly education) as partisan and—given the realities of the social order—fundamentally subversive."[54]

For Du Bois, a true education centered on self-cultivation that served as the necessary preconditions for lifelong learning and political agency. A true education yields, among other things, self-confidence and intellectual independence. Education was thus a permanent destabilizing force: "Education will always have an element of danger and revolution, of dissatisfaction and discontent."[55] For Du Bois, education should make one unfit to be a slave, as opposed to cementing those at the bottom into a fixed place.

For Du Bois, education was a weapon connected to political struggle. Oppressive regimes depend on a network of lies, mystifications, and brainwashing to socialize exploited and oppressed groups into accepting their poverty, marginalization, and powerlessness as natural, a result of individual choice, and a neutral consequence of a system that is proclaimed to be free and open to all individuals.[56] In this sense, educational institutions reflect and perpetuate reigning power relations. Du Bois exposed and criticized the widespread academic complicity in the degradation of African Americans.[57] Negative representations that ranged from the homogenization of an entire group of people, negative caricatures and stereotypes, and "scientific" or biological claims of inferiority/criminality were employed.[58] For Du Bois, "the exploitation and almost universal underestimation of Africans have led to wide denial of the very existence of their history and culture."[59] Without a history and culture of their own, African Americans' history and culture was written by their oppressors, erased, or ignored and then filled in when necessary by reigning prejudice.

It was absolutely essential in this regard for Du Bois to write the unwritten history of African Americans and disseminate this counter-propaganda throughout the United States and the world. For Du Bois, "little effort has been made to preserve the records of Negro effort and speeches, action, work, and wages, homes and families."[60] As the massive section of *Black Reconstruction* on white historical versions of the Civil War illustrate, history was used to distort not to educate.[61] Du Bois sought to correct accounts that ignored the contributions made by the former slaves to American democracy. With Du Bois, an undeniable connection exists between the representation of marginalized groups, pedagogy, and politics. Shifting one's perspective from the viewpoint of the dominant group to the viewpoint of the marginalized becomes a subversive act and condition of progressive social change. America's pedagogy of oppression and brainwashing based on the denial of black humanity had to be replaced by a pedagogy of revolt based on truth telling, positive representations of black culture, and the role black agency played in the transformation of the United States.

White Democracy, White Capitalism

Despite his defense of thoughtful revolt, Du Bois knew the chances for the successful social and political transformation of the United States were slim. Du Bois would nonetheless never give up. For Du Bois, a "religion of whiteness" (the conviction that "white" meant good, innocent, and pure) was an essential component of the American creed that cemented the racial caste system into place.[62] The legal construction of the white race in America gave the white majority a superiority complex. This complex was predicated on keeping former slaves in their place.[63] For Du Bois, "the masters feared their former slaves' success far more than their anticipated failure," because this would shatter the intellectual justification for the racial caste system.[64] Divided by race hatred as a way to redirect and transfer the glance of poor whites away from their capitalist exploiters, the white working-class and the Negro existed in a hostile symbiotic relationship. When African Americans were not being harassed by the police or lynched, "the Negro became Court Jester to the ignorant American mob."[65] The poor white South also played a strategic role in the perpetuation of the racial caste system. For Du Bois: "The poor white south—it became the instrument by which democracy in the nation was done to death, race provincialism deified, and the world delivered to plutocracy."[66] For Du Bois, fear of unemployment, not an innate racist gene, is what grounded the mob spirit against African Americans.[67]

For Du Bois, American democracy emerged as a static and intolerant political form. In terms of basic attitudes toward current and freed slaves, the psychology and intellectual disposition of Americans was the result of a long process of cultural, political, and social conditioning. As a result of their unlimited power over other humans, Southerners walked with their chests puffed out and with an arrogant strut. The Southerner expected, if not demanded, total deference and obedience:

> The psychological effect of slavery on the Southern planter was fatal. They expected deference and self-abasement; they were easily insulted and choleric. Their honor became a vast an awful thing, requiring wide and insistence deference. Such of them as were inherently weak and inefficient were all the more easily angered, jealous, and resentful; while the few who were superior conceived no bounds to their power and personal prestige. Nothing is so calculated to ruin human nature as absolute power over human beings.[68]

The weakest of the Southerners "were all the more easily angered." African Americans were the permanent targets of their resentment. This attitude toward African Americans was the fruit of deeply held assumptions that went at least as far back to the racist ideas and views of Thomas Jefferson, James Madison, George Washington, and others.[69]

Democracy conceived as healthy debate and criticism was massacred on the shores of the racial caste system. Capitalism exacerbated the problem. For Du Bois, "a dictatorship of capital was arising."[70] Du Bois continues: "Northern industry murdered democracy."[71] The entrenched "intolerance and arrogance of the South" combined with the "complacent Philistinism of the North" made political change unlikely.[72] Democracy depended on conflicting ideas for its life force but the American habituation to slothful mental and moral reflection debilitated it. Americans were "morally emasculated and mentally hogtied." Du Bois continues: the "healthy difference of opinion which leads to the discovery of truth under changing conditions" was stifled.[73]

Fear of Domestic and International Race Revolt

The unwillingness of whites to shift their perspective influenced how Du Bois presented the problem of race in his work. The specter of revolt, Du Bois thought, might provide the needed push for political change. This specter came from the domestic and international context. In addition to the connections between revolt, democracy, critique, and education that were central categories in Du Bois's work, he played on the white fear of a black revolt that existed in the United States.[74] As Du Bois puts it, "the memory of John Brown stands today as a mighty warning to his country."[75]

Du Bois thus summons the specter of an uneducated, angry, revenge-driven newly freed mass of armed strong black men who had nothing to lose: "There was the black man looming like a dark ghost on the horizon. He was the child of force and greed, and the father of wealth and war."[76] Even earlier than *Black Reconstruction*, though, Du Bois summoned the specter of violent revolt: "The fear of that great bound beast was ever there—a nameless, haunting dread that never left the South and never ceased, but ever nerved the remorseless cruelty of the master's arm."[77] Du Bois continues, "no secure civilization can be built in the South with the Negro as an ignorant, turbulent proletariat."[78] The extremes of the Negro problem were "careless ignorance and laziness" and "fierce hate and vindictiveness."[79]

Fear of revolt defined the identity of the Southerner and was a form of bad conscience that lurked just below the surface of the face of agrarian refinement. "It is not so much that they fear that the Negro will strike if he gets a chance," Du Bois claimed, "but rather that they assume with curious unanimity that he has reason to strike."[80] Du Bois forced the issue to a clear head: "You have no choice; either you must help furnish this race from within its own ranks with thoughtful men of trained leadership, or you must suffer the evil consequences of a headless misguided rabble."[81] Du Bois continues: "Men go wild and fight for freedom with bestial ferocity when they must—where there is no other way."[82]

In addition to these warnings about an angry black proletariat with nothing to lose rising up, the threat of revolt is also present and organizes the outlines of Du Bois's first major work. In *The Suppression of the African Slave-Trade to the United States of America, 1638-1870*, Du Bois makes it clear that a new perspective was needed to help America see itself through the eyes of the millions it continued to oppress. *Suppression* was Du Bois's doctoral dissertation at Harvard University, and though it was indeed written while at Harvard, it does not reflect the cultural elitism and extreme conservatism of the institution. Because *Suppression* was written in a detached social scientific style, this has the counterintuitive result of intensifying its subject. In a manner that is similar to *Black Reconstruction*, which draws attention to the global significance of the reconstruction of American democracy to include freed slaves, *Suppression* documents the international character of the slave trade and the essential role played by slavery in creating America as a land of unlimited exploitation. When the slave-trade was outlawed in the United States, American slave ships sailed on and employed the "fraudulent use of the flag."[83] That is, slave ships lowered the American flag and raised the flag of a different country, not out of allegiance to Spain or Portugal, but to avoid being inspected so human trafficking could continue unabated.[84] Given the immense profits of the slave trade, and the political power of the Southern states, the US federal government simply refused to enforce the legal statutes ending slavery. The political and economic context of the slave-trade provided the frame for a basic point Du Bois makes in *Suppression*. The presence of a servile class is a serious danger, especially during times of war and insurrection.[85] Since the servile class was defined as outside but lived inside the regime, slaves would have good reason to join the cause of an invader or become recruits for domestic revolutionaries. A recent international event was also a cause for concern.

"Discovered" by Christopher Columbus in 1492, San Domingo (known today as Haiti) served as colonial outpost and center of the slave trade for the Spanish, British, and French. As a result of the European "civilizing" mission, the native population on San Domingo was massacred (reduced from 500,000 to 60,000 in fifteen years) and African slaves were drained from Africa and shipped to the island.[86] Revolts on the island were not uncommon and were practiced in a variety of ways, including disruption at major ports and via poisoning.[87] The major revolt, however, flared up at the end of the eighteenth century, inspired by core ideals of the French Revolution, and led by Toussaint L'Ouverture. Initiated in 1791, and finally independent in 1804 as a result of defeating the British, Spanish, and French, Haiti was born, the name change signifying the black revolt. For Du Bois, the revolt of Haitian slaves led by "Toussaint the Savior," as he put it, "shook the world with bloody revolt."[88] Although violent outbreaks may have been infrequent and usually unsuccessful, Du Bois expresses the issue clearly: "The flare of Haiti lighted the night and made the world remember that these, too, were men."[89] Given the need to keep slaves in their place, it is not surprising that the United States refused to recognize Haiti after the slave revolt and only did so nearly seven decades later (in 1862) by President Lincoln.[90] Because of increasing cases of runaway slaves, uprisings on slave ships, the fact that the white population was outnumbered by slaves in South Carolina and Virginia, whites had good reason to fear slave rebellions and a vengeful massacre of the white oppressive class. Du Bois knew that drawing attention to the fires lit in the past by militant slaves had disturbing contemporary relevance.

Du Bois also argued that revolt was not a regional matter, as many white Northerners wanted to believe, but a geopolitical volcano.[91] The question of the future for Du Bois was "how best to keep these millions from brooding over the wrongs of the past."[92] White America, Du Bois believed, continued to avoid the truth: "Whether you like it or not the millions are here, and here they will remain. If you do not lift them up, they will pull you down."[93] The question of the enfranchisement of the former slaves was also a matter that Du Bois connected to the idea of revolt: "Given a mass of ignorance and poverty, is that mass less dangerous without the ballot?"[94]

Fear of "the great bound beast" was a permanent paranoia complex for white Americans and led to preemptive violence against African Americans.[95] When Du Bois addressed African Americans, he presented the political stakes: "American Negroes must themselves *force* their race into the new economic set up and bring with them the millions of West Indians and Africans or else drift into greater poverty until there is no resort but the last red alternative of revolt, revenge, and war."[96] For Du Bois, "such mental frustration cannot indefinitely continue. Someday it may burst in fire and blood. *Who will be to blame?*"[97]

According to Melvin Rogers, Du Bois "did not advance the threat of a race war and bloody violence to stimulate white Americans to action."[98] I disagree, because the evidence suggests otherwise. It is not that Du Bois promoted a race war, but Du Bois reminded white Americans that a race war was the natural result of bottled black resentment and the "mounting fury of shackled men."[99] The cause of the revolt Du Bois warned might someday come is how the dominant group was treating the oppressed. Oppressive practices push the oppressed to the point where a violent revolt is the only course of action available to them.[100] The way

Du Bois framed the problem of race was intended to stimulate white Americans to change.

Du Bois, however, was always careful about how he positioned himself in relation to radical positions. Du Bois feared that a revenge driven Fanonian style uprising would fail and invite a brutal backlash. The form of revolt Du Bois promoted was more radical than a spectacular one-time explosion of rage. A lifelong commitment to a thoughtful mode of revolt was the only path that made sense to Du Bois. Even so, at a rare moment—and placed in Du Bois's poem "The Riddle of the Sphinx"—intense rage lurked beneath his calm demeanor: "I hate them, Oh! I hate them well, I hate them, Christ! As I hate Hell. If I were God I'd sound their knell, This Day!"[101]

Revolt as a Way of Life

Nourished by the economic and political foundation of the country, and by a propaganda apparatus that assured white Americans former slaves were inferior, racism became, and to some extent remains, an unconscious and conditioned American reflex. Du Bois states: "The present attitude of whites is much more the result of inherited customs and of those irrational and partly subconscious actions of men which control so large a proportion of their deeds."[102] Just like Pavlov's salivating dogs, racism was triggered by cues that operated below the realm of cognitive awareness.[103] Hence, it would take time to route it out. "Attitudes cannot be changed," Du Bois claims, "by sudden assault."[104]

Du Bois gravitated to the idea of revolt broadly conceived as a result of his realization that no single strategy for political change was complete. Indeed, the reduction of politics to protest was naive because protest cannot be maintained indefinitely.[105] Relying on incremental reform to correct racial problems was also a dead end, because it was not possible to reform a political system that was fundamentally corrupt. Protracted struggle, education, activism, historical inquiry, truth-telling, critique, and a new perspective were needed. Even though Du Bois purchased a shotgun for self-defense and promised to "spray the guts on the grass" of anyone who attacked his family, he knew that armed resistance against the hostile white majority was a limited strategy for success. The situation was so dire that, as Du Bois puts it, there was even a "hopelessness of physical defense."[106] Running away was also limited due to the reach of the global capitalist-racist order. A new foundation and justification for political and economic life was needed to set the world on a life-affirming path. In the meantime, the only option was revolt as a way of life.

Revolt as a way of life was not a repeatable practice but a form of tactical political boldness and commitment to political change. Du Bois embodied revolt as a way of life in his voice as an author, in his appearance, as a political theorist, as a public intellectual, and stylistically in his writings. Yes, he was bookish and dressed in an elegant manner, but this was how Du Bois lived and practiced the contradiction that his being African American in the United States imposed on him. Du Bois defended the value of individual autonomy, but knew that for African Americans collective struggle was needed. Revolt as a way of life is thus an imperative of individuality as well as a call to cultivate collective political consciousness and solidarity grounded in a historical understanding of the history of people of color.

Fighting for political change was not a moment of conflict for Du Bois but a lifelong battle. For Du Bois, the "the real battle is a matter of study and thought; of the building up of loyalties; of the long training of men, of the growth of institutions. It is not a publicity stunt. *It is a life.*"[107] The liveliness of one's life was constituted by the depth of one's resistance to injustice. Revolt, then, was not a political position but the defining feature of one's identity, an identity that was itself in a state of permanent revolt. This involved actively resisting double consciousness, transcending self-hatred, disrupting stereotypes, and advocating political struggle by any and all means. Du Bois practiced revolt as a way of life to such an extent that he nearly refused to die: "At 75 my death was practically requested."[108] He lived twenty more years. And Du Bois would fight until the bitter end: "Either extermination root and branch or absolute equality. There can be no compromise. This is the last great battle of the West."[109]

Militant Citizens

Revolt as a way of life does not and probably will never receive universal acclaim. Let's turn to some critiques of it. Heinz Eulau's critique of the militant citizen allows us to grapple with the possible limits of this mode of confrontational citizenship.[110] For the World War II propaganda analyst for the US Department of Justice, assistant editor of the *New Republic*, and former APSA president, the militant's self-righteous indignation and employment of individual conscience as the supreme guide to political action blinds the militant to the "democratic conception of politics as a never-ending process of compromise and adjustment."[111] For Eulau, the militant's "individualism could not possibly find practical application."[112] The militant was more rhetorical and literary than political and it "remains unclear just what specific political means [the militant] considered appropriate to achieve objectives."[113] Nancy L. Rosenblum posits a similar critique of the militant.[114] Rosenblum claims that what interests the militant is "antagonism and uncompromisingness as a way of life."[115] For Rosenblum, the militant has a "romantic loathing of existing institutions."[116]

I disagree with Eulau's and Rosenblum's condemnation of militant citizenship because it closes a space for principled dissent and this has negative implications for a vibrant democratic society.[117] The opposition between the fanatical militant (revolutionary) and the reasonable citizen (reformer) that structures Eulau's and Rosenblum's critique of the militant risks obscuring and possibly negating precisely what is valuable about the life and work in Du Bois. The world is not as black and white, as Eulau and Rosenblum assume. Du Bois occupies a more nuanced political position than Eulau and Rosenblum allow, because he keeps reform and revolution on the table as viable political options without getting stuck on either side of the opposition.

By dismissing the militant citizen Eulau and Rosenblum's work easily slides into an ideological justification for the status quo, one where a pastoral imperative rules the day in which liberal ascetic priests calm the masses into passivity and experts and consultants barter and compromise about which incremental changes to make to public policy.[118] But in order to accomplish this, militant citizens have to be ignored and dismissed, or worse, purged, so true dialogue can take place. That is to say, the liberal public sphere depends on a Hobbesian moment of "casting out of civil society members who are cumbersome thereunto."[119] For Eulau and Rosenblum, the militant citizen's "reign of inner sensibility" is too much to take; her opposition to "actual laws and institutions" is abhorrent.[120] The militant's anti-institutionalism derives from "his simplistic understanding of politics, according to which no strategy besides personal outrage and self-assertion is imaginable."[121] The extremist, Rosenblum claims, "takes one idea or aim to its limit."[122]

As disruptive as militant citizens might be, the impatience Rosenblum has with principled dissent easily leads to justifications for the criminalization of dissent. Today, consider that the vague and endless "war on terror" is used to block and/or prevent peaceful protests, track the behavior and movement of dissenting individuals through sophisticated surveillance technology, and is employed to create a paralyzing culture of fear. Also consider that the only available political options for the American people are the Republican and Democrat political parties, and both promote endless war, the indefinite detention of terror suspects in secret prisons, extrajudicial murder, torture, and criminalize dissent.[123] Rosenblum's faith in the American party system, as are all faiths, is based on Rosenblum's blindness to the exclusions endemic to liberal institutions and a blindness to the power of concentrated wealth as a dominating force in US politics. Rosenblum also fails to see the value of dissenting individuals who upset politics as usual and challenge fundamental assumptions, even if these disruptive individuals might not have an alternative worked out in advance. To his credit, Eulau applauds the militant's "moral sincerity, his spiritual courage and his sense of genuine inquiry."[124] Rosenblum, in contrast, is not able to affirm anything about the militant's militant conscience.

At its worst, Rosenblum's opposition between the good (e.g., reasonable reform minded) versus bad (e.g., militant revolutionary) democratic citizen leads to a static form of self-congratulating liberal politics. Rosenblum claims, for example, that militants have "nothing new to teach," and they occupy the worst of two worlds insofar as the militant has "an absolutist ethic without any definite content" and "utility's permissiveness without its humane limitation—efficiency." For Rosenblum, "militancy is not an adequate way of understanding the political world." Militancy, for her, is "reaction, purely negative," wrought by "impotence and actual powerlessness."[125]

The case of Du Bois illustrates that a thoughtful form of militancy and revolt is possible. Revolt as a way of life broadens the field for political action beyond a liberal frame, but without becoming unreflective, dogmatic, and dismissive in the process. If the militant represents the worst of both worlds (at least according to Rosenblum), Du Bois represents the best of both. For Du Bois, discernment and judgment are essential to politics, but not if it leads to inaction and blindly accepting the so-called neutral and color blind status quo. Juridical freedom and the so-called color blind status quo have generated a racial incarceration state, sentencing disparities based on the color of skin, continuing police brutality, and a Black Lives Matter movement under President

Obama's watch.[126] Although it would be incorrect to classify Du Bois as an extreme militant, it would also be incorrect to say he was a safe and reasonable liberal subject. That is to say, Du Bois was an advocate of thoughtful revolt. In Du Bois's case, this involved a permanent oppositional stance to the political status quo as a lifelong commitment.

Response to Objections

It could be objected that revolt as a way of life is counterproductive, threatens democratic procedure, and could lead to violent repression against protestors. While these objections may at first glance seem to be legitimate, the African American experience illustrates that extra-institutional means to bring about political change can be more effective than institutional means.[127] If you are defined outside of the political system, it is not possible to work within the political system. Current discussions of race relations in America must be informed by the history of the tactics employed by former slaves to gain their freedom. Given the widespread denial about racism in America that goes up from police precincts in Baltimore, Maryland, through race-baiting tactics of white voters via the American party system, and to the Supreme Court's proclamation of the end of racism and promulgation of the doctrine of color blindness, Du Bois is helpful for triggering a change in perspective and forcing the issue of the United States' racist past and present apparent in unequal access to quality education, disproportionate poverty rates, and disproportionate incarceration rates for people of color.[128] This intellectual shift will likely be uncomfortable and disruptive. It will not be as disruptive in the long run as leaving the current racial crisis in the hands of politicians to work out procedurally (and/or ignore) and in the hands of a corrupt criminal justice system.[129] For African Americans, procedural democracy has been and still remains the death of real democracy. The criminal justice system in America has always been and remains a foundation stone of the racial order.[130]

It could be objected that I overestimate the role revolt as a way of life plays in Du Bois's work. I disagree. From Du Bois's claim that "John Brown was right," to the way Du Bois mobilizes the threat of black revolt throughout his work, from the global character of the fight for justice among people of color, to the role education plays in awakening militant self-consciousness, Du Bois practiced revolt as a way of life in a manner that was drawn out and was irreducible to any one-time heroic act of revolutionary activity.[131] The fact that Du Bois claims that African Americans must "cultivate a spirit of calm, patient persistence" in no way negates my claim.[132]

Finally, it could be objected that Du Bois only deployed black rage and revolt as a threat to the white establishment, which confirms the view that Du Bois was a political moderate. Would you rather deal with an armed angry black mob or a Harvard-educated cane wielding chap like me? It is true that Du Bois was different in appearance, demeanor, and disposition from the black submerged mass. This opposition, however, only exists on the surface, for Du Bois never distanced himself from the needs of the severely oppressed and never gave up on the mass militancy needed to bring an end to racial apartheid. That is to say, Du Bois rejected the opposition between reform and revolution. For him, both options were on the table. This is what makes the life and work of Du Bois a crucial component of confrontational citizenship.

Conclusion

Du Bois's carefully crafted defense of revolt as a way of life puts into question the argument that he was an elitist advocate of the talented tenth. Du Bois did not, as Martin Luther King Jr., suggests, "leave behind the 'untalented' 90 percent."[133] Du Bois states in unequivocal terms: "The work which lies nearest my heart is not that of the talented few in opposition to the needs of the submerged many."[134] The training of the talented few, though, was an important step to lifting up the submerged mass of black people. But so was creating the basis for global solidarity among people of color through a historical and theoretical understanding of race relations that could be put to use practically. Revolt was not a one-time moment of decisive action for Du Bois, but a lifelong struggle against America's political, economic, and racial dictatorship. Revolt has been a defining feature of African American political action because of the absence of other viable alternatives to bring about change. America, a place of "show and tinsel built upon a groan," a land of mendacity, indifferent to the plight of African Americans: "With such a foundation a kingdom must in time sway and fall."[135] Du Bois sought to give America a new future on a stronger foundation. For Du Bois, radical democracy and socialism were the crucial foundation stones needed for America's renewal.

An indicted criminal, denied a passport, called a dangerous person by Theodore Roosevelt, prevented for a time from leaving America, shunned by the academic establishment, forced to retire from Atlanta University, ultimately relocating to Ghana before his death shortly thereafter, Du Bois practiced revolt as a way of life.[136] Du Bois invented a language to talk about race in America, which threatened academic conventions, created his permanent employment problem, inflamed racist America, and required fierce independence. For his entire life Du Bois refused to back down: "One thing alone I own and that is my own soul."[137] Ironically, it was something artificial that set Du Bois on the path of revolt as a way of life: "Racial distinction based on color was the greatest thing in my life."[138] Du Bois continues: "I was by long education and continual compulsion and daily reminder, a colored man in a white world."[139] Perhaps white Americans simply could not see how the calculated destruction of African Americans was destroying democracy in America: "None are as blind as those nearest the thing seen."[140] Du Bois's gift to us today is the idea of revolt as a way of life, an idea that may give us a new set of eyes to see what is right in front of us. As Charles W. Mills puts it, "whites take their racial privilege so much for granted that they do not even see it as political, as a form of domination."[141] Once Americans learn how to see the race problem, perhaps they will learn how to speak about it as well. For as Du Bois puts it, "we're not dead yet. We are not going to die."[142] This refusal, this intransigence, this bleak but also noble defiance is what makes Du Bois's idea of revolt as a way of life a fundamental component of confrontational citizenship.

Chapter Five
Hannah Arendt on
Putting the Political Back into Politics

Introduction

As long as politics involves power relations, political resistance will be an inescapable feature of political life. Widespread political resistance can be a serious problem and threaten political order. Political resistance can also be a sign of a healthy polity and provoke needed political change. How regimes handle political resistance is a good indicator of their commitment to free speech, right of assembly, and redress of grievances. Hannah Arendt's (1906-75) work on political action has received ample attention.[1] The same cannot be said of her concept of political resistance.[2] The originality of Arendt's reflections on political resistance and the relevance of this political category today justify exploring the concept of political resistance in her writings. How should political resistance be conceptualized today? How can political resistance avoid taking counterproductive turns? Arendt answers these questions in creative ways.

Arendt's concept of political resistance is valuable because it overcomes either/or political dichotomies, including order/anarchy, law/violence, obedience/revolt, and expands the terrain of politics. For Arendt, political resistance must take the form of a double concept, as something that points in conflicting directions at the same time. Arendt's notion of political resistance as a double concept is a practical and theoretical construct that confronts the problem of power. It also provides a way to rethink the relationship between legal orders and challenges to them that overcomes the limits of contemporary liberal theory (e.g., John Rawls) and some of the ideas of Michel Foucault. The form of contemporary liberal theory advanced by Rawls overidentifies with the state.[3] Foucault goes to the other extreme and rejects the state as essentially disciplinary.[4] Arendt's concept of political resistance as a double concept demonstrates that it is possible to take a critical stance toward political institutions but without rejecting them. Hence, Arendt emerges as a defender of a unique type of political resistance that will be of interest to scholars reflecting on democratic citizenship, authority, and legitimacy who want to avoid either/or thinking and the intellectual exhaustion that accompanies it.

Resistance

Arendt did not write a text or essay explicitly on political resistance. Nor does she define once and for all what resistance is. Yet, the word appears frequently and at decisive moments in Arendt's early, middle, and later writings. Arendt privileges the idea of resistance because of the work it accomplishes on three different registers. For her, it involves political, intellectual, and existential dimensions. Resistance as a political concept names the refusal of the citizenry to completely identify with the political order. The refusal to identify lays the groundwork for the idea of resistance. Resistance is also a key component of the life of the mind. Specifically, Arendt maintains that trying to understand something requires a certain level of distance, if not resistance. Comprehension, Arendt states, involves "the facing up to, and resisting of, reality," an active refusal to be manipulated and deceived.[5] Existentially, political resistance creates and preserves spaces within which humans can act politically. This allows humans to appear in the world and fulfill their *telos* as political agents.[6]

Other references to political resistance in Arendt's work are not difficult to locate. Recall, for example, Arendt's praise for the French and Danish resistance movements to Nazi totalitarianism; her claim that civil disobedience was consistent with the letter and spirit of the US Constitution; the text she devoted to the concept of revolution; her defense of Hungarian resistance to Soviet domination; her favorable evaluation of the student movement in the 1960s; her book on defiant individuals; her support of violence against fascism; and the transgressive character of her conception of political action.[7] Clearly, Arendt had a sustained interest in political resistance that can be traced back to her earliest major texts.

As early as *The Origins of Totalitarianism*, for example, Arendt claims that a "new political principle," a "new law on earth" was needed to guarantee human dignity.[8] Arendt located a new political principle in the section of this text called "The Perplexities of the Rights of Man" and called it the "right to action."[9] Arendt's appeal to the "right to action" grew out of her critique of the nation-state, the emptiness of abstract human rights, and the emergence/production of new groups of people who were absolutely vulnerable as a result of their statelessness. Even after its appearance in *Origins*, Arendt's defense of the right to action continued to be a theme in her work, and was rooted in her belief that political action preserved human dignity by opening a space for freedom to appear. This prevents humans from only living life in the private realm and being reduced to a standing reserve for technological exploitation.[10] Arendt's investigation of the right to action required her to turn to and reconceive some of the foundational concepts and dichotomies of Western political thought. The one that is particularly significant in terms of the right to action and political resistance is authority.

Authority

For Arendt, and just about every other thinker in the Western tradition, a lack of authority leads to political instability. How to create and sustain authority in the body politic is a vexing political question. The concept of authority points to the problems of foundation, freedom, legitimacy, and obedience. In Arendt's essay, "What Is Authority?" she offers a genealogy of authority that traces its development from ancient Greece, Rome, and into modernity. Immediately, we learn that authority is not an easy term to define. As Arendt states, "the very term has been clouded by controversy and confusion"; "little about its nature appears self-evident or even comprehensible."[11] Exactly why this is the case is unclear but the fact remains: "We are no longer in a position to know what authority really *is*."[12] Arendt refuses to say what authority is in general and focuses on what authority was historically. But first, she deconstructs authority by distinguishing it from words that are mistaken for authority. Arendt insists on the importance of making distinctions because whatever fills the function of authority does not mean that it is authority. For her, authority is not the same as tyranny and violence, and authority is never only a matter of obedience. That is, authority is not whatever makes people obey.

Arendt dissects the concept of authority via dialectical analysis and a mode of negative presentation where clarifying what a concept is emerges through articulating what the concept is not. For Arendt, authority is not coercion, force, persuasion, power, and violence.

> Since authority always demands obedience, it is commonly mistaken for some form of power or violence. Yet authority precludes the use of external means of coercion; where force is used, authority itself has failed. Authority, on the other hand, is incompatible with persuasion, which presupposes equality and works through a process of argumentation. When arguments are used, authority is left in abeyance. Against the egalitarian order of persuasion stands the authoritarian order, which is always hierarchical. If authority is to be defined at all, then, it must be in contradistinction to both coercion by force and persuasion through arguments.[13]

That authority demands obedience is not a surprising claim. That authority lies between force and persuasion is more contentious. Before we examine Arendt's reconceptualization of authority, let's look at how authority has been conceived at a couple of important historical moments.

The tradition of Western political theory tends to view authority as something that provides the foundation for political orders from an external source. This removes it from the sphere of contestation and is the origin of authoritarian political orders. Arendt states: "The source of authority in authoritarian government is always a force external and superior to its own power."[14] Arendt flags Plato's *Republic* as a foundational text for the articulation of this mode of authority. Plato is significant because he "tried to introduce something akin to authority into the public life of the Greek polis."[15] Arendt does not point to the "Myth of the Metals" as the ground for authority, but the economy of rewards/punishments articulated in the enigmatic book ten of Plato's *Republic*. Arendt also refers to the philosopher's exclusive access to ideas as the source of political authority. This gave political authority both a mythical foundation and a punitive one. Since the hoi polloi (e.g., common people) cannot comprehend truth through reason, Plato ultimately invokes fear of punishment and rhetoric as a substitute for logical persuasion.

Rome was also decisive for Arendt in the development of authority insofar as the experience of creating a political foundation, Arendt states, "brought authority as word, concept, and reality into our history."[16] Authority, not violence, "ruled the conduct of citizens."[17] The source of authority was in the past and not in the realm of ideas and was sustained through the preservation and augmentation of the political foundation. This led to political stability: "Roman authority suggests that the act of foundation inevitably develops its own stability and permanence."[18] This confirms Arendt's claim that authority gives the world "durability," "groundwork," "permanence," and "reliability."[19] Rome perpetuated its authority through the cult of ancestors, attachment to precedents, and widespread belief in the sacredness of foundation.[20]

In her own time, Arendt held the view that authority was in a state of crisis that was "political in origin and nature."[21] Symptoms of the loss of authority in the twentieth century can be seen in a "general dissatisfaction, widespread malaise, and contempt for those in power."[22] Modernity is tantamount to the crisis of authority to such an extent that "we are no longer in a position to know what authority really *is*."[23] Retrieving a Greek or Roman notion of authority was not an option on both epistemological and practical grounds.

This is a problem because the presence or absence of authority is connected to the stability of a political regime. Indeed, the crisis of authority accounts for the frequency of revolutions in the modern age. The lack of authority, according to Arendt, has been "the curse of constitutional government in nearly all European countries."[24] Without authority, we must face the problem of living together with full force:

> Authority as we once knew it, which grew out of the Roman experience of foundation and was understood in the light of Greek political philosophy, has nowhere been re-established, either through revolutions or through the even less promising means of restoration, and least of all through the conservative moods and trends which occasionally sweep public opinion. For to live in a political realm with neither authority nor the concomitant awareness that the source of authority transcends power and those who are in power, means to be confronted anew, without the religious trust in a sacred beginning and without the protection of traditional and therefore self-evident standards of behavior, by the elementary problems of living-together.[25]

In these two closing sentences in the essay "What Is Authority?" Arendt maintains that authority has been lost and that this loss confronts us with the most fundamental problem of political life. Without authority, the intersubjective basis of politics is shipwrecked; bonds of solidarity connecting citizens with each other that result from the attachment to and reenactment of political foundation lose their force. Although Arendt concludes "What Is Authority?" on this pessimistic note, this is not a sign that she has given up on authority. The challenge becomes recovering authority as a political concept suited to the contemporary context. That Arendt responds to this challenge is clear by analyzing the relationship between the right to action, political resistance, and authority. As we shall see, the degeneration of authority is arrested through a dialectical movement where authority is constituted via active resistance to it. For Arendt, political obedience involves distance and resistance to the source of authority that requires obedience.

Putting the Political Back into Politics

Arendt was convinced that conceiving authority and political resistance in mutually exclusive ways was a mistake. But thinking two things simultaneously (e.g., obedience and resistance) that are usually conceived as opposites is contradictory. How is it possible to be both for and against the same thing? Arendt insists that we must put into question the logic and deductive modes of the common world that give us simplistic either/or dichotomies, because this prevents us from fashioning political concepts consistent with the right to action. We need to respond to the world with new ideas, not "with preformed judgments, that is, with prejudices."[26]

As the innovative and wide-ranging character of Arendt's oeuvre demonstrates, thinking about politics must be a permanently reactivated involvement in the world that responds to the fault lines of the historical moment, not something that submits to "the coercive character of logical argumentation."[27] It is a mistake, for example, to construe political thinking as a form of cognition that imposes dead political categories on actual political events in order to make sense of them. The "tyranny of logicality" in the "mind's submission to logic" at work in the "compulsory process of deduction" is the furthest thing from the spontaneity and creativity that innovative political thought requires.[28] For Arendt, the crisis of authority requires inventing a new way of thinking about politics that would in turn lead to new political practices. It was necessary, in the words of Arendt, to "think against the tradition while using its own conceptual tools."[29] The master's weapons could and must be wielded against the master. In a move similar to but ultimately different from Heideggerian *Destruktion* because it had a political not an existential outcome, Arendt fused contradictory political imperatives together without annulling either side of the opposition in order to intensify a foundational political problematic.

The fusion of contradictory political imperatives puts the political back into politics and is central to Arendt's recovery of political authority, the revolutionary spirit, and her critique of legal orders. Let's start with authority. For Arendt, "authority implies an obedience in which men retain their freedom."[30] Arendt does not reject political obedience in the name of freedom, nor does she ping-pong in the opposite direction and appeal to a hierarchical order that would demand obedience. Both freedom and obedience must work together, or at least coexist simultaneously. Authority is not authoritarian but *implies* obedience in ways compatible with political freedom. As Arendt famously puts it, "the *raison d'être* of politics is freedom."[31] Yet, political life would be impossible without obedience: "Obedience is a political virtue of the first order, and without it no body politic could survive."[32] But as Arendt suggests in *Eichmann in Jerusalem*, complete obedience dehumanizes.[33] Arendt simultaneously brings together and separates what are normally viewed as opposites, freedom and obedience. Obedience is both necessary for sustaining a political order and problematic because it can snuff out the critical faculties and the right to action. The recovery of authority as a political concept requires a way of thinking capable of seeing beyond either/or political oppositions that give us restricted possibilities and unhelpful polarities.

Let's turn to the revolutionary spirit. For Arendt, recapturing the spirit of revolution also requires a new style of political thinking: "To recapture the lost spirit of revolution must, to a certain extent, consist in the attempt at thinking together and combining meaningfully what our present vocabulary presents to us in terms of opposition and contradiction."[34] Arendt was referring to the concern with stability that is often viewed as antithetical to the spirit of the new. The revolutionary moment contained both moments (e.g., disruption and stability) and this was the foundation of its authority. For Arendt, "they [authority and obedience] were not mutually exclusive opposites but two sides of the same event" in the act of foundation.[35] For Arendt, we need to move beyond thinking in "pairs of opposites" that pit agents of change against those fearful of it.[36] Political stability, for Arendt, was the result of putting the regime perpetually into question via political resistance as a way to create a vibrant and living form of political stability.

Arendt's rejection of either/or political thinking also plays itself out in terms of her defense of a vibrant political culture and can be found in *Crises of the Republic*. She states: "Dissent implies consent, and is the hallmark of free government; one who knows that he may dissent knows also that he somehow consents when he does not dissent."[37] Viewing dissent and consent together is yet another strategic move on Arendt's part. Getting stuck on either side would, in the case of consent, trigger an overidentification with the status quo and lead to political passivity. In the case of dissent, it would engender a counterproductive antiposition.

Arendt's rejection of either/or political thinking is also apparent in her critique of legal orders. Legal orders tend to move relatively slowly when it comes to change, restrict the space for citizen participation, and view political resistance as a threat to order. Although Arendt was critical of the conservatism of legal orders, she also praised legal orders, criticized the "contempt for law" and "motion mania" of totalitarian regimes, endorsed the execution of Adolf Eichmann by a political state, and claimed that "the space between men as it is hedged in by laws, is the living space of freedom."[38] Arendt refuses to be simply "for or against" legal orders. Arendt does not condemn juridical institutions, and she avoids the trap involved in the reduction of political life to a legal framework for the resolution of conflict for good political reasons. Reducing political life to juridical-political institutions consolidates the order/anarchy opposition and constricts the political sphere to the point of suffocation. Institutions protect humans, but Arendt knows political institutions are also capable of annihilating humans. She states: "Institutions left to themselves without control and guidance by men, turned into monsters devouring nations and countries."[39] For Arendt, political institutions also threaten political freedom.

> Freedom can be guaranteed by laws even less than justice; a legal framework that would attempt to insure the permanence of freedom would not only kill all political life, but would abolish even that margin of unpredictability without which freedom cannot exist.[40]

Legal orders serve a stabilizing function. Legal orders establish predictability and regularity. But legal orders tend to be quite conservative. Legal orders never initiate real political change. For Arendt, "law can indeed stabilize and legalize change once it has occurred but the change itself is always the result of extra-legal action."[41] Political change may be the result of extralegal action but, just like for obedience and freedom, Arendt is wary of taking this position too far. She avoids getting stuck in yet another either/or political opposition between pure legality and extra-legal action. For Arendt, legal orders are both a positive condition of a politics of freedom but law can also "kill all political life."[42]

As we have seen, the recovery of political authority, revolutionary spirit, and vibrant political culture required a new way of thinking about politics that overcomes the tendency to reduce politics to a series of binary oppositions. Arendt's work *On Revolution* takes this theoretical and political strategy further. As we shall see, Arendt's work on revolution addresses the question of the legitimacy of a regime grounded in revolution, deepens her claim that regimes need to incorporate opposing political principles within themselves, and points the way to an alternative form of the state. Arendt was trying to articulate a position that avoided the conservatism of legal orders as well as the instability of total anarchy and totalitarianism.

Revolution

Arendt's analysis and critique of the American, French, and Russian revolutions in *On Revolution* adds important dimensions to the foregoing discussion of political resistance, authority, and the right to action. In revolutionary situations, the stakes for political life are high. The overthrow and negation of a political regime is always an easier task than the construction of a better alternative. For Arendt, the first task of revolution is making a constitution. This is a challenge because it raises questions about the legitimacy of the new regime. How can the new order establish its legitimacy, one might ask, if it is based on the rejection of the legitimacy of its predecessor? To what would it appeal? For Arendt, all legality is essentially illegal: "Those who get together to constitute a new government are themselves unconstitutional, that is, they have no authority to do what they have set out to achieve."[43] That is to say, all regimes are stuck in a self-contradiction.[44]

Framing a constitution is only part of the problem in a postrevolutionary situation. The attempt to preserve the revolutionary spirit, the second task of revolution according to Arendt, intensifies the problem of the authority and legitimacy of a regime grounded in revolution. As long as constitutions allow the survival of the revolutionary spirit in the regime, political orders acquire legitimacy. When political orders break the link with energy from below as a constant source of vitality, that is, when the revolutionary becomes a conservative the day after the revolution, regimes lose their authority and legitimacy. Arendt's rejection of either/or political thinking surfaces yet again. For Arendt, it is necessary to be a bit conservative and revolutionary simultaneously. We need to augment, conserve, and preserve those aspects of a regime that facilitate the right to action and challenge the elements that deny it. For this to happen, Arendt claims, "we must have a new concept of the state."[45]

Arendt came close to articulating this new concept of the state in her reflections on political resistance, authority, and revolution. For Arendt, political regimes should be constructed in ways that permit permanent political struggle, contain institutions at odds with themselves, and support a vibrant democratic political culture. All political regimes are essentially arbitrary, "all authority in the last analysis rests on opinion" and Arendt insists that they must be permanently challenged precisely because of this, in order to continually establish and reestablish their authority and legitimacy.[46] While the Weimar legal theorist Carl Schmitt (1888-1985) came to a similar conclusion about the arbitrary character of political orders, Schmitt looked to the sovereign to decide on the exception and ward off political instability in critical situations.[47] Arendt was not as obsessed as Schmitt with political disorder and saw a positive role for both the legal order and democratic challenges to it.

The lesson we can learn from Arendt is clear. In order for a regime to be a real political community, it must never consolidate and enclose its revolutionary beginning in hierarchical differentiations between rulers and ruled. Let's recall one of Arendt's definitions of freedom: "To move in a sphere where neither rule nor being ruled existed."[48] Arendtian political resistance creates and preserves this egalitarian sphere beyond the shadow of Schmitt's sovereign politics. Sovereignty was not the solution, in fact, sovereignty was the real enemy. For Arendt, "if men wish to be free, it is precisely sovereignty they must renounce."[49] Hence, Arendt insists on the value of both institutions and counterinstitutions in the same polity. Arendt even calls for "the establishment of civil disobedience among our political institutions" and suggests the need for a "new constitutional amendment" to ensure it.[50] This position encapsulates

Arendt's defense of legality, her affirmation of political resistance, her recognition of the paradox of democratic authority, her commitment to the revolutionary spirit even after the revolution, and her call for a style of political thinking that expands political possibilities and overcomes the either/or political dead-ends of many forms of contemporary political theorizing.

Arendt Beyond Rawls and Foucault

Let's bring Arendt into dialogue with John Rawls (1921–2002) and Michel Foucault (1926–84), in order to draw out the originality of Arendt's position and demonstrate how it goes beyond the work of Rawls and Foucault. Rawls has had a significant impact on the theoretical landscape since the publication of *A Theory of Justice* in 1971, and in his subsequent writings that addressed the concerns of his critics and led to a greater clarification of his theoretical vision in *Political Liberalism*.[51] Rawls's goal of creating a fair and stable political order with well-functioning institutions is a noble aspiration. Nonetheless, his core assumptions about politics have made many critics wonder about the trade-offs involved with justice as fairness. For Rawls, well-designed institutions eliminate the need for a counterinstitution. Since the result of rational deliberation in Rawls's original position is unanimity, this renders any subsequent resistance irrational.[52] In a well-ordered Rawlsian society, Rawls claims "arbitrary authority has disappeared."[53] Power relations disintegrate and then evaporate in the acid bath of rational interlocution. Rawls's discussion of civil disobedience is particularly troubling. For Rawls, "the injustice of a law is not, in general, a sufficient reason for not adhering to it."[54] Even if institutions are flawed, Rawls counsels passivity as the reasonable and civil solution: "The duty of civility imposes a due acceptance of the defects of institutions."[55] Rawls suppresses political conflict with an apolitical discourse of rationality, promulgates the illusion that political orders can exist without power, and fashions citizens who are unable to speak the language of protest.

In stark contrast to Rawls, Foucault is so critical of institutions that he recommends their total rejection. Before I develop my critique of Foucault, it is important to note that there is much to praise in Foucault's work, including his rejection of the docile subjectivity of the Rawlsian sort, his savage critique of domination, his analysis of power at the micro- and subpolitical levels, and his work on behalf of prison inmates, the mentally ill, and other marginalized groups. As opposed to arguing for a massive overhaul of the social and political order, Foucault turned to the self's capacity to fashion itself aesthetically as a critical political strategy for liberation and individual autonomy amid the unfreedom of late modern societies.[56] In terms of political resistance, Foucault put into question traditional assumptions about agency and argued that power itself generates resistance: "Where there is power," he maintains, "there is resistance." Since "power is everywhere," just about everything should be resisted.[57]

Nevertheless, in an interview, "On Popular Justice: A Discussion with Maoists," Foucault argues for the "elimination of the juridical apparatus."[58] Foucault's commitment to exposing power and his skepticism about legal orders is justified, but this skepticism prevents him from articulating what a better political order might be. Foucault states: "I think that to imagine another system is to extend our participation in the present system."[59] Although resistance may be a central theme in Foucault's work, he limits or restricts resistance to the micro- or subpolitical level and fails to see how institutions can be designed to facilitate their own transformation. Although Foucault's intensification of the sense of oppression in previously unexamined areas of life has had a beneficial impact on struggles for freedom, Foucault's turn away from the state and concepts like authority, legitimacy, and sovereignty restricts his political relevance to aesthetic self-creation, autonomy, and individual liberation.[60]

Unlike Foucault, Arendt's conception of political resistance as a double concept overcomes either/or political dichotomies and navigates the chasm between consent/dissent, order/anarchy, freedom/obedience, and revolution/restoration. Arendt opposes the rejection of the legal order as disciplinary as a political stance, as well as the overidentification with any political order. The subversion of institutional self-identity as a strategy to open spaces for political action, struggle, and resistance was a more promising avenue for Arendt than the conclusion that domination was inescapable (e.g., Foucault), or that well-designed institutions alone held the answer to all of our problems (e.g., Rawls), or that a strong sovereign Hobbesian leader was the answer to the problem of political legitimacy in the twentieth century (e.g., Schmitt). The lessons of the twentieth century, including genocide, totalitarianism, global destruction, loss of home, the banality of evil (e.g., Adolf Eichmann), and the birth of the masses lacking any sense of judgment, taught Arendt that it was as much of a mistake to blindly trust the state as it was to reject it altogether. For Arendt, there might still be poetry after Auschwitz but it would have to be one that memorialized the horrors of the twentieth century, refused the romantic escape into the aesthetic realm, rejected the will to domination in Schmittian sovereignty, permanently criticized the legal order, and fashioned core political concepts in contradictory ways to prevent them from being co-opted by counterrevolutionary forces that declare war on their own people.

Conclusion

In contrast to Foucault's celebration of political resistance without limits, his turn to aesthetic self-creation, and his rejection of legal orders as inescapably disciplinary; and in contrast to Rawlsian justice as fairness without dissent, power, and political struggle, Arendt gives us political resistance as a double concept, as something that confronts the problem of power and for strategic reasons points in conflicting directions at the same time. Rawls's happy embrace of institutions untainted by power effectively eliminates the significance of the category of political resistance from his thought. Foucault placed the question of resistance at the center of his work, but by focusing on the micro-logical dimension to resistance he tended to ignore how political resistance might alter the political order as a whole. Arendtian resistance overcomes the limitations of both Rawls and Foucault because it demonstrates that it is possible to take a critical stance toward institutions but without rejecting them; that authority can best be perpetuated through resistance to it; that political resistance and the right to action protect humans from oppression; and that it is a mistake to either overidentify with or reject the state.[61]

It could be argued that Arendt's model or "concept" of political resistance as a double concept, one that incorporates antithetical aspects into it, is contradictory, makes the formation of a democratic will impossible, and undermines the authority of the state. I disagree. What we lose in efficiency and democratic will formation, we gain in a more open process for democratic struggle and decision making. This keeps politics actual, undermines institutional authoritarianism, and builds the authority and legitimacy of a political order over time. It could also be objected that the presence of institutions and counterinstitutions in the same polity eliminates political predictability. Again, I disagree. Arendt strikes a far better balance on this than both Rawls and Foucault—the former overemphasizing institutional regularity at the expense of democratic unpredictability, the latter valorizing all forms of resistance to the detriment of any settled political practices. Unlike Rawls who eliminates space for resistance and Foucault who embraces all forms of resistance, Arendt puts forth political resistance as a double concept, as something context sensitive and irreducible to any known political position or program. In this sense, political resistance is a practice not a program. Intellectually, political resistance as a double concept overcomes the simplistic either/or mode of political theorizing that give us unbridgeable dichotomies and restricted political possibilities and expands the ways we think about politics. Politically, political resistance as a double concept leads to the permanent critique of the state and intensifies the possibility for positive political change and the renewal of political life.

Chapter Six
Gloria Anzaldúa Singing the Song of Herself

Introduction

Generally speaking, individuals have to fight to advance and protect their political and economic interests. In the United States, you can vote, join an interest group, and get involved in politics. If an interest group that furthers what you want does not exist, you can create one that does. If you are unable to support a political candidate, you can run for political office yourself. On face value, this sounds great. However, all of these options assume that the political system is open to everyone and treats everyone the same way. Historically, this has not been the case, especially for women of color.[1] In the United States, women of color have been positioned outside of the political sphere, denied political voice, and excluded from participating. How can the public (including women of color) gain greater voice and empowerment in the context of unequal access to the political sphere, neoliberal hegemony, political dysfunction, patriarchy, racism, and the corporate domination of the political realm?

Gloria Anzaldúa (1942–2004) has a unique answer to this question. For her, self-craft is the starting point for productive political engagement for groups (in particular, women of color) who have been historically marginalized. For Anzaldúa, self-craft covers a range of practices including loving oneself and letting oneself be, finding one's voice as an author, taking pride in one's identity, truth-telling, being a bridge for others, and becoming a militant political agent. Self-craft emerges as a prerequisite for productive political engagement and key component of confrontational citizenship that lays the groundwork for the birth of new forms of solidarity and community.

Not everyone, though, is a fan of self-craft, or what is often called identity politics. Thinkers like Arthur Schlesinger Jr., Samuel P. Huntington, and Allan Bloom view identity claims as un-American, leading to social chaos, and risk plunging us into hell.[2] Other authors are also skeptical about identity politics. Identity claims disrupt overlapping consensus (e.g., John Rawls), are depoliticizing (e.g., Wendy Brown), and are a threat to participatory politics grounded on commonality (e.g., Sheldon Wolin).[3] Interestingly, Anzaldúa dodges these critiques because she creates a new type of self that leads to a more welcoming collectivity for women of color than ones predicated on "getting over" one's ethnic/racial background. Because she avoids extreme positions (e.g., American nationalism on one side; Chicano nationalism on the other), Anzaldúa emerges as an important theorist of an activist politics, freedom, and identity formation. She brings together without final reconciliation the competing demands of individual voice (self-craft) and collective solidarity (us-craft).

In this regard, Anzaldúa's work can be situated within a body of research that defends the political significance of identity. Susan Bickford, for example, argues that "group identities may be cherished as a source of strength and purpose." Identity, Bickford continues, can "serve as a vital motivation in our political lives." Group identities, finally, "can make political action possible."[4] Given Anzaldúa's work on hybrid cultural formations and identity as a source of political empowerment, Anzaldúa is an important interlocutor in ongoing discussions about the political character of culture and individual identity. Reflecting on the particular (herself) is a strategy to fashion a noncolonial universal and nonoppressive basis for solidarity with others. The politics of self-craft emerges as her most important contribution to radical political thought and supplements the other components of confrontational citizenship analyzed in this book (e.g., hatred, rage, revolution, revolt, etc.).

The Poetics and Politics of Everyday Life

In her groundbreaking work *Borderlands/La Frontera*, Anzaldúa addresses the historical, cultural, social, economic, sexual, and political situation of Mexican Americans in the United States and in the borderlands.[5] Anzaldúa grew up in the borderlands, namely, Hargill, Texas, and explains: "Hatred, anger and exploitation are the prominent features of this landscape."[6] As a child, Anzaldúa was bused twenty miles from Hargill to Edinburg, Texas, to attend school. She graduated from Edinburg High School in 1962. Then she attended Pan American University (now called University of Texas, Rio Grande Valley), earning a BA in English, art, and education in 1969. Anzaldúa entered the University of Texas at Austin as a graduate student in literature and education and earned her master's degree in these fields in 1973. As a Chicana lesbian from a working-class background, Anzaldúa did not have an easy time surviving inside or outside of her community. Within the Latino/a community, Anzaldúa was an outsider because she refused to conform to the gender roles ascribed to women. In the Anglo world, Anzaldúa was also an outsider as a member of a permanently suspect conquered population, sexual minority, and racial other. She responded to this imposed marginalization with creativity and the politics of self-craft. To this day, the relative neglect of Anzaldúa among political scientists is a sign that she is either still unknown or that she is regarded as a marginal thinker without much relevance for contemporary political thinking.[7] As we shall see, this is an unfortunate oversight given the wide range of pressing political issues Anzaldúa negotiates in her writings pertaining to the political, sexual, and ethnic/racial oppression of Latinos/as as well as her path-breaking work on identity formation.

Historically, Mexican Americans were a conquered population who were given US citizenship by the Treaty of Guadalupe-Hidalgo in 1848 (for Puerto Ricans, the Jones Act of 1917 imposed a unique version of US citizenship on them), classified as white by the US Census Bureau, but remained a group with an uneasy and at times tense relationship with the hegemonic Anglo majority. Even today, Latinos/as suffer from poverty, incarceration, and low educational achievement at disproportionate rates.[8] Forced to assimilate; terrorized by the Texas Rangers, local police, and border patrol; lynched; stereotyped as lazy, stupid, and fit only for manual labor; criminalized, exploited economically, and interned in *barrios* and *colonias* as a result of legal segregation and racism, Latinos/as have been and in certain areas remain an arguably internally colonized population in the United States.[9] Even today, Mexican Americans continue to be aliens within the body politic, foreigners in their native land, depicted as dormant criminals, rapists, and the ever-encroaching unassimilable "brown tide."[10] The everyday experiences of Latinos/as living in the United States within this cultural, social, political, and economic context (with special attention given to Latinas in the borderlands region) became the subject matter of Anzaldúa's writing.

As opposed to invoking the discourse of universality, Anzaldúa identified the ways in which one's place and concrete situation in the world bends, constrains, and contorts the self in accordance with cultural expectations, legal status, norms regulating sexual practices, and economic opportunity. Anzaldúa's best-known book in this regard is *Borderlands/La Frontera: The New Mestiza*. In describing her book, she states that it is one that "speaks of my existence," and is designed to convey a feeling of being "excruciatingly alive."[11] It was the book, moreover, where Anzaldúa found her voice as an author, as it was the outlet where she began to make sense of her hybrid life and experiences living on both sides of the border as well as carrying the border on her back and in her flesh. By writing about her life (self-craft), Anzaldúa was able to share these experiences with others and thereby create the basis for a collective solidarity anchored in these shared experiences. For her, the border was more than a militarized checkpoint. It was a "historical and metaphorical site."[12] The borderland, for Anzaldúa, was also a "bleeding wound," "a vague and undetermined place," and a "third country" that constituted her hybrid identity.[13] Finally, the borderland was a zone inhabited by one of the most exploitable and exploited populations on the planet as a result of arbitrary political designations (e.g., shifting enforcement of the border) and desperate lives lived on the edge of starvation.

Borders, of course, have a material dimension apparent in border guards, checkpoints, and fences/walls. Borders also had an ontological dimension. "Borders are set up," Anzaldúa explains, "to distinguish *us* from *them*."[14] "*Los atravesados*," Anzaldúa continues, live here: "the squint-eyed, the perverse, the queer, the troublesome, the mongrel, the mulatto, the half-breed, the half-dead; in short, those who cross over, pass over, or go through the confines of the 'normal.'"[15] This was the political-psychological context (e.g., the imposition of a colonized self that is then internalized to produce shame and self-hatred) Anzaldúa engaged and sought to transform via the written word.

In addition to her own writings that served as an outlet for her voice and process for the creation of her unique identity, creating spaces for others was also how Anzaldúa reached out to other women of color who never thought of themselves as writers. Inventing and reinventing oneself emerged as a strategy to escape oppressive characterizations and to claim one's life. To this end, Anzaldúa edited several books, including *This Bridge Called My Back: Writing by Radical Women of Color* (with Cherríe Moraga) and *Making Face, Making Soul: Haciendo Caras, Creative and Critical Perspectives by Feminists of Color*. Anzaldúa's book *This Bridge Called My Back* draws attention to multiple forms of oppression faced by women of color by including a variety of perspectives of women traditionally denied voice. By including their voices and perspectives in this volume, the writers become bridges for other women who might benefit from learning about women who struggle to make sense of their lives and marginalized status. Anzaldúa's book *Making Face, Making Soul, Haciendo Caras* also addresses the forms of oppression faced by women of color. Like self-craft, "making face" refers to the joy of actively re-creating one's identity free from internally and externally imposed masks that result from self-hatred and hegemonic negative stereotypes.[16] As Anzaldúa states, "I want the freedom to carve and chisel my own face."[17] Our faces are not of our own making: "White culture and its perspectives are inscribed on us/into us."[18] Anzaldúa continues: "We are 'written' all over, or should I say carved, and tattooed with the sharp needles of experience."[19] A narrow range of personalities that in turn became the "essence" of their identity were imposed on Latinas by the Latino and Anglo communities.[20] For Anzaldúa, Latino/as need to "unlearn the *puta*/virgin dichotomy."[21] Latinas could do more than lie on their backs in a whorehouse or prostrate themselves to patriarchal representations of the divine and male enforcers of patriarchal structure in Catholic churches. As Anzaldúa puts it, "the struggle of the *mestiza* is above all a feminist one."[22]

All of Anzaldúa's writings contained components that were personal, political, and global. Reflecting on her childhood, Anzaldúa learned she was a problem: "Nothing in my culture approved of me."[23] Anzaldúa had, in her own words, "the mark of the Beast."[24] Anzaldúa also sensed her parents' disapproval ("by the worried look on my parents' face I learned something was wrong with me") and took solace in reading ("very early on I started reading Nietzsche"), as both a form of escape ("books saved my sanity") and as an act of resistance to the communal norms and externally imposed personalities that trapped Chicanas into preordained roles: "Nun; prostitute; mother."[25] Anzaldúa did not mince words in terms of her views on her own culture: "My culture cripples its women."[26] Latinas were also oppressed by the dominant Anglo culture, where they were invisible as human agents while doing back-breaking work as farm workers, underpaid maids, waitresses, and childcare workers; or caricatured and hypervisible in the media yet voiceless as welfare recipients and hypersexualized predators.[27]

Under these conditions involving multiple forms of oppression, survival in the United States and borderlands required a "fierceness of spirit," which is an essential component of the type of confrontational citizenship Anzaldúa practiced.[28] This fierceness of spirit, which implied being untamed and intractable, was for Anzaldúa both the essence of her identity ("there is a rebel in me"), and fueled the creative process where languages were mixed, academic rules were broken, and disciplines were shattered.[29] Anzaldúa struggled to find her own voice as an intellectual committed to social justice, because traditional academic styles and disciplines did not provide her an outlet. While she was as student at Pan American University, for example, she was required to take several classes intended to grind away her Spanglish accent. Once Anzaldúa moved on to the University of Texas at Austin, she discovered Chicana studies and literature did not exist and was told by her academic advisers to pick another topic. Anzaldúa fought these voice inhibiting norms: "My whole struggle is to change the disciplines, to change the genres, to change how people look at a poem, at theory or at children's books. So I have to struggle between how many of these rules I can break."[30] Anzaldúa also had to fight her culture, which tried to annihilate her voice and "take away our ability to act."[31] Resistance was her response: "My Chicana identity is grounded in the Indian women's history of resistance."[32] Anzaldúa continues: "The personal and cultural narratives are . . . impassioned and conflicted engagements in resistance."[33]

Political Writing

Anzaldúa had an intense and evolving relationship to language as a mode of oppression and instrument of liberation. Writing becomes a liberating political act when it empowers the writers to become the authors of their own lives (self-craft) and intervene in the world to open this option for others. This requires the author to abandon the temporary but ultimately false comfort of self and externally imposed stereotypes and to become an agent of self-determination. Early on, Anzaldúa was not able to publish her written work ("they wouldn't publish me"), as a result of her critique of Latino *machista* culture, her defiant voice as an author, and her commitment to truth-telling: "My mouth was a mother-load."[34] Anzaldúa also felt the anger generated by marginalization ("I was angry and I am still angry"), but avoided the trap of alcohol, drugs, and violence as a way to cope with it.[35] "The bottle, the snort, the fist, the needle," Anzaldúa suggests, were forms of reaction to oppression for Latinos, but ultimately led to the annihilation of the self: "All reaction," Anzaldúa claims, "is limited by and dependent on what is reacting against."[36] Rage was also a defensive mechanism to hold the world at bay, a form of "auto-cannibalism."[37] Rage drove others away and was a way to fortress the self against exposure and vulnerability.[38]

For Anzaldúa, writing was how she transformed her anger into a process of self-overcoming and regeneration. Writing was a form of self-craft, that is, a mode of coming to terms with her lived experience and a metapolitical practice. That is to say, Anzaldúa struggled to come to terms with her experiences living on/near the border as an internally colonized subject. She turned to language to bring herself back to life: "Naming is how I make my presence known, how I assert who and what I am and want to be known as. Naming myself is a survival tactic."[39] As an outlet for her voice, writing was also a metapolitical practice.

Writing was a metapolitical practice because it created the conditions for political agency. In this sense, writing was how Anzaldúa reclaimed herself from obliteration. Writing was also an act central to the creation of *mestiza* consciousness because it allowed Anzaldúa to overcome enforced silence. To this end, Anzaldúa playfully violated norms of the tongue (she rejected the command to speak "pure" English or "pure" Spanish) through the creation of a *mestiza* language. Writing was a form of militancy but also an index of exposure, of "how much nakedness I achieve."[40] Writing involved a lot of "squirming" (like "being queer") and being vulnerable and "spreading one's legs."[41] For Anzaldúa, language was not a neutral instrument of communication. It could hold one back and be yet another instrument of oppression. Speaking or writing in clichés, for example, was the index of thoughtlessness and one's resistance to change.[42] For Anzaldúa, language is a political mechanism of control that falsifies the world and positions oppressed groups as permanent targets of linguistic domination. The Spanish language, for Anzaldúa, was a weapon used against women: "We are robbed of our female being by the masculine plural." She continues: "Language is a male discourse."[43]

In a unique combination of the insights of Friedrich Nietzsche, Frantz Fanon, Paulo Freire, and radical feminism that ties together the "linguistic turn," decolonization theory, revolutionary pedagogy, queer theory, and feminism, Anzaldúa turned to language as a political force: "Writing and speaking are political acts that spring from the impulse to subvert, resist, educate, and make changes."[44] Anzaldúa had to write or she would have shriveled up and died: "Writing saved my life," and in the process of saving her life she also created "a language of rebellion" to reclaim her agency through language.[45] The only thing that could save Anzaldúa from the horror of her reality was protest, revolt, and defiant resistance via the written word: "Why am I compelled to write," she asks? "Because I have no choice. Because I must keep the spirit of my revolt and myself alive."[46] Writing, if properly enacted, was a "deliberate and desperate determination to subvert the status quo."[47] But one has to be "stubborn, preserving, impenetrable as stone, yet possessing a malleability that renders us unbreakable."[48] Finally, Anzaldúa's work, as she puts it, is a "conscious rupture with all oppressive traditions of all cultures and religions," in order to live a better life with others in a transformed reality.[49]

Culture of Resistance

Anzaldúa's concept of culture as something that "touches," "edges," and "straddles" divergent areas without annulling the distinctiveness of each, while also producing a third unreconciled zone, continues the theme of resistance to domination but in the cultural sphere.[50] For Anzaldúa, culture and identity are entities that are permanently contested and ongoing formations without conclusion. Anzaldúa's identity is a creative, if not a fugitive, construct: "My identity is always in flux."[51] Culture for Anzaldúa also escapes rigid classification and is conceived of as an open creative process that interrupts a feeling of belonging and orientation. Anzaldúa argues that "the feeling of not belonging to any culture at all" and that "to be disoriented in space is the normal way of being for us *mestizas* living in the borderlands."[52]

Via self-craft, Anzaldúa fashioned and re-created herself as something new. But Anzaldúa was not a radical individualist. Coalitions and allies were needed to contest oppressive traditions since cultures and traditions are collective and not individual constructs. For example, Anzaldúa argues that "we need to allow whites to be our allies."[53] Anzaldúa notes that "it is not that I reject everything that has to do with white culture. I like the English language, for example, and there is a lot of Anglo ideology that I like as well. But not all of it fits with our experiences and cultural roots."[54] Anzaldúa continues:

> As a *mestiza* I have no country, my homeland cast me out; yet all countries are mine because I am every women's sister or potential lover. (As a lesbian I have no race, my own people

disclaim me; but I am all races because there is the queer of me in all races.) I am cultureless because, as feminist, I challenge the collective cultural/religious male-derived beliefs of Indo-Hispanics and Anglos; yet I am cultured because I am participating in the creation of yet another culture.[55]

Anzaldúa's new culture would not replicate the exclusions and closures of nationalist communal belonging because "the new *mestiza* has a 'plural personality.'"[56] Cultivating a plural personality, Anzaldúa believes, increases the likelihood of receptivity and sensitivity to others.

Since Anzaldúa could not change the world by herself alone, Anzaldúa called for a "sociality of resistance."[57] Building coalitions and alliance work was necessary for this but it was not easy work because it is "the attempt to shift positions, change positions, reposition ourselves regarding our individual and collective identities."[58] This was uncomfortable because it undermined common modes of understanding and hierarchical formations: "Coalition work is about individual voices being heard not as a figure-head speaking."[59] Through the fusion of a creative spirit and the spirit of resistance in the context of both personal and historical knowledge of oppression, Anzaldúa builds a mode of resistance based on knowing the past: "We must know our history of resistance."[60] In this regard, Anzaldúa's life experiences led her to become political and reinvent the meaning of the political.[61] Creativity was how it manifested in the written word and had a political meaning: "Creative acts are forms of political activism employing definite aesthetic strategies for resisting dominant cultural norms."[62] As I have previously noted, the political dimension in Anzaldúa is a result of how she channels lived experience into her reflections on identity (self-craft) and the demand for social justice. Anzaldúa developed a new way of being that opened the possibility of connections with others but without annulling what was unique about each singular person. This approach overcomes the hypocrisy of the discourse of universality that only masquerades as universal while serving and perpetuating the interests of specific groups.[63]

Freedom

If writing and resistance are two mutually reinforcing moments in Anzaldúa's work, the word *freedom* is a unifying theme that arguably brings all of these pieces together. Anzaldúa, for example, claims she chose to be queer.[64] Anzaldúa also demands the freedom to chisel her own face.[65] Hence, Anzaldúa transgresses the narrow roles prescribed for Latinas. Anzaldúa is free to write bi- or even trilingually, and she is free to have a "wild tongue." What type of freedom is this? It would be a mistake to read all of these gestures as a form of rugged individualism, a form of "butching" up the self in order to become invulnerable, impenetrable, and untouchable; a Chicana sovereign Kantian lord of the universe, as it were.[66] By delving into her own autobiography and redefining what freedom might mean in a transformed reality, Anzaldúa acquired the capacity to forge connections with others, but the condition of this was her total vulnerability. This departs from conceptions of freedom conceived on the model of the sovereign subject who objectifies everything external to him and exploits the world to maximize self-interest.[67] Freedom, for Anzaldúa, depends on vulnerability and overcoming the subject/object dualism.[68]

In this regard, Anzaldúa has a complex, and arguably superior, notion of the will, freedom, and the self than that of Chicano nationalists.[69] Reflecting on the process of writing a book, Anzaldúa muses that "this whole thing has a mind of its own . . . with minimal direction from my will."[70] Additionally, by sharing the most private details of her struggle to live as a person with dignity in the very contexts that seek to annihilate the self, vulnerability becomes, ironically, Anzaldúa's most powerful weapon.[71] That is, vulnerability becomes the foundation on which alliances and solidarity with others can be created for the purposes of fighting for one's dignity. This possibility is foreclosed if the relation we have with ourselves (one of domination and repression) is generalized and dictates how we relate to others. In a moment of self-diagnosis, Anzaldúa states: "I spent the first half of my life learning to rule myself."[72] The *mestiza*, in contrast, makes "herself vulnerable to foreign ways of seeing and thinking."[73] She is "weaponless with open arms."[74] Putting down our arms (guns) and simultaneously opening our arms is central to both loving ourselves (singing the song of ourselves [drawing on a phrase from Walt Whitman]) and existing alongside others in loving and nonviolent ways.

Self-craft, that is, Anzaldúa's ongoing and never completed work on the self, was a precondition to enter and inhabit the transformed reality that is the product of theorizing the border and herself:

My 'awakened dreams' are about shifts. Thought shifts, reality shifts, gender shifts: one person metamorphoses into another in a world where people fly through the air, heal from mortal wounds. I am playing with my Self, I am playing with the world's soul, I am the dialogue between my Self and *el espíritu del mundo*. I change myself, I change the world.[75]

Anzaldúa's work on the self was, to express it again, not a narcissistic gesture or a bottomless plunge into the abyss and fixation on one's wounds and scabs but the starting point of Anzaldúa's revolutionary activity.[76] To this end, the most amazing thing Anzaldúa did, at least in her own mind, was to write: "Writing is the most daring thing I have ever done and the most dangerous."[77] Writing was the ultimate manifestation of her freedom. Anzaldúa's autobiographical work allowed her to refashion herself. Hence, it saved her life: "The writing is my whole life, it is my obsession."[78] Anzaldúa's writings also had a global significance for women of color and all people. Anzaldúa's writing created an opening for others to see their own experiences within a broader network of oppressive practices that one need not accept. To the extent Anzaldúa changed herself, as the quote above indicates, she changed the world.

Given the role culture, resistance, freedom, writing, and reclaiming the dignity of the self in a world bent on violating it, Anzaldúa can arguably play a pivotal role in the development of militant agency and a "migrant way of being."[79] For Maria Lugones, "Anzaldúa's *Borderlands* is a work creating a theoretical space for resistance."[80] Creating a space for resistance involves the creation of agency. Contestation and resistance only make sense within the context of oppression. Anzaldúa provides this context in autobiographical and historical form. Anzaldúa is angry and this anger is grounded in the experience of marginalization and oppression. But the self or identity conception that results from the experience of oppression is not fixed and static but is "a kind of equilibrium."[81] Anzaldúa channels her anger into literary-political creative acts so that she can corroborate her freedom and simultaneously sustain her vulnerability. Anzaldúa sings the song of herself not in a vacuum but as an impassioned cry to others to reclaim their dignity, write their own counternarrative, and to live alongside others with a gentle and loving spirit. Anzaldúa does not provide a static/fixed "us" versus "them" identity that was a defining feature of Chicano nationalist radical politics but, in line with Jacques Derrida's insight that *what is proper for a culture is to not be identical to itself*," Anzaldúa opens up identity formation to what makes it alive, historical, and capable of continuous change.[82]

Beltrán's Critique of Anzaldúa

Not all scholars find Anzaldúa's theoretical dance between her experiences as a working-class lesbian Chicana living in the borderlands, self-craft, and appeal to hybridity to be politically productive. Cristina Beltrán's critique of Anzaldúa is arguably the most direct and sustained challenge to Anzaldúa's new mestiza identity and consciousness. To be more specific, Beltrán argues that Anzaldúa's appeal to hybridity "becomes a foundational or fixed identity that forecloses more creative and productively defiant approaches to identity and subjectivity."[83] For Beltrán, "Anzaldúa veers from the productive possibilities of contingency and crossings toward the solace of epistemic privilege. And it is this double gesture—this contradiction—that lies at the heart of *Borderlands/La Frontera*."[84] Beltrán continues: "Chicano nationalists produced a politicized subjectivity during the Chicano Movement that emerged as the basis for recent notions of hybridity put forward by writers like Gloria Anzaldúa."[85]

Beltrán goes on to argue that Anzaldúa portrays the art of the West as monolithically bad and non-Western cultures are monolithically good.[86] Beltrán also argues that Anzaldúa privileges the experience of marginal subjects with the solace of "epistemic privilege" via "*La facultad.*"[87] The appeal to an epistemic privileged position would sound something like this: "You can never know what I know because you have not experienced what I have been through." Additionally, Beltrán argues that Anzaldúa's language of borders implies "stability on either side."[88] For Beltrán, Anzaldúa creates a sense of commonality and shared epistemology that undercuts the potential for disagreement amongst border subjects. There is also a "privileging of the indigenous side of *mestiza* identity."[89] Anzaldúa, finally, constructs a "dominant narrative of subjectivity in which some subjects represent multiplicity and insight while others signify unenlightened singularity."[90] Anzaldúa retreats, in the words of Beltrán, from the radical implications of *mestizaje*. Ultimately, Anzaldúa's approach to theorizing *mestizaje* in Chicano political discourse is "unsuccessful."[91]

Even though Beltrán's critique is carefully argued and draws on evidence that supports her claims, Beltrán's engagement with Anzaldúa is at best a misreading. To be more specific, Beltrán misses Anzaldúa's entire thesis that complicates this interpretation, including Anzaldúa's critique of dualistic thinking, Anzaldúa's work on coalition politics, and her historical/fluid conception of identity (self-craft). Additionally, Beltrán arguably holds Anzaldúa up to a potentially unreasonable standard of political purity in the sense of expelling identity from the equation of political subjectivity (even though Anzaldúa develops a new mode of identity that arguably avoids the pitfalls Beltrán criticizes) that has the consequence of dismissing the aspects of Anzaldúa that are central to a revitalization of radical citizenship and rethinking of Chicana feminism. I find Yvonne Yarbro-Bejarano's view of Anzaldúa much more compelling than Beltrán's. Anzaldúa, according to Yarbro-Bejarano, could be accused of a "romanticized linking between Chicanos and indigenous cultures." However, for Yarbro-Bejarano, Anzaldúa invokes the indigenous in the name of the "construction of an inclusive and multiple identity" not an exclusionary and singular Chicano identity.[92]

Self-craft, that is, narrating the experience of personal oppression/struggle is where political theorizing begins for Anzaldúa as a way to rebuild her agency, resist oppressive traditions, and trigger collective resistance. Without rebuilding her identity by establishing her voice and interpreting her life in ways that validate her experiences, Anzaldúa would lack the context/location from which to contest oppression.[93]

In addition to the type of critical autobiography she practices, Anzaldúa's writing style is also a mode of resistance. Anzaldúa's work breaks norms of academic discourse. Like Nietzsche, Anzaldúa is poet, historian, artist, madwoman, Antichrist, and activist, but she is arguably more radical than Nietzsche.[94] How? Anzaldúa mixes languages and overcomes herself as a way to connect with others while avoiding Nietzsche's nostalgia for aristocracy, tragedy, and radical individualism. Switching codes, mixing English, Castilian Spanish, North Mexican dialect, "Tex-Mex," and Nahuatl in the spoken and written word force the issue of Anzaldúa's resistance to Anglo domination by not only refusing to erase parts of herself in the shakedown of assimilation, but by creating her own language ("language is a homeland") that was highly personal but also comprehensible to others: "I am my language."[95] Anzaldúa's new language, though, would not be a sovereign gesture: "There is no one Chicano language just as there is no one Chicano experience."[96] In this way, contestation is Anzaldúa's *modus operandi* in terms of linguistic practices and writing style (and her being, for that matter), but Beltrán has a difficult time seeing this. In keeping with her commitment to *mestiza* consciousness and modes of being, Anzaldúa had multiple faces and, contra Beltrán, Anzaldúa fashioned hers (via self-craft) in ways that broke with the conservatism of Chicano nationalism.[97] In the process Anzaldúa opened Chicana identity to something connected to the past but without being completely determined by the past. Contra Beltrán, Anzaldúa draws on but does not replicate the ideological assumptions of the Latino authors Anzaldúa in part bases her work on.[98]

True, Anzaldúa is indebted to the militant radicalism of the Chicano movement, but she moves beyond the nationalist and patriarchal dimensions of it by theorizing the experiences of women of color on the border in order to create modes of identity that are fluid, flexible, and open; identities that are more of a crossroads than an end point.[99] Identity, for Anzaldúa, should not close one down but open one up and establish connection with others. Anzaldúa states: "All blood is intricately woven together."[100] Beltrán sees Anzaldúa as ultimately falling back into the same forms of fixed identity of the Chicano movement. For Beltrán, "Anzaldúa is too invested in earlier nationalist narratives of *mestizaje* and their conception of monolithic stable Anglo subjects."[101] For Beltrán, there is a lack of a space for contestation in Anzaldúa because of this.[102] This view is at best an overstatement and a misreading. If one takes into account the following citation by Anzaldúa, Beltrán seems to miss the entire point. As Anzaldúa puts it, "I don't have any real 'original Mexican' roots."[103] Anzaldúa's work thus breaks with the discourse of Chicano nationalism, and it is a foray into the intersections between words as weapons of domination (Nietzsche), decolonization theory (Fanon), revolutionary pedagogy (Freire), cultural hybridity (Derrida), feminism, queer theory, and Chicana studies.

Nevertheless, it could be objected that self-craft can be easily co-opted to fit into a neoliberal discourse of the adaptable, instrumental, and predictable self who self-invents to self-benefit. Also, that self-craft lacks a normative component. That self-craft, finally, is not really that threatening to anything. I disagree with these objections. First, self-craft is the path to solidarity. Self-craft is ultimately a social practice that builds communities capable of resisting diffuse forms of neoliberal oppression. Self-craft also emboldens historically marginalized groups to come together, stand up, and protest. In this way, self-craft is embedded in a larger political context and is positioned against neoliberal conceptions of the self. Second, self-craft does not lack a normative edge. It creates revolutionary forms of subjectivity that open a new world beyond the cruelty, exclusion, and violence of neoliberalism. This is based on constantly shifting positions and affirming the fissures/borders that constitute identity as opposed to building walls to create closed forms of the self that render solidarity impossible. Third, self-craft is threatening because it empowers previously marginalized groups to come together to protest and resist neoliberal oppression.

Conclusion

Andrew L. Barlow argues "globalization's tendency to marginalize or exclude people of color has given new life to ethnic community formation and resistance."[104] Tack on what Étienne Balibar calls the violent suppression of the poor as the new basis for neoliberal capital accumulation and an explosive political situation is created.[105] As the political order becomes more repressive as a way to hold together a society splitting into the superrich and the rest of us, the working poor and ethnic minorities are pitted against each other in a battle for survival. Their mutual hostility is generated through the manipulation of hatred via media images that perpetuate stereotypes about brown and black people, academics and politicians who exploit and target people of color to rebuild a lost sense of white identity and national unity, increasingly repressive social policy that *racializes* criminality, and a war against immigrants being waged on the US-Mexico border and throughout the country.

As time goes on, we are learning that the border is no longer confined to a specific geographical location as a result of the presence of various forms of border patrol and state/federal police everywhere.[106] Anzaldúa shows us how norms act as omnipresent border patrol agents that inhabit our minds, our bodies, our sense of political possibility, and attempt to crush us under the weight of patriarchal, racist, and heteronormative hegemony.

Every day, we are bombarded with racially coded expressions that masquerade as color-blind and race neutral (e.g., "welfare," "good schools," "crime," "undeserving poor") as a way to engender racial hatred (albeit in subtle ways), to prevent working-class solidarity with ethnic/racial groups.[107] Given this, collective action against current political and economic elites will continue to be unlikely unless a broad alliance can be formed between a divergent set of groups with a focus on how the current political and economic system can be transformed to benefit all people, not just the top 1 percent. But this would involve drawing on modes of ethnic and racial political resistance already in place and *politicizing* identity in line with the suggestions made by Anzaldúa as the precondition for broad-based collective solidarity. The argument that identities are only social constructions may be accurate, but it would be irresponsible to downplay the material components of oppression that result from these socially constructed categories that disproportionately impact people of color.

Let's go back to the question I posed at the beginning of this chapter. How can the public (including women of color) gain greater voice and empowerment in the context of unequal access to the political sphere, neoliberal hegemony, political dysfunction, patriarchy, racism, and the corporate domination of the political realm? Marx's critique of capitalism and conception of a homogenous revolutionary proletariat may be part of the answer, but it is not a complete one as a result of the lack of differentiation within the concept of the proletariat and Marx's arguably Eurocentric perspective.[108] Michael Hardt and Antonio Negri's "multitude" improves on Marx insofar as Hardt and Negri explore global resistance movements capable of action in common without annulling internal difference in order to challenge the decentered sovereignty of corporations and international institutions.[109] Even though Anzaldúa draws on a different historical and political context to derive her conclusions, she articulates a complementary position to Hardt and Negri that is worth exploring.

A broader base for collective resistance against current political and economic institutions that includes women of color is needed today. This base for resistance can come from "the third space" Anzaldúa creates— the "interstice that allows contradictions to coexist in the production of a new element."[110] Anzaldúa offers a creative way to politicize identity as a way to create a basis for collective solidarity and to create an explosion of militant resistance against an oppressive and antidemocratic global political order. In this sense, Anzaldúa's creative version of Chicana feminism as a multidimensional practice of resistance and contestation is the key for collective resistance against the neoliberal nightmare. In the case of Anzaldúa, self-craft and singing the song of herself is also a song about others. Self-craft as a mode of protest against hegemonic norms pulls the self out of the abyss of shame and self-hatred and becomes the basis for new modes of collective solidarity.

Consider, for example, Black Lives Matter (BLM). This movement has assembled a broad coalition of individuals and groups to fight the horrific persecution and oppression of people of color, specifically, young black males. Created in 2012, BLM eschews narrow nationalism and connects struggles "across race, class, gender, nationality, sexuality, and disability" (as stated on the BLM website). Today, BLM is impossible to ignore. Their intersectional strategy has been effective.[111] The fact that BLM has been met with a significant amount of hostility testifies to the fact that the United States political system is threatened by people of color, especially the ones who draw attention to current racist practices. When people of color announce themselves as full and equal citizens in extra-institutional political spaces, they are met with the repressive apparatus of the state (e.g., militarized police forces).

Consider, moreover, the alliance forged between US veterans and water protectors at Standing Rock Indian reservation.[112] These examples demonstrate that identity claims are not only compatible with action in concert but may also represent the spark capable of triggering broader forms of collective mobilization in the name of a better future. Through Anzaldúa's unique form of identity politics, she opens spaces for new forms of political agency. Anzaldúa charts a way for groups who have been historically excluded to advance and protect their political and economic interests. She thereby expands the range of practices that constitute democratic and confrontational citizenship.

Chapter Seven
Paulo Freire and the Pedagogy of Revolt

How individuals define politics, or what they learn to count as politics, is arguably a political matter. Consider, for example, the incomprehension of the upper class when the lower class take to the street and fight the police in extreme moments of social unrest.[1] This action is not political, the rich might say, it is criminal! Clearly, one's standpoint compels one to view some things as properly political and other popular manifestations as asocial, criminal, or insane.[2] Another way of putting this is to say day-to-day politics lives off of the erasure of the political assumptions already presupposed in a political regime. Individuals and groups that are marginalized yet demand fundamental change will be ignored, denounced, imprisoned, and in extreme cases, killed. Given this, expanding the parameters of what counts as politics is a subversive act. The conceptual expansion of politics gives previously excluded groups a way to make sense of their reality so that they may struggle to change it.

Educational institutions are one of the arenas where the battle over the expansion and contraction of the meaning of politics is waged. At least since Plato who grounded his ideal state on a rigorous series of tests as well as a myth of legitimation (e.g., "myth of metals") to justify hierarchical political-philosophical rule in the *Republic*, educational institutions have not been neutral spaces for the mere acquisition of knowledge.[3] Rather, educational institutions are political because they operate within a field of broader power relations.[4] Through control of the curriculum, establishing correct parameters for teaching and research, alignment with corporate objectives, and promulgating professional norms, educational institutions arguably reflect and reinforce the power relations of the given political order.[5] Educational institutions also justify and thereby attempt to defuse the volatility of hierarchical rule and the unequal distribution of wealth/privilege. The use of violence to beat a population into submission usually signifies the failure of educational (and other ideo-logical) institutions to do their work. If it is true to say that educational institutions have historically been conservative institutions designed to perpetuate the political status quo, how might educational institutions be transformed to become sites of revolutionary thinking and change? How might the neoliberal university engender the radical critique of its own presuppositions and open utopian vistas for imagining alternatives to current political and economic arrangements? These questions require us to examine how the pedagogical intersects the political, the global, and the discipline of political science. These questions require us to take a look at the writings of Paulo Freire.

Even though Paulo Freire's work starts from a space seemingly distant from the political realm (e.g., pedagogy), the educational activist and theorist Freire provides a critical understanding of education that has revolutionary implications for our understanding of politics as well as for the transformation of political science education. Via dialogic praxis, the reinvention of power, and permanent revolution, Freire over-comes the "iron law of oligarchy" in the classroom and polity. He thereby reconnects local political struggles to the utopian aspiration for democ-racy without leaders. Freire is thus a thinker from whom we have a lot to learn, especially in the field of political science which has yet to affirm Freire's political-pedagogical insights as a way to open and advance a world beyond the neoliberal nightmare of permanent war, growing inequality, political corruption, and prison as a way of life.

There have been many good studies of Freire's work on pedagogy, but the majority of this research has been conducted in fields other than political science.[7] What distinguishes my interpretation of Freire from these treatments of him is my emphasis on (1) Freire as a political theorist and (2) how he can put the political into political science via pedagogy. Freire's utopian hopefulness can also help us think our way out of the contemporary impasse in political theory where it is fashionable to argue that we are living in a nightmare where, as Wendy Brown puts it, the "*demos* have been undone," but no options are articulated to challenge this.[8] Freire's work can also enrich the conversation about pedagogy as more political scientists express interest in and conduct research on teaching and learning. Freire, finally, is also helpful for exposing the complicity of at least part of the discipline of political science with the political status quo.[9]

Paulo Freire

The Brazilian global educational activist Paulo Freire (1921-97) should be counted among the few individuals in the twentieth century who fundamentally changed how the political realm is experienced and perceived by those on the bottom of the political order. This was the result of Freire's experiences working with the illiterate in the former slave colonies in South America, in particular, Brazil; his time living in the United States and in Europe during his exile; his international travel as a public intellectual; and his stint as secretary of education for the city of São Paulo, Brazil. In terms of intellectual influences, Freire was a dialectical thinker who fused Kantian universalism with the humanism of the early Marx. He connected both aspects in a form of popular *paideia*, signifying intellectual emancipation for the people and commitment to the revolutionary transformation of society.[10] For Freire, educational practices are a way to build organized popular power capable of confronting and overthrowing oppressive political orders. Freire is relevant today because of this, as well as the fact that he illuminates the political implications of education in ways that were previously unrecognized that are a direct consequence of his time working with illiterate adults in the Third World.[11] Freire thus rewrites Kant's "An Answer to the Question: 'What Is Enlightenment?'" for those who have been left out of or beat down by the new neoliberal global political order.[12]

Freire was formally trained as a lawyer (although he never practiced law). His commitment to radical democracy, a nondogmatic Marxist critique of society, and the defense of identity politics is clear throughout his writings and leads to a position not of just denouncing injustice but of "announcing a new utopia."[13] Freire is thus a utopian thinker from whom we have a lot to learn because he fused critique with the discourse of hope. As Cornel West puts it, Freire fused "social theory, moral outrage, and political praxis."[14] As the working conditions for educators deteriorate as a result of budget cuts, the corporatization of higher education, and rule by shortsighted opportunistic administrators, Freire is a model intellectual for showing how to hold onto one's integrity and commitment to revolutionary change while working for neoliberal educational institutions.[15]

In terms of his political biography, Freire was interrogated and imprisoned in a tiny cell for approximately three months by the Brazilian military junta that seized power in 1964.[16] Why? Because Freire taught the lower classes how to read and understand their place on the bottom of society as a result of the legacies of colonialism and political decisions of the reigning elite. Even after he left Brazil, Freire's reputation as an educational revolutionary, much like Che Guevara's, often preceded him. Freire was prevented from entering Haiti, and he was arrested in Gabon, Africa. After sixteen years in exile, he returned to Brazil in 1980, and continued his work on the humanization of the classroom space.

"I'm Neutral"

Freire's reflections on the interrelationship between the political and educational spheres begin with his rejection of the discourse of scientific neutrality (and the pursuit of objective knowledge) among scholars and educators in the humanities, social sciences, and education departments. For Freire, the belief in intellectual neutrality flags a specific vision of politics and life premised on the assumption of the legitimacy of the status quo. To adopt an uncritical mind-set to the status quo is inescapably a way of supporting the status quo. Freire states: "Claiming neutrality does not constitute neutrality; quite the contrary, it helps maintain the status quo."[17] Freire continues: "All educational practice implies an interpretation of man and the world."[18] Because of this, educational practices (e.g., teaching style and definition of research) are inescapably infused with political and value commitments. As Peter McLaren puts it, "*the pedagogical* is implicated in *the political*."[19] The attempt to negate the political and value-laden character of educational practices would not only represent a negation of life but would also be an outright lie.[20] Freire states, "I could never treat education as something cold, mental, merely technical, and without soul."[21] For Freire, education for student and teacher alike involves the whole person—their life history, their political commitments, and their aspirations: "Our presence in the world, which implies choice and decision, is not a neutral presence."[22]

In any academic discipline, but especially the social sciences, the fixation on method, technique, and the belief in objective knowledge sidesteps the fundamental issue, namely, the problem of power as it plays out in the relationship between education and the broader society.[23] At its worst, the fixation on method generates noncritical, descriptive, and arguably ideological academic disciplines as a result of the de facto endorsement of the political status quo.[24] As Freire states, "no educational practice takes place in a vacuum."[25] For Freire, "the so-called neutrality of science is nothing more than a necessary myth of the ruling classes."[26] A politically relevant teaching practice and research project, according to Freire, would fuse a critique of power with a hopeful vision for social and political change, and foreground the question of whose interests are being served as a result of what is taking place in the classroom and whose interests are being served by what is appearing in print in academic books and journals.[27]

Because Freire experienced firsthand the role education played and continues to play in the domination of the impoverished populations of colonies and former colonies, the classroom must be viewed as a realm of politics. Consider, for example, that the classroom continues to be used as a weapon against the poor to keep them in their place (e.g., via high-tech surveillance in schools; permanent police presence; patriotic rituals [e.g., flag salute]), disseminates ideological narratives (parading as objective) about why some people are poor and others are rich and rhetoric about equal opportunity.[28] The classroom can also be deployed and mobilized to further the fight against the past and present legacies of colonialism, rule by the few, and for progressive social and political transformation. Because of this unconventional and provocative position, many doubted, as Freire claimed, "whether or not I am an educator."[29] This doubt or reservation about Freire being an educator was itself a political move, though. All education/research is inescapably political as a result of the way problems are framed, the questions that are asked, and whose research is included in or excluded from the discussion.[30]

The acknowledgment of the political significance of research, teaching, and education does not mean that all positions are reduced to the level of opinion and that no one is right or wrong about anything.[31] Some arguments are qualitatively better than other arguments, even if all arguments ultimately lack an absolute basis. Freire's rejection of neutrality simply means facing up to the fact that everything that takes place within educational institutions has political implications, that knowledge is always situated in a historical context, and that no decision is ever made in a sphere untouched by power. Freire wants educators and scholars to embrace "epistemological distance" as a check on "aggressive rationalism" where a methodological fixation on trees risks blinding one to the larger forest of power.[32] Freire's rejection of positivism as the ideology of the reigning elite should not be construed as a rejection of rigorous academic work. He isn't stuck in a simplistic binary. Freire explains: "My position is to be in sympathy with both commonsense and a rigorous academic approach."[33]

Freire's true educator, that is, one committed to creating a society that allows all humans to flourish, would not indoctrinate students to follow a particular party line. As Freire puts it, "no one can unveil the world for another."[34] By avowing the political character of educational institutions as a force for progressive social and political change, and simultaneously rejecting the imposition of a counterhegemonic dogma on the minds of students, Freire constructs a hopeful vision for political change based on a critical theory of power and a utopian vision of a new type of political order. Freire thus engages in a metapolitical project in the Kantian sense of working on the conditions of possibility for the emergence of radical political subjectivity, but avoids the Leninist dictum of a self-appointed elite that leads the people to the promised land.

For Freire, the decisions educators make (or simply accept and practice as a result of habit and professional norms) must be brought to the level of political consciousness. Freire thus backs educators into a political-existential corner where educators are required to be more explicit about the political implications of classroom practices (e.g., how one teaches), the political implications of the content of what is taught (e.g., what one teaches), and the core assumptions and political implications of a particular research project (e.g., vision for political change). It is hard to imagine, for example, that students are being educated to be democratic citizens in classes organized on the basis of lecture for the entire class period, where teachers deposit knowledge into the heads of students who sit there passive and silent. Students cannot be liberated, Freire proclaims, with the "instruments of domestication."[35]

It is also hard to imagine that students will understand anything significant about American democracy by memorizing the functions of political institutions and sidestepping how capitalism limits, if not negates, rule by the people. Yet the relationship between the American political state and capitalism is virtually ignored by nearly every standard textbook on American politics for first year university students.[36] It is also hard to imagine that objective research is being carried out when the scholars conducting the research assume that inequality is inevitable, rule by the enlightened few is wise, and that the masses are destined to be ignorant and impoverished.[37] As Freire states, "it is naïve to expect the dominant classes to develop a type of education that would enable subordinate classes to perceive social injustices critically."[38] Finally, it is hard to imagine that a scholar is serving a valuable role as a member in a democratic society when they state about their research, as UCLA professor of political science Lynn Vavreck does, that "it's not the job of the scholars conducting the work to explain it."[39]

For Freire, there is no escape from the educational-existential decision. Either one sides with the political status quo (even if by default), or one positions oneself in the classroom as a force for social and political transformation. Whereas John Dewey posits the integrative value of education on young people in *Democracy and Education*, Freire as a result of working with the "wretched of the earth" in the Third World, viewed education as a vehicle for the recuperation of the humanity of the oppressed and for the revolutionary transformation of society.[40] If educators merely replicate via habit the content requirements of their academic discipline, condition students to adapt and integrate themselves to the status quo, and preoccupy themselves solely with methodology, Freire argues that they are instruments of domination for the ruling class. What matters for him is how educational institutions position students as political subjects. For Freire, "the important thing is to place men in conscious confrontation with their problems, to make them agents of their own recuperation."[41] As the reader may have guessed, Freire becomes a political target as a result of his ideas, which, as he states, "do not benefit the interests of the dominant class."[42]

It would be a mistake, however, to reduce Freire's political position to a sort of reverse indoctrination, where the progressive ideas the educator identifies are simply pounded into the brains of students. Freire states: "Treating schools as non-neutral spaces does not mean turning them into a political base for the party in power."[43] He also claims that "what is impermissible is for teachers to impose on their pupils their own 'reading of the world.'"[44] For Freire, the Right and Left are in some ways the same insofar as they use schools as propaganda sites for the political indoctrination of young people.

The Right imposes and generalizes a dictatorship of the marketplace and eliminates from students the capacity to dream of an alternative to the neoliberal political and economic status quo. The Left's mistake, for Freire, "has always been their absolute conviction of their certainties, which makes them sectarian, authoritarian, and religious."[45] For Freire, Marxists also need to get over their "smug certainty."[46] Freire thus rejects all party lines and attempts to make the political significance of education explicit through an egalitarian-dialogic approach to teaching that is dedicated to recuperating the humanity of students. This requires something deeper than merely inverting hierarchy, imposing a model for correct thinking onto students, demonizing others, and restricting the realm of acceptable thoughts. Rather, it starts by rejecting the discourse of neutrality and positivism as ideologies of the ruling class. It also starts by rejecting the fundamentalism of the Right and Left and the "arrogance of administrators."[47] Finally, it requires having faith in the people irrespective of their social class and previous conditions of physical and mental servitude. "Trusting the people," Freire proclaims, "is the indispensable precondition for revolutionary change."[48]

Illiteracy

Reading and writing are not neutral activities but are connected to politics, questions of power, and political struggle.[49] Freire's interest in adult literacy grew out of his firsthand experience working with rural farm workers and urban slum dwellers in South America. Literacy was a political issue not in some broad existential sense but because literacy was a requirement for voting in Brazil as outlined in the 1891 Brazilian Constitution, and like all literacy tests, it was designed to be failed.[50] Hence, illiteracy is a political and structural problem insofar as some groups are positioned in the social order in ways that prevent them from having and/or acquiring the capacity to read and name the world. In this sense, illiteracy is a form of socially engineered paralysis of the political imagination and sign of political disempowerment.

In "Literacy and Destitution," Freire continues these themes and argues that literacy is not just about reading and writing (e.g., learning one's ABC's) but is a broader political issue that is connected to struggles for social and political transformation.[51] Freire's concept of literacy as something broader than a minimal capacity to grasp abstract symbols or rhythmically sing the sounds of consonants to include a basic understanding of politics, or what is often called political literacy, is particularly relevant to the United States and other advanced industrial societies. Consider, for example, that today millions of people in advanced industrialized democracies have their attention directed to a variety of spectacles (e.g., sporting and media events), and seem to be swimming in oceans of information via talk radio and headline news. [52] These *technologistas*, who might crash into you because they are texting while driving, or who you might bump into on the street or in an airport because they walk with their heads permanently tilted downward, also blog, text, tweet on Twitter, post "selfies" and "usies" on Facebook, send videos on Snapchat, count their followers on Instagram, and chase Pokéman. It would be a mistake, though, to define literacy as the quantity of information one is exposed to, transfers, and can absorb.[53] In the face of literally oceans of information, an uninformed electorate paralyzed by the strange combination of profound ignorance and self-satisfied arrogance in the world's "leading" democracy continues to stare political scientists in the face.[54] Freire's work on literacy is important for understanding the broader social and political forces that have produced this strange form of oligarchic corporate democracy with uninformed/misinformed, somewhat cynical, and self-satisfied citizens in the United States.[55] The political significance of sleepwalking *technologistas* is troubling because they are vulnerable to misinformation, propaganda, and the inflammatory rhetoric of demagogue-entertainers who promise them freedom via debt, peace through war, and identity by way of walls and the sacrifice of the immigrant other.

Contra conceptions of literacy construed as the minimal knowledge needed to read and write, Freire's concept of literacy is political because it reclaims language from abstract, static, and reified formulations and situates words in contexts that illuminate broader power relationships. For Freire, "problems of language always involve ideological questions and, along with them, questions of power."[56] Words, for Freire, are not neutral but weapons within highly charged political contexts that are connected to the social control of marginalized populations. Since illiteracy is a structural problem, the project of literacy must put an end to the structures that generated the problem. For Freire, "illiteracy is one of the concrete expressions of an unjust social reality."[57] Hence, literacy and political agency work together. For Freire, literacy is a route to the "invention of citizenship."[58] It did not make a difference whether the invention of citizenship would take place in remote villages in South America, alongside the Rio Grande in south Texas, or in schools in Long Beach, CA. In every case, literacy was a question of the social and political understanding and possible transformation of an unjust reality. The teaching style and specific examples used in the classroom for the project of literacy must confront the structures of power that shape the life chances and intellectual horizons of impoverished people, not hide these power relationships behind myths about the slow but inevitable spread of democracy, the growing inclusion of underrepresented groups in the political process, minimal civilian casualties in war as a result of "smart bombs," national unity, and the United States as the greatest peace-loving country in the history of the world.

Fundamental Inversion

The type of critical pedagogy formulated by Freire required a fundamental inversion pertaining to the way educators and students conceptualized the learning process. The questions Freire asks are not whether students are learning, not whether our measurements for learning are accurate, not whether students are being adequately prepared for the workplace, not whether there are enough writing assignments, not whether the latest "best practices" are employed, and not whether tests are being used to maximize learning.[59] Freire asks, first, who are the students in terms of their lived experience, socioeconomic class, and access to the political sphere? As Stanley Aronowitz aptly puts it, Freire helps students "achieve a grasp of the concrete conditions of their daily lives."[60] For Freire, "the educator must begin with the educands' 'here' and not with her or his own."[61] One must, Freire asserts, "get close to the language and syntax of the audience."[62] For Freire, there is a "need for educators to soak up as it were the culture of the popular masses."[63] This knowledge allows the educator to form an intersubjective connection with students so a new type of learning can take place.

This new type of learning must help students gain a political understanding of their daily lives. For the majority of people on the planet, everyday life is structured by exploitation, unequal power, privilege, exclusion, and domination that is enforced through the internalization of codes dictating acquiescence and social deference, and ultimately backed up with violence. For Freire, anything that prevents students from acquiring a political understanding of their lived experience is an oppressive mystification, an ideological tactic of domination, and the devaluation of the humanity of students. In contrast to vocational pedagogical approaches based on teaching students to adapt to and find a place within the political and economic status quo, critical pedagogy helps students forge connections between their lives and broader social and economic conditions for the purpose of the revolutionary transformation of society. Students are thereby given and simultaneously give themselves the capacity to "intervene in their context."[64] Critical pedagogy boils down to the self-acquisition of political consciousness, or to what Freire calls *conscientização*, which he defines as the "awakening of critical awareness."[65]

The failure to know who one is teaching in terms of their socioeconomic location in society would thus make it impossible to teach students in any meaningful sense of the term: "Unless educators expose themselves to the popular culture across the board," Freire asserts, "their discourse will hardly be heard by anyone but themselves."[66] Learning about the daily lives of students, in particular, how students are already political beings is the first step to Freire's political understanding of teaching. The reinvention of the power relation in the classroom between teacher and student on the basis of the dialogic encounter and problem-posing pedagogical practice is the second step, and sets the stage for the emergence of collective solidarity and a newly acquired political consciousness.[67] For Freire, "dialogue in any situation demands the problematic confrontation of that very knowledge in its unquestionable relationship with the concrete reality in which it is engendered and on which it acts in order to better understand, explain, and transform that reality."[68]

Freire's theory of dialogue rejects the view that the teacher talks and "teaches" and the student listens and "learns." For Freire, this view objectifies students and renders dialogue impossible. Freire also rejects a Socratic dialogic-intellectual approach, not because Socrates concluded his dialogic encounters by saying that he "knows nothing," which renders Socrates unteachable at a certain level, but because Socratic intellectualism avoided the "man-world relationship."[69] That is, Socrates failed to illuminate how one's place in the world impacts and constricts one's intellectual horizons. In contrast to Socratic intellectualism, Freire prefers "reciprocal learning between teachers and students."[70] This cannot be led by the sovereign-teacher-educator, but names a dialogic practice based on the mutual analysis of the contexts in which teachers and students live so that these contexts can be challenged and transformed. Via dialogic praxis, students become "agents of their own recuperation."[71] To prevent dialogue from becoming a ruse of power, dialogue for Freire is not about speaking "to" someone (e.g., a hierarchal and vertical relationship), but "with" another person (e.g., a horizontal encounter compatible with solidarity).[72] *Philia* provided the necessary intersubjective emotive bridge between teacher and student that enables mutual learning: "It is not possible to be a teacher without loving one's students."[73]

Pedagogy and Revolt

Freire's pedagogy of revolt is based on dialogue, a critique of power, the constitution of radical agency, and revolution conceived as a recurring event. Freirean dialogue is a key component of the reinvention of power as a nonreactionary force because it permanently keeps a space open for listening, learning, and communion with the oppressed. The reinvention of power also plays itself out in the transformation of the self-identity of educational practitioners. To be a teacher requires a metaphorical martyrdom, the "death of the teacher," as it were: "The educator for freedom has to die as the exclusive educator of learners."[74] The "death of the teacher" emerges as the precondition for the birth of the confrontational citizen. Freire thus performs the deconstruction of educational institutions via teaching practices that open a new horizon for the emancipatory project. Let's chart the steps needed to make this happen.

First, the social relations of domination in educational institutions that mirror the relations of domination in the society at large have to be analyzed and undermined. Much like Michel Foucault's genealogical analysis of how punishment renders the body docile in *Discipline and Punish*, Freire was similarly interested in the ways that students are "positioned" and become objects of power when they enter the classroom.[75] Located ambiguously between the family and the workplace, educational institutions attempt to contain social problems and shape students to fit into preordained occupational roles. Through a protracted conditioning process, students learn that they are required to be silent when the teacher enters. For most of the day, students sit while instructors stand. The classroom space is also structured in a hierarchical manner with an invisible yet concrete wall between students and teacher that mirrors and reinforces the hierarchical character of churches, the workplace, the courtroom, soccer teams, the cheerleading squad, and just about every aspect of life in a hierarchal society. The classroom also spatially organizes bodies via strict rules of placement, posture, hygiene, attire, and consciousness.[76] All of this is intended to constitute "readiness for learning," which resembles a strange immobilizing and infantilizing form of domination.

Just like workers, students are constituted as a mass and simultaneously individualized via specific classroom practices. Teachers discipline students through public humiliation, expulsion, evaluation according to "objective" criteria, surveillance, classification, constant comparison, and referring students to the appropriate disciplinary authorities (e.g., medical, psychological) when necessary. Workers face termination and starvation if they violate the norms of docility and submissiveness in the workplace. In classrooms, students enter a field where they are held accountable for their performance of unspoken educational rituals, including punctuality, memorization, orderly classroom conduct, following instructions, adherence to deadlines, and evaluation. But the constant evaluation of students, for Freire, has nothing to do with education. It is about "punishment."[77] Once the social relations of domination in education institutions are illuminated, the content of what is taught acquires a new level of significance.

That is to say, the classroom must be transformed into a space where the contradictions of the society at large are ventilated and are subjected to critical analysis through the introduction of appropriate learning materials and teaching style. For Freire, the learning process is not a disembodied pursuit of "facts" but a visceral experience: "I have a right to be angry and to express that anger," he proclaims.[78] Given the legacy of colonial domination outlined by Eduardo Galeano's *Open Veins of Latin America: Five Centuries of the Pillage of a Continent*, education should be profoundly disturbing and upsetting.[79] This is precisely what Freire injects into the curriculum via critical pedagogy. In this sense, critical pedagogy gnaws at the foundations of oppressive political orders, "like a pack of rats," and positions students in a manner to hasten their collapse.[80] Education is thus an enactment and rehearsal of revolution.[81] For Freire, the classroom is a space of revolutionary struggle and revolt insofar as it is a location where students reclaim their humanity via a critical understanding of their place in the world. The real teacher had to occupy an ever shifting location to accomplish this, though. As Freire puts it, the teacher is both inside and outside the system: "I have been trying to think and teach by keeping one foot inside the system and the other foot outside."[82] In addition to his commitment to dialogue and the "death of the teacher," this inside-outside position flags Freire's attempt to reinvent power that never sets itself up against an outside.

In contrast to sovereign power, this new mode of Freirean power is one that "does not fear to be called into question and does not become rigid for the sake of defending the freedom already achieved."[83] If there is going to be a revolution worthy of the name, Freire insists, it must be one that is a "continuous event."[84] Taking power via a spectacular overthrow of an oppressive regime reflects a superficial understanding of the problem of oppression and yearning for popular rule. For Freire, the real challenge was to "reinvent power."[85] The starting place for this was in the classroom via a protracted pedagogical-political experiment in self-rule, dialogue, and revolution conceptualized and practiced as a continuous event. The type of democracy Freire had in mind would not represent constituents. It would resist institutional form and permanently disrupt the tendency to become an oligarchy. Democracy, for Freire, is not a form but the perpetual enactment of a people's revolt against centralized power in the classroom and outside of it in the polity. For Freire, "I prefer rebelliousness because it affirms my status as a person who has never given in to the manipulations and strategies designed to reduce the human person to nothing."[86] It is through rebellion, Freire asserts, that we can "affirm ourselves."[87]

But rebellion must go further and become revolution as a continuous event. This is grounded in collective agency and the formation of a political identity. Freire states: "Without a sense of identity there is no need for struggle. I will only fight you if I am very sure of myself."[88] Freire continues: "At no time can there be a struggle for liberation and self-affirmation without the formation of an identity, and identity of an individual, the group, the social class."[89] Consider, for example, the following Arizona law that maps with brutal clarity the connection between politics and the challenge of emergent political identity, as well as the significance of Freire's argument.

Arizona's 2010 House Bill 2281 eliminated ethnic studies programs and indicates that the state has an interest in the proper (meaning political) socialization of young people and in restricting the meaning of politics and collective struggle so that it corresponds with official non-threatening definitions and understandings. To be more specific, House Bill 2281 explicitly forbids "ethnic solidarity" and promotes "treatment of pupils as individuals."[90] It thus imposes via the elimination of ethnic studies programs the adoption by Latino/a students of an American individualistic identity premised on the negation of a historical understanding of the treatment of the conquered Mexican population and theft of Mexican territory.[91] However you slice it, Bill 2281 signifies a fear of a racialized crisis emerging in the United States, and the belief that this can be contained through curriculum control.[92] Although House Bill 2281 targets Latino/a students, the logic of it can be easily generalized to fit other ethnic/racial categories perceived as a threat to current distributions of power. As racial unrest in response to persistent police brutality continues to plague American cities, the question seems to be how effective this form of curriculum control will be for the pacification of the disenfranchised and dispossessed over the long term.

Democracy without the Demos?

Freire's work illuminates the interrelationship between curriculum control and the need to negate emergent political struggle in this recent Arizona law. Bringing Freire into dialogue with Wendy Brown illustrates how our sense of political possibility is not always imposed on us but is also the result of specific political-theoretical choices and commitments. Undeniably, Wendy Brown has had a significant impact on contemporary political theorizing.[93] Brown's *Undoing the Demos: Neoliberalism's Stealth Revolution*, which deepens themes developed in "American Nightmare," makes a compelling case that the bases to contest neoliberalism are being systematically undermined on a global level.[94] This reflects, as Brown states, the "vanishing value and lexicon for public things."[95] Our predicament, Brown asserts, is one of "unavowed exhaustion and despair in Western civilization." For Brown, we have entered a "civilizational turning point."[96] A "soft and total" form of governing has emerged.[97] "Humanity," Brown proclaims, "will have entered its darkest chapter ever."[98]

Brown's claims fit well within one of the major narratives of decline in political theory, that of Sheldon Wolin (other narratives of decline are articulated by Jean-Jacques Rousseau, Edmund Burke, Friedrich Nietzsche, Martin Heidegger, Leo Strauss, Hannah Arendt, and others).[99] As one of the leading students of Sheldon Wolin, Brown also shares Wolin's assumption that the political has been increasingly displaced by economic discourse, or absorbed into nonpolitical institutions and activities, but Brown radicalizes Wolin's view with the work of Herbert Marcuse and Michel Foucault.[100] The inescapable consequence of starting with Wolin's decline narrative about the displacement of the political, the "fugitive" or nonexistent character of democracy, and vision of the practice of political theory as bound by the historical terms of discourse, is a strange form of conservatism, which manifests itself as nostalgia or despair, or in the case of Wendy Brown, both.[101] Please allow me to develop this point in greater detail.

In her effort to grasp the present, Brown demonstrates that the capacity to contest neoliberalism is paralyzed by a series of legal, economic, and political decisions that entrench the power of the reigning corporate elite and program the majority of the population for powerlessness and destitution, on the one hand, or to consumption (mistakenly penned freedom), on the other.[102] For Brown, everything that at one point in time was conceived as belonging to the domain of the political has been transferred to the economic realm. *Homo politicus* has morphed into *homo oeconomicus*, where one's "friends and family" represent a business opportunity to make a quick buck or get a referral discount on one's cable television bill. Despite Brown's provocative critique, which reminds the reader of Herbert Marcuse's *One-Dimensional Man* where economic rationality reigns supreme, Brown runs into a political-theoretical dead-end as she nears the conclusion of her book.[103] According to Brown, the only forms of struggle against neoliberalism left standing today are "action as reaction" and possibly the form of genealogical critique practiced by Brown. The result, as Étienne Balibar claims in his recent discussion of Wendy Brown's work, is an apocalyptic leftist version of the "end of history."[104] In Brown's critique of neoliberalism, according to Balibar, Brown neutralizes the field of antagonism and makes it impossible to reconfigure past models of struggle and political engagement to fit new contexts. Brown's neoliberal subject does not struggle against neoliberalism because the neoliberal subject does not know what struggle is, how to engage in it, and no viable options remain for fighting back. Such is our predicament during this "civilizational turning point."

In contrast to Brown who adopts Wolin's narrative of decline but runs into a theoretical dead-end in the leftist "end of history" thesis, and in contrast to behavioralism, which turns out to be establishment ideology masquerading as scientific neutrality, Freire puts forward a vision of a new type of Leftist, one who is located in the classroom, who is not naive about power but is still filled with utopian hope, one who is able to explain why research is relevant to the lives of people, and one who is dedicated to social and political transformation inside and outside of the classroom.

Unlike Brown, Freire keeps history open to novelty and invention and Freire rejects nostalgia that "nullifies tomorrow."[105] If behavioral political science skirts the issue of politics via the discourse of neutrality, the version of political theory peddled by Wendy Brown undermines the bases for political struggle as a result of genealogical critique, a totalizing narrative of decline, and a static and closed philosophy of history. Does it make any difference if one laments (e.g., the Left) or welcomes (e.g., the

Right) the "end of history"? However you slice it, the result is the same. The present is the horizon for the future so get used to it. For both the Left and Right lured to sleep in the "end of history" thesis, political struggle is unnecessary, impossible, and pointless. Freire, in contrast, was driven by the prospect of social and political transformation, creatively appropriated the intellectual resources at his disposal and forged something new, fused this mix of Marxist humanism, postcolonial theory, and existentialism with the lessons Freire learned from working with illiterate farm workers and slum dwellers in South America, and he stands before us as a utopian political theorist committed to the fight for social justice. And yet, given the minimal attention dedicated to pedagogy by most political scientists, I would bet that if you asked a random behavioralist political scientist at APSA if they had read Freire's work on the political significance of pedagogy and incorporated it in some way into their teaching and research, you would be greeted with a blank stare.

Conclusion

But does the fact that Freire wrote for a Third World context limit the applicability of his ideas to other contexts? The answer is no. Freire states that "any ideas coming from another part of the world cannot be simply transplanted."[106] Freire also claims that "there is a universal dimension to what I have been writing about education."[107] Is it not the case, though, that Freire's work operates according to a simplistic either/or and us/them understanding of the world, and it might not always be as clear cut as Freire seems to think? Perhaps the "banking model" of education is not always oppressive and counterrevolutionary. Perhaps dialogue in the classroom is not always desirable and possible at every moment. However, Freire's dichotomy between liberating and oppressive education is nonetheless helpful for making basic distinctions, especially for new and inexperienced educators that may not realize that the rhetoric of learning cloaked over institutions of higher education conceal the fact that educational institutions are big businesses and have ideological agendas.[108]

When President Obama claims that it is not a student's "color" or the "income of their parents" that is the most important factor determining their success in "A Blueprint for Reform" but "the teacher standing at the front of the classroom," Obama seems to be embracing a Freirean position. On closer examination, Obama has a rather narrow historical sensibility and is setting teachers up for failure.[109] In one swoop of the pen, Obama not only makes teachers responsible for overcoming the legacies of racism and economic inequality, but he also denies the power of past oppression (not to mention current forms) on the present and future. In addition to calling for a new type of educator, the work of Freire brings the legacies of past and current oppression into the lesson plan, the life-contexts of students become the text, dialogue the method, democratic nonreactionary power the practice, self-liberation the goal, facilitated by the ultimate disappearing act of the teacher as the authoritative dispenser of knowledge, and all of this geared to the broadest possible humanization of society.

In conclusion, Freire as a political theorist is a viable alternative to the narratives of decline of Sheldon Wolin and Leo Strauss that have served as a grounding assumption for several generations of US political theorists. Freire's work is also an alternative to behavioral political science as establishment ideology. Freire also opens a vector that stays clear of Wendy Brown's apocalyptic leftist "end of history" thesis. How, one might ask? Freire's work expands the dialogue about the types of pedagogy needed to rebuild our democracy, and the type of academic and professional institutions that need to be in place to sustain this project over the long term. Finally, Freire's work requires political scientists and political theorists to look into the existential mirror and ask: "Who do I serve?"

Conclusion
The Right of Resistance

Political resistance is the condition of possibility of every regime as well as the condition of its potential transformation and/or annihilation. Resistance to domination has played a central role in defining the scope and limits of citizenship. From the abolitionist movement in the United States and its songs of freedom, the underground railroad, anti-Apartheid movement, Spanish *Indignados*, Occupy Wall Street, Black Lives Matter, Arab Spring, antiglobalization movements, water protectors, and massive anti-Trump protests, the tension between those who occupy centers of power and those denied access to them continues to be a pressing issue in contemporary politics that can fundamentally alter our conceptions of citizenship in productive ways.

Liberal theory does not offer us a way to understand new forms of resistance, rebellion, and revolt in our time and has an impoverished conception of citizenship. Through its attachment to rights, shared values, constitutionalism, the discourse of universality/color blindness, defense of the two-party system, and singing the song of representative democracy, liberal theory has severed the connection between citizenship and resistance and in the process this has led to closed forms of political power, the narrowing of political discussion, and the reification of state power. It is difficult to avoid the conclusion that liberal theory is little more than an apology and/or ideological justification for the status quo. Liberal theory has obscured the significance of political resistance for citizenship, community, and democratic politics at a time when the political sphere is becoming increasingly disconnected from energy from below, which is only exacerbating current levels of political discontent. Liberals have given us the dream of a political order grounded on consensus, floating above the problems of power, privilege, and inequality. This is a dream for a world without politics conceived as political struggle. The disappearance of the people from the practice of state power threatens democratic accountability and political legitimacy.

With the collapse of communist regimes, the utopianism of the Left has been reduced to a murmur. Since Enlightenment rationality has been revealed as yet another mode of domination, it is not clear where the Left should turn to justify the project of emancipation, or even what form it should take.[1] Both theoretically and politically, Leftists have crash-landed on the boulevard of broken dreams, huddling together for warmth, as progressive energy dims. The apocalyptic turn in Wendy Brown's political theory mirrors the end-of-history proclamation of neoconservatives.[2]

The disappearance of coherent opposition to neoliberalism and state power could not have come at a worse time given the fusion of politics and paranoia in response to 911. Preemptive wars, silencing of dissent, cynical interpretations of American constitutional law that expand the power of the state, rise in religious fundamentalism, and a climate of fear and surveillance are the signs of the times. Tack on the self-congratulatory rhetoric about the "end of history" and victory of market capitalism and it's enough to make any self-respecting critically oriented intellectual shudder.

Both the disarray of the Left and the current political context that denies the possibility of a viable alternative to current economic and political arrangement make the concepts of revolt, rebellion, and revolution particularly important today. My study has sought to expand the political imagination and push democratic theory beyond its current location. Popular dissatisfaction with politics, political institutions, and political leaders is undeniable today. The elucidation of the concepts of revolt, resistance, and rebellion can clarify the full range of options available to citizens in order to intelligently challenge abuses of state power. Historically, confrontational citizens have played a pivotal role in widening the parameters of discussion and transforming who is allowed to participate in politics. The confrontational citizen is not a criminal but a utopian figure of a new political order that has yet to come. Significant political change is possible. This change will be, as it always has, the result of confrontational modes of citizenship.

The expression confrontational citizenship used throughout this study has been invoked to refer to a skeptical, active, informed, defiant, dissenting, and critical mode of citizenship, not knee-jerk activism, frenzied subjectivity, and belligerent extremism. Revolt as a way of life, as the chapter on Du Bois demonstrated, involves thoughtfulness. Hatred and rage can lead to strategic forms of political engagement, as long as they are deployed dialectically. Confrontational citizenship does not occupy one side of the opposition that conceives democracy as either a moment of interruption and formlessness (e.g., Sheldon Wolin) or as a moment of form, stability, and consensus (e.g., John Rawls).[3] Rather, confrontational citizenship is a double contradictory imperative that, as demonstrated in the chapter on Hannah Arendt, creates authority only to the extent that this authority cancels itself out as a form of domination that demands obedience.[4] In the deployment of hatred and rage, confrontational citizenship involves a dialectical movement that generates creative responses to injustice. As an identity claim, confrontational citizenship creates the basis for collective solidarity. As a form of pedagogy, confrontational citizenship names and enacts the recovery of the humanity of the oppressed in their capacity for self-articulation. As a strategy for substantive social and political transformation, confrontational citizenship requires a Kantian moment of thinking without the constraint of rules in order to lay the groundwork for critical and creative modes of thought and political engagement.

The order of right and its keyword *citizenship* has always meant the consolidation and institutionalization of certain relations of power, and in the case of Thomas Hobbes, purging the political order of conflict and controversy so that subjects could safely pursue their private interests, although these subjects would also be politically disempowered while under watch of the sovereign's eye and clenched fist. Can the order of right be an order of resistance to its own antidemocratic institutional consolidation? As I argued in my chapter on Arendt, I believe it can, but we have to be creative and think ourselves out of unhelpful binaries and a cramped political imagination.

Confrontational citizenship is affirmative, critical, and utopian. It affirms political invention, creativity, and humor. Hence, it resists the apocalyptic turn in the work of Wendy Brown and Giorgio Agamben.[5] Confrontational citizenship is critical insofar as it provides the historical and theoretical contexts that open spaces for struggle and generate modes of political subjectivity that have the fire to embrace confrontation as a way of life. The defense of agonistics and contestation are good first steps but they need to go further.[6] Contestation occurs within settled political spheres. In contrast, confrontational citizenship operates within, but also exceeds the boundaries of, the political and creates broader and wider spaces for political struggle. Finally, confrontational citizenship is utopian insofar as it fights for a better world beyond the current neoliberal nightmare of racialized mass incarceration, endless war, annihilation of the environment, concentration of wealth in the hands of the few, and political corruption.

Confrontational citizenship and the right of resistance are geared to opening a space for political transformation and the permanent refounding of the political sphere. Citizenship is the origin of all political legitimacy.[7] But legitimacy and authority become oppression and domination as a result of the capture of political energy within institutions, procedures, and settled practices that benefit entrenched groups at the expense of everyone else. Confrontational citizenship is thus a way of life that involves learning to speak and learning to name in ways that are antagonistic to conventional patterns of speaking, thinking, and being. Hardt and Negri's recent work is productive in this regard because it avoids the apocalyptic turn in Leftist theorizing, foregrounds the antagonistic dimension of politics, demonstrates how the production of subjectivity is the essential terrain of politics, embraces insurrectionary perspectives, and analyzes the current political moment as a moment of crisis on the brink of political change as a result of the failure of unilateralism, growing inequality, and financial collapse.[8]

The work of Étienne Balibar also constitutes a creative and provocative response to the current political and economic moment. Throughout all of Balibar's work, but especially in some of his more recent publications, he explores the possibility of radical social and political transformation. For Balibar, all political orders are held together by an unstable network of forces, relations, and institutions that more or less constitute political stability without ever being able to absolutely guarantee it. To this end, Balibar unleashes via dialectical analysis the antinomies contained in core political categories (e.g., the main ones being constitution and insurrection; institution and counterinstitution), so that both poles of the binary may be repoliticized.[9] Balibar deconstructs political categories to excavate the forms of struggle that created them but that have been erased by historical sedimentation, social stabilization, and political exclusions. "An imprescriptible moment of an-anarchy," Balibar claims, "has to be constantly reactivated precisely if the institution is to be political."[10] The political project, for Balibar, is one of refounding and renewal via historical recovery of raw energy in our inherited political language and concepts and engagement with the political and economic fault-lines of the contemporary moment. For Balibar, "the foundations of modern nation-states are to be found in insurrections, declarations of independence, or constitutions of peoples."[11]

History is not over for Balibar but is a permanent struggle for emancipation. Citizenship names the site of this struggle: "The battle against the denial of citizenship is indeed the vital heart of the politics of emancipation."[12] Balibar thus explores the metapolitical conditions for a repoliticization of the political, or what he calls, "a politics of politics, which aims at creating, recreating, and conserving the set of conditions within which politics as a collective participation in public affairs is possible."[13] A good dialectician, Balibar avoids the identification with either pole of the binary. Procedural conceptions of democracy, for Balibar, reflect "society's blindness to its own bases."[14] There is no political status quo, moment of stasis, equilibrium, and stability to the political world. "Equaliberty" is Balibar's double concept (e.g., dialectical praxis) meant to disorganize and transform political orders in progressive directions.

Balibar's work is a good supplement to confrontational citizenship. I oppose the one offered by Rogers M. Smith. Smith claims that Americans must "recognize their civic history and destiny as their own collective enterprise." Smith continues and states that Americans must "consider themselves part of a special historical collectivity of immense significance for themselves and humanity."[15] This sort of grandiose self-evaluation is at best a distraction, at its worst a form of political obfuscation. Confrontational citizenship puts citizens on a different trajectory, where the concluding moment of stability that generates a reverential backward-looking glance to the past is never as important as the permanent struggle for the expansion of the practices that constitute citizenship and thus the boundaries of the political.

To this end, the core points of this study have been the following:

1. Intense emotions (e.g., anger, hatred, and rage) are good as sources of political motivation and the creation of political subjectivity, but they must be deployed dialectically. Fear and anger have been used by conservatives to create scapegoats, obfuscate class rule, mask inequality, and create a need for a strong leader. The Left needs to tap into popular hatred and rage against corporate and political elites for the purposes of social and political transformation.

2. The identification of the political/economic enemy is required to clarify the terms of political struggle and clarify required courses of action. As Machiavelli makes clear, political and economic elites are the real problem. Hating the class enemy is important, but the strategic deployment of humor increases the likelihood of popular mobilization against corrupt elites.

3. Political identity (properly understood) is good and a necessary component in the creation of political coalitions and a social base for political change. The claim that all identities are only social constructions risks depoliticizing, dehistoricizing, and leveling identity formations, and thereby deprives historically marginalized groups the energy that fuels political engagement. The view that identity claims undermine the possibility of action in concert is inaccurate, given the new ways identities are being conceptualized and the intersectional collectivities that continue to emerge.

4. Elite rule conceptions of politics lead to political corruption. Widespread citizen participation/confrontation is necessary to promote a responsive political sphere, prevent corruption, and increase political legitimacy. Authority is strengthened when it is challenged, as long as it changes in response and does not respond in a reactionary manner.

5. An explicit utopian orientation in democratic theory is needed as fuel for political engagement. As a result of its anti-utopian orientation, democratic theory risks being an ideological justification of the political status quo.

6. A commitment to revolutionary change need not involve violence. Kant shows how thinking without the constraint of rules can open a productive moment of revolutionary anarchism that is creative, not violent.

7. Critique is not enough. Confrontational citizenship is not an antiposition but a defense of creative modes of political engagement and social transformation. History is not

over but kept alive via the reactivation of old struggles, the birth of new forms of struggle, and a vision of permanent struggle as the basis for the political order. Revolt is not a one-time spectacular demonstration but must be conceived of as a way of life.

8. Political education, creativity, and pedagogy are essential components for struggle and confrontation as a way of life. Widespread political literacy is also an indispensable condition for social and political transformation. A pedagogy of revolt ensures that democracy will be more than an empty word.

9. Institutions and counterinstitutions keep the political connected to the people. The overidentification with institutions, law, and order negates the political. Creative ways to lodge permanent revolution into political foundations, political institutions, and political concepts are needed. The demonization and/or rejection of political institutions is as politically counterproductive as the overidentification with political institutions.

Of course, the risk is that nothing happens, nothing changes, and we die in a state of despair. The message of confrontational citizenship, however, is ultimately a hopeful and utopian one. It names some of struggles that took place in the past and ones taking place today, the fault lines that have emerged, and tries to indicate how the polity can be changed in positive directions. Confrontational citizenship is a way of life, a way of being, a permanent fight that, at the end of the day, gives us hope that the people can make enlightened decisions about the quality and direction of public life. This, of course, can never be guaranteed. Irrespective of what the outcome might be, however, we are going to have to fight for any and all real political change. Confrontational citizenship is thus the unsurpassable horizon of our time. It names the indispensable role protest plays in making regimes accountable to the people and creating political regimes where life is worthy of being lived.

Notes

Preface

1. Limited political options as a result of an entrenched two-party system, domination of the political sphere by right-wing corporate interests, elections that are more of a spectacle than a check on the reigning elite, mass incarceration, growing economic inequality, permanent war, extra-judicial indefinite detention of suspects, environmental decimation, refugee crises, and student debt to straitjacket young people to submitting to the status quo. For some of these and related problems see Jane Mayer, *Dark Money: The Hidden History of the Billionaires behind the Rise of the Radical Right* (New York: Doubleday, 2016); Naomi Klein, *The Shock Doctrine: The Rise of Disaster Capitalism* (New York: Metropolitan Books, 2007); Michelle Alexander, *The New Jim Crow: Mass Incarceration in an Age of Colorblindness* (New York: The New Press, 2012); and Cornel West, *Democracy Matters: Winning the Fight Against Imperialism* (New York: Penguin, 2004).

2. See William E. Connolly, *Capitalism and Christianity, American Style* (Durham, NC: Duke University Press, 2008).

3. Jeb Bush says Americans "need to work longer hours" to earn more. *Guardian*, July 9, 2015.

4. *Gallup*, "Trust in Government," accessed February 9, 2016.

5. Aristotle, *Politics*, trans. Reeve (Indianapolis, IN: Hackett Press, 1998), p. 73.

6. Chris Hedges, *Wages of Rebellion: The Moral Imperative of Revolt* (New York: Nation Books, 2015), p. 1. Giorgio Agamben also states: "The concept of 'citizen' is no longer adequate for describing the social-political reality of modern states"; *Means without Ends: Notes on Politics*, trans. Binetti and Cesarino (Minneapolis, MN: University of Minnesota Press, 2000), p. 23.

7. Jacques Rancière, *Disagreement: Politics and Philosophy*, trans. Rose (Minneapolis, MN: University of Minnesota Press, 1999).

8. See Paul Magnette, *Citizenship: The History of an Idea*, trans. Long (Colchester, UK: European Consortium for Political Research, 2005). See also Aristotle's *Politics*, 1998.

9. Rogers M. Smith, *Civic Ideals: Conflicting Visions of Citizenship in U.S. History* (New Haven, CT: Yale University Press, 1997), p. 1.

10. As Jodi Dean argues, the appeal for more democracy only serves to entrench the powers that be. See Jodi Dean, *Democracy and Other Neoliberal Fantasies: Communicative Rationality and Left Politics* (Durham, NC: Duke University Press, 2009).

11. For Frances Fox Piven, "it is in fact precisely at the moments when people act outside of electoral norms that electoral-representative procedures are more likely to realize their democratic potential," in *Challenging Authority: How Ordinary People Change America* (New York: Rowman & Littlefield, 2006), p. 2.

12. Étienne Balibar, *Citizenship*, trans. Scott-Railton (Cambridge, UK: Polity Press, 2015), p. 2.

13. Frances Fox Piven and Richard A. Cloward, *Poor People's Movements: Why They Succeed, How They Fail* (New York: Vintage Books, 1977), xi.

14. See, for example, the work of Nancy Rosenblum, in particular, *On the Side of Angels: An Appreciation of Parties and Partisanship* (Princeton, NJ: Princeton University Press, 2010) for a caricature of the extremist.

15. Jason Frank, *Constituent Moments: Enacting the People in Post-revolutionary America* (Durham, NC: Duke University Press, 2010). Frank states: "This double inscription of the people enables what I call constituent moments, when the underauthorized—imposters, radicals, self-created entities—seize the mantle of authorization, changing the inherited rules of authorization in the process" (p. 8).

16. Wendy Brown, *Undoing the Demos: Neoliberalism's Stealth Revolution* (New York: Zone Books, 2015). Simon Critchley, *Infinitely Demanding: Ethics of Commitment, Politics of Resistance* (London, UK: Verso, 2007).

17. Wendy Brown, *Undoing the Demos*, pp. 41, 110.

18. Simon Critchley, *Infinitely Demanding*, pp. 2, 37.

19. See Amy Gutman and Dennis Thompson, *Why Deliberative Democracy?* (Princeton, NJ: Princeton University Press, 2003); Michael Morrell, *Empathy and Deliberation: Feeling, Thinking, and*

Deliberation (University Park, PA: Pennsylvania State University Press, 2010).

20. See Jürgen Habermas, *Between Facts and Norms: Contributions to Discourse Theory of Law and Democracy*, trans. Rehg (Cambridge, MA: MIT Press, 1998).

21. Francis Fox Piven, *Challenging Authority: How Ordinary People Change America*, p. 146.

22. See William E. Connolly, *Ethos of Pluralization* (Minneapolis, MN: University of Minnesota Press, 1995); Bonnie Honig, *Political Theory and the Displacement of Politics* (Ithaca, NY: Cornell University Press, 1993).

23. Chantal Mouffe, *Agonistics: Thinking the World Politically* (New York: Verso, 2013).

24. See Nancy Rosenblum, *On the Side of Angels: An Appreciation of Parties and Partisanship*, 2010; Paul Starr, *Freedom's Power: The True Force of Liberalism* (New York: Basic Books, 2007); Chandran Kukathas, *The Liberal Archipelago: A Theory of Diversity and Freedom* (New York: Oxford University Press, 2003); *Liberalism and the Moral Life*, Ed. Rosenblum (Cambridge, MA: Harvard University Press, 1989).

25. See Ian F. Haney López, *White by Law: The Legal Construction of Race* (New York: New York University Press, 1996).

26. See Jeffrey M. Jones, "In U.S., New Record 43% are Political Independents," *Gallup*, January 7, 2015. For Jones, "These changes have left both parties at or near low points in the percentage who identify themselves as core supporters of the party." On whether Americans trust government to do what is right, 37 percent of individuals polled claimed "not very much." *Gallup*, "Trust in Government," accessed February 9, 2016.

27. See Robert B. Reich, *Saving Capitalism: For the Many, Not the Few* (New York: Alfred A. Knopf, 2015), p. 180.

28. See Étienne Balibar, *Equaliberty*, trans. Ingram (Durham, NC: Duke University Press, 2014); see also Jacques Rancière, *Disagreement: Politics and Philosophy*, trans. Rose (Minneapolis, MN: University of Minnesota Press, 1999). Chantal Mouffe, *Agonistics: Thinking the World Politically* (New York: Verso, 2013). Michael Hardt and Antonio Negri, *Commonwealth* (Harvard, MA: Belknap Press, 2009). Although I am influenced by her work, I disagree with Mouffe's critique of the Occupy Movement as a symptom of neo-liberalism as well has her claim that Michael Hardt and Antonio

Negri are ultimately naïve messianic thinkers whose faith in the absolute democracy of the multitude blinds them to the need for agonistic engagement with existing institutions.

29. In this sense, the canon of political theory is not adequate. See George Kateb who argues the opposite in "The Adequacy of the Canon"; *Political Theory* 30 (2002): 482–505. See Mary Hawkesworth for a critique of traditional ways of practicing political theory in "From Constitutive Outside to the Politics of Extinction: Critical Race Theory, Feminist Theory, and Political Theory," *Political Research Quarterly* 63 (2010): 686–96.

Introduction

1. Evidence that the current political and economic system is rigged to benefit the few is clear to see in the recent government bailout of the US financial sector. Reckless financial sector practices were rewarded by US politicians via the Emergency Economic Stabilization Act of 2008, proposed by Secretary of the Treasury Henry Paulson (e.g., former Goldman Sachs chief executive) and signed by President George W. Bush, which authorized the use of $700 billion of public funds to be used to bailout the banks and provide massive bonuses for the criminals running the banks while ordinary people lost their jobs, houses, and retirement funds. See Stephen Bernard, "Bailed out Banks Gave Millions in Executive Bonuses, NY AG Report Shows," ABC News, accessed February 4, 2016. See also Robert Reich on the recent abuses of the US corporate-political class in *Saving Capitalism: For the Many, Not the Few.* Neoliberal economic policy (e.g., supply-side economics) premised on the idea that the best way to help everyone is to give more money to the rich has required a long-term propaganda campaign. For the doctrine of free market fundamentalism, see Milton Friedman, *Capitalism and Freedom* (Chicago, IL: University of Chicago Press, 2002). For an analysis and critique of neoliberalism see David Harvey, *A Brief History of Neoliberalism* (Oxford, UK: Oxford University Press, 2005).

2. William E. Connolly's "agonistic respect" that strives for an "ethics of engagement" does not generate the types of confrontational political subjectivity defended here. See William E. Connolly, *The Ethos of Pluralization* (Minneapolis, MN: University of Minnesota Press,

1995), xix. For Connolly, we need to foster an "ethos of reciprocal forbearance and responsiveness" (xxiii). In my view, Connolly's "agonistic respect" is not confrontational enough.

3. Cheryl Hall, *The Trouble with Passion: Political Theory Beyond the Reign of Reason* (New York: Routledge, 2005), p. 3. For Hall, "passion is one of the most important things in the world because it can inspire people to act, to reach 'across the chasm' to the gods/good, to make a difference in the world" (p. 5). See also George E. Marcus, *The Sentimental Citizen: Emotion in Democratic Politics* (University Park: PA: Pennsylvania State University Press, 2002).

4. Michael E. Morrell, *Empathy and Democracy: Feeling, Thinking, and Deliberation.* John P. McCormick, *Machiavellian Democracy* (Cambridge, UK: Cambridge University Press, 2011).

5. See Chantal Mouffe, *The Democratic Paradox* (London, UK: Verso, 2000). The class bases of the enemy is what prevents my position from mirroring Carl Schmitt's amorphous political enemy that could include anyone. See Carl Schmitt, *The Concept of the Political,* trans. Schwab (Chicago, IL: University of Chicago Press, 2007).

6. See "Introduction" in *Deliberative Democracy: Essays on Reason and Politics,* Eds. Bohman and Rehg (Cambridge, MA: MIT Press, 1997), iv.

7. Amy Gutmann and Dennis Thompson, *Why Deliberative Democracy,* p. 7.

8. Chantal Mouffe's work is good on the identification of the enemy but she does not mobilize the range of perspectives employed here and she lacks a strong utopian dimension to her thinking. See Mouffe, *The Return of the Political* (New York: Verso, 1993). See also Chantal Mouffe, *Agonistics: Thinking the World Politically* (London, UK: Verso, 2013). In *Agonistics,* she states: "A well-functioning democracy calls for a confrontation of democratic political positions" but this is "regulated by a set of democratic procedures accepted by the adversaries" (pp. 7, 9). Mouffe restricts the terrain of politics by her claim that adversaries share an acceptance of the rules of the game. What are you to do if, like Frederick Douglass, you are defined outside of the game?

9. Arthur M. Schlesinger Jr., *The Disuniting of America: Reflections on a Multicultural Society* (New York: W. W. Norton & Company, 1998).

10. See John Rawls, *A Theory of Justice.* See Sheldon Wolin "Democracy, Difference, and Re-Cognition" in *Fugitive Democracy and Other Essays,* ed. Xenos (Princeton, NJ: Princeton University Press,

2016). Wendy Brown, *States of Injury: Power and Freedom in Late Modernity* (Princeton, NJ: Princeton University Press, 1995); William E. Connolly, *Ethos of Pluralization*; Cristina Beltrán, *The Trouble with Unity: Latino Politics and the Creation of Identity* (Oxford, UK: Oxford University Press, 2010).

11. See Joseph Schumpeter for a conception of rule by elites in *Capitalism, Socialism, and Democracy* (New York: Harper & Row, 1976). See also Robert Dahl, *A Preface to Democratic Theory* (Chicago, IL: University of Chicago Press, 2006). I discuss Samuel P. Huntington's and Carl Schmitt's contempt for democracy in my chapter on hatred. Many deliberative theorists and advocates of civic republicanism are also not critical enough of the exclusions already structured into existing institutions and they end up endorsing, by choice or default, rule by elites. See also William A. Galston who states: "Liberal constitutionalism both specifies basic liberties and tries to keep them outside the normal processes of democratic revision"; *The Practice of Liberal Pluralism* (New York: Cambridge University Press, 2005), p. 33.

12. Rogers M. Smith, *Civic Ideals: Conflicting Visions of Citizenship in U.S. History* (New Haven, CT: Yale University Press, 1997), p. 505.

13. Étienne Balibar, *Masses, Classes, Ideas: Studies on Politics and Philosophy Before and After Marx*, trans. Swenson (New York: Routledge, 1994), p. 211.

14. Ian Shapiro, *The State of Democratic Theory* (Princeton, NJ: Princeton University Press, 2003), p. 4.

15. Shapiro, *The State of Democratic Theory*, 2003, p. 4.

16. Michaele L. Ferguson, *Sharing Democracy* (New York: Oxford University Press, 2012). See Holloway Sparks, "Dissident Citizenship: Democratic Theory, Political Courage, and Activist Women," *Hypatia* 12, no. 4 (1997): 74-110.

17. Michaele L. Ferguson, *Sharing Democracy*, pp. 6, 131, 159, 163.

18. See Richard Rorty, *Achieving Our Country: Leftist Thought in Twentieth Century America* (Cambridge, MA: Harvard University Press, 1999), where he castigates the Left for its obsession with theory and pines for a more "reformist and pragmatic Left" (p. 103).

19. John Medearis, *Why Democracy is Oppositional* (Cambridge, MA: Harvard University Press, 2015).

20. Steven Johnston, *American Dionysia: Violence, Tragedy, and Democratic Politics* (New York: Cambridge University Press, 2015).

21. Johnston, *American Dionysia*, pp. 32, 33, 10.

22. William A. Galston, *The Practice of Liberal Pluralism*, pp. 33, 97, 128, 151, 165.

23. For a classic antimajoritarian statement and rejection of participatory democracy see James Madison, *Federalist 10*. Postcolonial theory offers an enlarged perspective for articulating alternative forms of political subjectivity and resistance. See Frantz Fanon, *The Wretched of the Earth*, trans. Philcox (New York: Grove Press, 2004).

24. Wendy Brown, *Undoing the Demos: Neoliberalism's Stealth Revolution*. See also Giorgio Agamben whose work has made us realize that concentration camps are everywhere, but he does not propose ways to contest the reduction of the human to bare life. See Giorgo Agamben, *Homo Sacer: Sovereign Power and Bare Life*, trans. Heller-Roazen (Stanford, CA: Stanford University Press, 1998); Giorgio Agamben, *State of Exception*, trans. Attell (Chicago, IL: University of Chicago Press, 2005).

25. Giorgio Agamben, *Homo Sacer: Sovereign Power and Bare Life*.

26. This nostalgia can be found in Harvey C. Mansfield, *Manliness* (New Haven, CT: Yale University Press, 2007). The backward-looking glance implied by Donald Trump's slogan "Make America great again" implies that something in the past was great that has to be retrieved and revived. Just like the person who utters the slogan, the lack of content is the content.

27. August Nimtz argues that revolutionary strategy should be the core political focus of our time. Even though I disagree with parts of his interpretation of Lenin, Nimtz is on the right path in terms of the centrality of revolutionary strategy as a political-pedagogical undertaking. See August H. Nimtz, *Lenin's Electoral Strategy from Marx and Engels through the Revolution of 1905: The Ballot, the Streets—or Both* (New York: Palgrave Macmillan, 2014) and August H. Nimtz, *Lenin's Electoral Strategy from 1907 to the October Revolution of 1917: The Ballot, the Streets—or Both*, New York: Palgrave Macmillan, 2014).

Chapter 1

1. See Carl Boggs, *Imperial Delusions: American Militarism and Endless War* (New York: Rowman & Littlefield, 2004) and *Empire Versus*

Democracy: The Triumph of Corporate and Military Power (New York: Routledge, 2011); Sheldon Wolin, *Democracy Incorporated: Managed Democracy and the Specter of Inverted Totalitarianism* (Princeton, NJ: Princeton University Press, 2008); Joseph Nevins, *Operation Gatekeeper: The Rise of the "Illegal Alien" and the Making of the U.S.-Mexico Boundary* (New York: Routledge, 2002); Andrew L. Barlow, *Between Fear and Hope: Globalization and Race in the United States* (New York: Rowman & Littlefield, 2003); Michelle Alexander, *The New Jim Crow: Mass Incarceration in the Age of Colorblindness* (New York: The New Press, 2012); Katherine Beckett, *Making Crime Pay: Law and Order in Contemporary American Politics* (New York: Oxford University Press, 1997).

2. See Murray Edelman, *Constructing the Political Spectacle* (Chicago: University of Chicago Press, 1988).

3. See Shan Li, *Los Angeles Times*, "Bodyguard Business is Booming," December 18, 2010. See also Edward J. Blakely and Mary Gail Snyder, *Fortress America: Gated Communities in the United States* (Washington, DC: Brookings, 1997). Wendy Brown argues that one of the effects of de-democratization is the production of a neoliberal subject "on the model of the entrepreneur and consumer." This neoliberal subject is indifferent to "veracity and accountability in government." See "American Nightmare: Neoliberalism, Neoconservatism, and De-Democratization," *Political Theory* 34, no. 6 (2006): 705. Although I agree with aspects of her critique, the nightmare will only come to an end when an effective countermovement fights back.

4. See Wolin, *Democracy Inc.*, x.

5. Hatred is arguably a safe academic piñata. The following research on hatred explores the counterproductive aspects. See David P. Levine, "Hatred of Government," *Administrative Theory & Praxis* 20, no. 3 (1998): 345–362; Edward L. Gleaser, "The Political Economy of Hatred," *Quarterly Journal of Economics* 120, no. 1 (2005): 45–86; Stephen Gwynn, "Hatred," *North American Review* (October 1923): 529–36; David W. Petegorsky, "The Strategy of Hatred," *Antioch Review* 1, no. 3 (1941): 376á88. For Aristotle, hatred is a cause of revolutions in monarchies. See Aristotle, *Politics*, ed. and trans. Ernest Barker (New York: Oxford University Press, 1958), p. 240. Immanuel Kant argues hatred violates the duty to the moral law. See Kant, *Metaphysics of Morals*, trans. Gregor (New York: Cambridge

University Press, 1991), pp. 251-53. For Friedrich Nietzsche, hatred is a component of slave morality. See *On the Genealogy of Morals*, trans. Kaufmann and Hollingdale (New York: Vintage, 1989). For Sigmund Freud, "hate . . . always remains in an intimate relation with the self-preservation instincts"; citation in Erich Fromm, *The Anatomy of Human Destructiveness* (New York: Henry Holt, 1973), p. 488. For Gustave Le Bon, crowds entertain violent and extreme sentiments: "Antipathy almost as soon as it is aroused is transformed into hatred"; see Le Bon, *The Crowd: A Study of the Popular Mind* (Mineola, NY: Dover, 2002), p. 38. Finally, hatred of the colonizing oppressor plays an important role in revolutionary struggle for Frantz Fanon: "The colonized subject identifies his enemy and casts all his exacerbated hatred and rage in this new direction." See *The Wretched of the Earth*, trans. Philcox (New York: Grove, 2004), p. 31.

6. The Hate Crime Statistics Act of 1990 defines a hate crime as a crime which "manifests prejudice based on race, religion, sexual orientation, or ethnicity." Studies on the rise of the extreme right and increases in hate crimes are important but risk perpetuating the tendency to see hatred as always counterproductive. As I argue in this article, hatred of the ruling class can lead to greater accountability and less oppressive political regimes.

7. See Philip Pettit, *Republicanism: A Theory of Freedom and Government* (New York: Oxford University Press, 1999), Pettit, *A Theory of Freedom: From the Psychology to the Politics of Agency* (New York: Oxford University Press, 2001); J. G. A. Pocock, *The Machiavellian Moment: Florentine Political Thought and the Atlantic Republican Tradition* (Princeton, NJ: Princeton University Press, 1975); and Quentin Skinner, *Machiavelli: A Very Short Introduction* (New York: Oxford University Press, 2000).

8. See Leo Strauss, *Thoughts on Machiavelli* (Chicago: University of Chicago Press, 1958); Ryan Balot and Stephen Trochimchuk, "The Many and the Few: On Machiavelli's 'Democratic Moment,'" *Review of Politics* 47, no. 4 (2012): 559-88. Balot and Trochimchuk "reject the idea that Machiavelli's central thrust is prodemocratic" (p. 559); Harvey Mansfield, *Machiavelli's Virtue* (Chicago: University of Chicago Press, 1966).

9. See Yves Winter, "Plebeian Politics: Machiavelli and the Ciompi Uprising," *Political Theory* 40, no. (2012): 736-66; Miguel Vatter,

Between Form and Event: Machiavelli's Theory of Political Freedom (Dordrecht, Netherlands: Kluwer, 2000); and Vatter, "The Quarrel between Populism and Republicanism: Machiavelli and the Antinomies of Plebeian Politics," *Contemporary Political Theory* 11, no.3 (2012): 242-63. Vatter misses the double nature of Machiavelli's politics and overlooks the instances when Machiavelli sees a positive role for the rule of law and political institutions as a way to manage hatred. Winter's populist and egalitarian reading of Machiavelli is an important contribution but downplays the double nature of Machiavelli's political thinking by seeing an uprising as a defining moment of Machiavelli's thought. John P. McCormick flags the importance of hatred but contains hatred in institutions because it may destabilize political life. See McCormick, *Machiavellian Democracy* (New York: Cambridge University Press, 2011). My interpretation of Machiavelli is thus positioned between Vatter (2000; 2012) and Winter's (2012) work, on one side, and McCormick's (2011), on the other, insofar as I argue that two incompatible imperatives exist simultaneously in Machiavelli. The first one is based on the need for flexibility, the rejection of legal limits, and the value of extra-institutional violence against elites as a way to satisfy popular hatred. The second one sets legal limits on political conduct and values institutional channels for venting popular hatred. These contradictory aspects are not reducible to one political position but nonetheless establish the political essence (conceived of as an antinomy) of Machiavelli's thinking that is grounded on the effective deployment, management, and venting of political hatred.

10. Machiavelli, *Prince*, trans. Bull (New York: Penguin, 2003); *Discourses*, trans. Walker (New York: Penguin, 2003). Machiavelli also discusses hatred in "History of Florence" and in "Tercets on Ambition" in *Machiavelli: The Chief Works and Others*, 3 vol., trans. Gilbert (Durham, NC: Duke University Press, 1989).

11. The centrality of hatred in Machiavelli is missed by interpretations that cast him as an immoralist, radical republican, democrat, proto-fascist, and pluralist. For Machiavelli as an immoralist, see Leo Strauss (1958). For Machiavelli as a radical republican, see Mary Dietz, "Trapping the Prince: Machiavelli and the Politics of Deception," *American Political Science Review* 80, no. 3 (1986), pp. 777-99. For Machiavelli as a democrat, see McCormick (2011).

For Machiavelli as a proto-fascist, see Hanna Fenichel Pitkin, "Meditations on Machiavelli" in *Feminist Interpretations of Niccolò Machiavelli*, ed. Falco (University Park, PA: Pennsylvania State University Press, 2004). For Machiavelli as a pluralist, see Isaiah Berlin, "The Originality of Machiavelli" in *Against the Current: Essays in the History of Ideas* (Princeton, NJ: Princeton University Press, 2001). Louis Althusser provides the most thorough discussion of hatred in Machiavelli in comparison to other scholarly studies. However, I disagree with Althusser's contention that Machiavelli develops a prince-populace relation with fear but without hatred. For Machiavelli, hatred is an ineradicable component of political life. See Louis Althusser, *Machiavelli and Us*, ed. Matheron, trans. Elliott (New York: Verso, 1999).

12. Althusser, *Machiavelli and Us*, pp. 100–101.

13. In the "History of Florence," Machiavelli claims tyranny generates hatred. Speaking for a Signor, Machiavelli writes: "In the midst of universal hatred no security is ever to be found, because you do not know from where the evil is going to come; and he who fears all men cannot secure himself against anybody, because those who are left are more fiery in their hate and more prepared for vengeance" (p. 1124).

14. "Tercets on Ambition," in *Machiavelli: The Chief Works and Others*, pp. 735–36 (emphasis added).

15. Ibid., 736–39.

16. According to Machiavelli, "the feelings of enmity and hate [are] so often caused by suspicion" ("History of Florence," p. 1384).

17. Machiavelli, *Prince*, p. 28. Hatred can work in the opposite direction and lead to self-destruction: "Conspiracies . . . give princes reasons for being afraid; fear gives him reasons for making himself safe; making himself safe gives him reasons for doing harm. Hence, feelings of hatred result from them, and in time often his downfall"; "History of Florence," p. 1384.

18. Machiavelli, *Prince*, p. 67.

19. Ibid., 64.

20. Ibid., 71.

21. Ibid., 34, 70.

22. Ibid., 70.

23. Ibid., 59.

24. Ibid., 33.

25. Ibid., 51, 48, 25, and 8.
26. Ibid., 64.
27. Ibid., 65 and 63.
28. Ibid., 68. According to Machiavelli, when a prince arms his people, he arms himself: "By arming your subjects you arm yourself; those who were suspect become loyal, and those who were loyal not only remain so but are changed from being merely your subjects to being your partisans" (*Prince*, p. 67).
29. Machiavelli, *Prince*, p. 34.
30. Ibid., 53.
31. Ibid., 62.
32. Ibid., 63.
33. Ibid., 58.
34. Ibid., 61.
35. Ibid., 59.
36. Ibid., 58-59.
37. Ibid., 65.
38. Machiavelli, *Discourses*, p. 114.
39. Machiavelli, speaking for Neri in the "History of Florence," writes: "An old love or an old hate cannot by new benefits or new injuries easily be cancelled" (p. 1261).
40. See McCormick, *Machiavellian Democracy*.
41. Machiavelli, *Discourses*, p. 156.
42. Machiavelli, *Prince*, p. 25 (emphasis added).
43. McCormick, "Machiavellian Democracy: Controlling Elites with Ferocious Populism," *American Political Science Review* 95, no. 2 (2001): 308.
44. So horrifying, in fact, that Immanuel Kant granted the death penalty to anyone who attacked the head of state "on the pretext that he has abused his authority." *Metaphysics of Morals*, trans. Gregor (New York: Cambridge University Press, 1991), p. 131.
45. Machiavelli, *Prince*, p. 23. See also Allie Terry, "Donatello's Decapitations and the Rhetoric of Beheading in Medicean Florence," *Renaissance Studies* 23, no. 5 (2009): 609-38 for an analysis of violent political turmoil and factional strife in Florence. See also Bruce Buchan, "Duo pezzi in su la piazza: The Death of the Body Politic in Western Political Theory," *South Atlantic Quarterly* 110, (2011): 901-15.
46. Machiavelli, *Prince*, p. 81.

47. See Pitkin, *Fortune Is a Woman: Gender and Politics in the Thought of Machiavelli* (Berkeley, CA: University of California Press, 1987), p. 138.

48. Instead of being rewarded for his trickery, the schoolmaster's two faces were slapped. In this sense, the schoolmaster is arguably a metaphor for fortuna.

49. Machiavelli, *Discourses*, p. 461.

50. Ibid.

51. Ibid. (emphasis added).

52. For a painting that depicts this incident see Nicolas Poussin's *Camillus and the Schoolmaster of Falerii*, c. 1635. Pasadena, CA. Norton Simon Museum.

53. The schoolmaster incident is neglected by most commentators on Machiavelli. There are a couple of exceptions. For a brief discussion of the beating of the schoolmaster, see Paul J. Rasmussen, *Excellence Unleashed: Machiavelli's Critique of Xenophon and the Moral Foundations of Politics* (Lanham, MD: Lexington Books, 2009). See also Vickie B. Sullivan, "In Defense of the City: Machiavelli's Bludgeoning of the Classical and Christian Traditions" in *Instilling Ethics*, ed. Thompson (Cumnor Hill, UK: Rowman & Littlefield, 2000), pp. 39–59.

54. For the political significance of humor, see Simon Critchley, *On Humour* (New York: Routledge, 2002). For Critchley, "jokes tear holes in our usual predictions about the empirical world. We might say that humour is produced by a disjunction between the way things are and the way they are represented in the joke, between expectation and actuality" (p. 1).

55. The lesser violence inflicted on the schoolmaster contradicts Freud's hypothesis that the individual throws off repressed instinctual impulses while in a group which may unleash extreme violence. See Sigmund Freud, *Group Psychology and the Analysis of the Ego*, trans. Strachey (New York: W. W. Norton & Co, 1959).

56. What if the populace mistakes the good judgment of elites for oppression, that is, what if the populace imagines they are being abused and oppressed when in fact leaders are working for the common good and are incorrectly accused of corruption? Machiavelli addresses this issue. True, the people can be mistaken and they have a hard time generalizing but the "populace does not make mistakes about particulars" and is "guilty of fewer faults

than is the prince" (*Discourses*, pp. 229, 260). That is to say, the people are not mistaken and know when they are being oppressed. And the people, Machiavelli states in one of his proclamations that place the idea of collective political resistance at the heart of his work, wish only "not to be oppressed" (*Prince*, pp. 33, 34). The nobles, in contrast, have an "excessive demand to dominate" (Discourses, p. 214).

57. See Pettit (1999, 2001); Pocock (1975); Skinner (2000).

58. Winter, "Plebeian Politics: Machiavelli and the Ciompi Uprising," *Political Theory* 40, no. 6 (2012): 749.

59. Machiavelli, *Discourses*, p. 132.

60. McCormick advocates institutional mechanisms for voicing popular animosity against elites in order to restore political accountability. For him, the entwinement of social conflict and institutional design is needed. McCormick also calls for a constitutional amendment that creates a People's Tribune via a random selection process with a wealth cap on participants. This is intended to build class consciousness and intensify popular resentment against elites for the purposes of elite surveillance. Whereas I see value in the moment of extra-institutional popular hatred against elites exemplified in the non-lethal beating of a despised schoolmaster, McCormick wants to generate and channel popular hatred through institutions to put a check on retributive cruelty and defensive ferocity. McCormick is aware that no political institution is beyond misuse. However, McCormick's institutional bias leads him to the belief that a "virtuous magistrate must remind the people that they make better and more just decisions when they gather, deliberate and decide in assembly than when they scream, shout and lash out as a disorganized mob in the street." With this quote, McCormick has restated the fantasy of mob violence of the Cambridge School that is used as a scare tactic to insist that institutional assemblies are superior to any other available option for popular political participation. For McCormick, either we have ordered problem-solving dialogue in an assembly or street anarchy where the masses run amok. This opposition does not accurately reflect Machiavelli's view, because Machiavelli does not rule out extra-institutional political violence as a mechanism to ensure elite accountability. See McCormick, "Subdue the Senate: Machiavelli's 'Way of Freedom' or Path to Tyranny?" *Political Theory* 40, no. 6 (2012): 729.

61. The problem of governance in the United States stems from what Huntington identified as an "excess of democracy" in *The Crisis of Democracy: Report on the Governability of Democracies to the Trilateral Commission* (New York: New York University Press, 1975), p. 123.

62. Schmitt, *The Concept of the Political*, trans. Schwab (Chicago: University of Chicago Press, 1996), p. 27 (emphasis added).

63. Huntington, *The Clash of Civilizations and the Remaking of the World Order* (New York: Simon & Schuster, 1996/2011), p. 20.

64. Huntington, *The Clash of Civilizations and the Remaking of the World Order*, p. 20.

65. Ibid. 21.

66. Huntington, *Who Are We? The Challenges of America's National Identity* (New York: Simon & Schuster, 2004), p. 365.

67. Huntington states: "The fundamental source of conflict in this new world will not be primarily ideological or primarily economic. The great divisions among humankind and the dominating source of conflict will be cultural." See "The Clash of Civilizations?" *Foreign Affairs* 72, no. 3 (1993): 22.

68. Ange-Marie Hancock, *The Politics of Disgust: The Public Identity of the Welfare Queen* (New York: New York University Press, 2004).

69. Self-hatred by the poor results from the internalization of the ideology of neoliberalism, which measures a human's worth by an economic matrix.

70. Huntington's title *Who Are We?* is deceptively simple, for it posits as a question something that Huntington already knows in advance. Huntington's static "we" simultaneously creates the true American as well as the domestic foreigner, who, as unassimilable, emerges as a paradoxical construction, as a hereditary immigrant. See Étienne Balibar, *Equaliberty: Political Essays*, trans. Ingram (Durham, NC: Duke University Press, 2014), p. 246, for an analysis of the political construction of hereditary immigrants.

71. Huntington, "The Clash of Civilizations?" p. 22. See also Patricia Cohen, "Oxfam Study Finds Richest 1% Is Likely to Control Half of Global Wealth by 2016" in the *New York Times*, January 19, 2015.

72. See Michael J. Shapiro, "Samuel Huntington's Moral Geography," *Theory & Event* 2, no. 4 (1999): para. 3.

73. Ian F. Haney López, *White by Law: The Legal Construction of Race* (New York: New York University Press, 1996). According to López,

races are social constructions that become real as a result of legal decisions: "The courts were responsible for deciding not only who was White, by why someone was White" (p. 3).

74. The discourse of "normality" can be called on to put a pseudo-scientific stamp on the condemnation of internal enemies as sexual deviants, insane, born criminals, abnormal, and mentally deficient in need of therapeutic-pharmacological treatment and imprisonment. See any of Michel Foucault's major books for his analysis of the discourse of normality as a practice of power.

75. Huntington, *Who Are We?* xvii. He continues: "My selection and presentation of evidence may well be influenced by my patriotic desire to find meaning and virtue in America's past and in its possible future" (ibid.).

76. Video games such as *Call of Duty* provide young people with the necessary social conditioning for the dehumanization and annihilation of the enemy/other. The films *Black Hawk Down* (2001) and *American Sniper* (2014) continue the theme for adults. See *Call of Duty*, David Vonderhaar et. al. (Los Angeles, CA: Infinity Ward, 2003); *Black Hawk Down*, dir. Ridley Scott (Santa Monica, CA: Revolution Studios, 2002); and *American Sniper*, dir. Clint Eastwood (Hollywood, CA: Warner Brothers, 2014).

77. In *Discourses*, Machiavelli claims it is useful and necessary for republics to "provide legal outlets for anger" (p. 125).

78. Machiavelli, *Discourses*, p. 112.

79. For Machiavelli, "the quarrels between the nobles and the plebs were the primary cause of Rome's retaining her freedom" (*Discourses*, p. 113).

80. In addition to extra-institutional acts of violence against elites, legal outlets are also needed for popular hatred against elites as well as for the ambitions of the populace (*Discourses*, pp. 125, 114). Without them, a political regime becomes a breeding ground for conspirators and assassins. Machiavelli also argues that a regime should be reconstituted every five years so that the original terror of the founding can impress on citizens their forgotten duties (*Discourses*, p. 388). The nonlethal and extra-institutional punishment of elites can also renew corrupt political orders.

81. Strauss states: "The philosophers and the demos in the sense indicated are separated by a gulf; their ends differ radically. The gulf can be bridged only by a noble rhetoric" (*Thoughts on Machiavelli*, 1958, p. 296).

82. Machiavelli, *Discourses*, p. 254.
83. Machiavelli, *Prince*, pp. 33, 34.

Chapter 2

1. For the Jacobins, the revolutionary elite embodies the people and smashes the old political order. See *Robespierre: Virtue and Terror,* trans. Howe (New York: Verso, 2007). See also Sophie Wahnich, *In Defence of the Terror: Liberty or Death in the French Revolution,* trans. Fernbach (New York, NY: Verso, 2012). See also William W. Sokoloff, "Jacobinism," *The Encyclopedia of Political Thought,* ed. Gibbons (Hoboken, NJ: Wiley-Blackwell, 2014).
2. Kant states that thinking freely leads to acting freely. See Kant, "Answer to the Question: What Is Enlightenment?" in *Kant, Political Writings* ed. Reiss, trans. Nisbet (New York: Cambridge University Press, 1991), p. 55, 59.
3. See John Rawls, "Justice as Fairness: Political not Metaphysical" in *Philosophy and Public Affairs 14* (1985): 223-51.
4. The expression civilizing revolution is a formulation I borrow from the work of Étienne Balibar. See Balibar, "Outlines of a Topography of Cruelty: Citizenship and Civility in the Era of Global Violence," *Constellations* 8 (2001): 15-29.
5. See Immanuel Kant, *Education,* trans. Churton (Ann Arbor, MI: University of Michigan Press, 1960), p. 6.
6. Kant's work on revolution and political resistance in this text is often invoked to illustrate the Prussian's opposition to radical political transformation. See Christine M. Korsgaard, *The Constitution of Agency: Essays on Practical Reason and Moral Psychology* (New York: Oxford University Press, 2008), pp. 233-62. Lenval Callender argues Kant does not condemn all resistance but only resistance conducted by violent means and resistance directed toward the forcible overthrow of a constitution. See Lenval A. Callender, *Kant and Revolution* (Bury St. Edmunds, UK: Arima Publishing, 2011), pp. 11, 60.
7. Kant, *Metaphysics of Morals,* 1991, ftn. 132.
8. Kant, *Metaphysics of Morals,* 1991, ftn. 132.
9. Kant, *Perpetual Peace and Other Essays,* trans. Humphrey (Indianapolis, IN: Hackett Press, 1988), p. 129.
10. Kant, *Conflict of the Faculties,* trans. Gregor (Lincoln, NE: University of Nebraska Press, 1992), p. 182.

11. For a discussion of these themes see H. S. Reiss, "Kant and the Right of Rebellion," *Journal of the History of Ideas* 17 (April 1956): 179–92; Dale Jacquette, "Kant on Unconditional Submission to the Suzerain," *History of Philosophy Quarterly* 13 (January 1996): 117–31; Lenval A. Callender, *Kant and Revolution*, (Bury St. Edmunds, UK: Arima Publishing, 2011); Lewis W. Beck, "Kant and the Right of Revolution," *Journal of the History of Ideas* 32 (July–September 1971): 411–22; Sidney Axinn, "Kant, Authority, and the French Revolution," *Journal of the History of Ideas* 32 (July–September 1971): 423–32; Robert S. Taylor, "Democratic Transitions and the Progress of Absolutism in Kant's Political Thought," *Journal of Politics* 68 (August 2006): 556–70; Christine Korsgaard, "Taking the Law into Our Own Hands: Kant on the Right to Revolution," *Reclaiming the History of Ethics: Essays for John Rawls*, ed. A. Reath, B. Herman, and C. Korsgaard (Cambridge, UK: Cambridge University Press, 1997).

12. See Hans Reiss, "Postcript" in *Kant: Political Writings*, ed. Reiss, trans. Nisbet (Cambridge, UK: Cambridge University Press, 1991), pp. 263–64.

13. Kant, *Metaphysics of Morals*, 1991, p. 159.

14. Kant, "Answer to the Question: What Is Enlightenment?" 1991, p. 55.

15. Kant, "Answer to the Question: What Is Enlightenment?" 1991, p. 55; emphasis added.

16. Kant, "What Is Orientation in Thinking?" in *Kant: Political Writings*, ed. Reiss, trans. Nisbet (New York: Cambridge University Press, 1991), ft., p. 249.

17. Arendt, *Lectures on Kant's Political Philosophy*, Ed. Beiner (Chicago, IL: University of Chicago Press, 1982), p. 45.

18. Arendt, *Lectures on Kant's Political Philosophy*, 1982, p. 38. Korsgaard claims "Kant's attitudes towards revolution, both in his work and in his life, are notoriously paradoxical" in *The Constitution of Agency: Essays on Practical Reason and Moral Psychology* (New York: Oxford University Press, 2008), p. 235.

19. Arendt, *Lectures on Kant's Political Philosophy*, 1982, p. 52.

20. See Romand Coles, *Rethinking Generosity: Critical Theory and the Politics of Caritas* (Ithaca, NY: Cornell University Press, 1997), p. 69.

21. Callender correctly argues that Kant's reflections on self-emancipation, a major theme of "An Answer to the Question: What Is Enlightenment?" are essential for understanding Kant's views on

revolution. According to Callender, "Kant does have a consistent and defensible view of revolution," in *Kant and Revolution*, pp. 6,106.

22. Kant, "Answer to the Question: What Is Enlightenment?" 1991, p. 54.

23. Kant, "Answer to the Question: What Is Enlightenment?" 1991, p. 55.

24. Kant, "Answer to the Question: What Is Enlightenment?" 1991, p. 55.

25. For the counterconcept of genius, see Avital Ronell, *Stupidity* (Chicago, IL: University of Illinois Press, 2002). For Kant, "deficiency in judgment is just what is ordinarily called stupidity, and for such a failing there is no remedy" in Kant, *Critique of Pure Reason*, trans. Smith (New York: St. Martin's Press, 1965), p. 178. As a result of the emphasis on singularity and commonality in his concept of genius, Yu Liu argues that Kant's concept of genius leads to a new theory of politics. However, this idea is not developed. See Yu Liu, "Celebrating both Singularity and Commonality: The Exemplary Originality of the Kantian Genius," *International Philosophical Quarterly* 52, No. 1 (March 2012): 99-116.

26. There is a structural link between revolutionary action and practical reason in Kant since both require the human agent to be free and a law unto oneself. It is well known that Kant accords primacy to practical reason. Kant states that "freedom constitutes the keystone of the whole structure of a system of pure reason." So long as the human agent could resist the domination of sensibility as a determinant of conduct, the human was free and self-legislating as opposed to a slave to the realm of sensibility. See Kant, *Critique of Practical Reason*, trans. Gregor (New York: Cambridge University Press, 1997), p. 3.

27. Arendt, *Lectures on Kant's Political Philosophy*, 1982, p. 13. See also Miguel Vatter who states: "Kant's system of law relies on an account of reflective judgment developed in his *Critique of Judgment*" in "The People Shall Be Judge: Reflective Judgment and Constituent Power in Kant's Philosophy of Law," *Political Theory* 39 (2011): 750.

28. See Jean-François Lyotard, *Lessons on the Analytic of the Sublime*, trans. Elizabeth Rottenberg (Stanford, CA: Stanford University Press, 1994); Julia Kristeva, "Is there a Feminine Genius?" *Critical Inquiry* 3 (2004): 493-504; Hannah Arendt, *Lectures on Kant's Political Philosophy* (Chicago, IL: University of Chicago Press, 1982); Linda Zerilli, *Feminism and the Abyss of Freedom* (Chicago, IL: University of Chicago Press, 2005).

29. Although Eva Schaper offers an accurate account of genius, and correctly flags the innovative character of Kant's work, the political

import of the concept of genius is neglected. See Eva Schaper, "Taste, Sublimity, and Genius: The Aesthetics of Nature" in *The Cambridge Companion to Kant*, ed. Paul Guyer, (New York: Cambridge University Press, 1992).

30. Kant, *Anthropology from a Pragmatic Point of View*, trans. Dowdell (Carbondale, IL: Southern Illinois University Press, 1978), p. 129. Kant was explicit about the need for a revolution in the inner make-up of the human agent: "That a human being should become not merely *legally* good, but *morally* good and thus in need of no other incentive to recognize a duty except the representation of duty itself—that, so long as the foundation of the maxims of the human being remains impure, cannot be effected through gradual *reform* but must rather be effected through a *revolution* in the disposition of the human being. And so a 'new man' can come about only through a kind of rebirth, as it were a new creation and a change of heart" in Kant, *Religion with the Boundaries of Mere Reason*, trans. and eds. Wood and Giovanni (New York: Cambridge University Press, 1998), p. 67-68.

31. See Paul Guyer, "Kant's Conception of Fine Art," *Journal of Aesthetics and Art Criticism* 52 (Summer 1994): 280. See also Guyer "Feeling and Freedom: Kant on Aesthetics and Morality, *Journal of Aesthetics and Art Criticism* 48 (Spring 1990): 137-46.

32. Kant, *Critique of Judgment*, trans. Pluhar (Indianapolis, IN: Hackett Press, 1987), p. 176.

33. Jacques Derrida, *Geneses, Genealogies, Genres, & Genius: The Secrets of the Archive*, trans. Beverly Bie Brahic (New York: Columbia University Press, 2006), p. 3.

34. John Stuart Mill defended genius in "On Liberty." Mill states: "I insist emphatically on the importance of genius." See J. S. Mill, "On Liberty" in *On Liberty and Other Writings*, ed. Collini, (New York: Cambridge University Press, 2005), p. 65. Nietzsche praised Plato in "The Greek State" as a thinker who organized a political order around the goal of producing the genius: "Every man is only dignified to the extent that he is a tool of genius." See Nietzsche, "The Greek State" in *On the Genealogy of Morality*, ed. Ansell-Pearson, trans. Diethe (New York: Cambridge University Press, 1994), p. 185. In "Schopenhauer as Educator," Nietzsche also claimed that humans evade their genius as a result of societal pressure. For him, the goal of all culture should be "the production of genius" that

is, the creation of true humans. See Nietzsche, "Schopenhauer as Educator" in *Unfashionable Observations*, trans. Gray (Stanford, CA: Stanford University Press, 1995), p. 190.

35. See Giorgio Tonelli, "Kant's Early Theory of Genius (1770-1779): Part II," *Journal of the History of Philosophy* 4 (July 1966): 222.

36. See Gerard, Alexander, *An Essay on Genius* (London, UK: W. Strahan, 1774).

37. Kant, *Critique of Judgment*, 1987, p. 174.

38. Kant, *Critique of Judgment*, 1987, p. 181.

39. Kant, *Critique of Judgment*, 1987, p. 181-82.

40. Kant, *Critique of Judgment*, 1987, p. 174.

41. Kant, *Critique of Judgment*, 1987, p. 177.

42. Kant, *Critique of Judgment*, 1987, p. 187.

43. Kant, *Critique of Judgment*, 1987, p. 186.

44. Kant, *Critique of Judgment*, 1987, p. 187, emphasis added. It is important to note that the German word *der Zwang* has several meanings, including constraint, compulsion, and force. The verb form *zwingen* means to compel and to force. See Immanuel Kant, *Kritik der Urteilskraft* (Frankfurt am Main, Germany: Suhrkamp Verlag, 1974), p. 255.

45. Kant, *Critique of Judgment*, 1987, p. 187.

46. Kant, *Critique of Judgment*, 1987, p. 161.

47. Kant, *Critique of Judgment*, 1987, p. 130.

48. See Coles, *Rethinking Generosity*, 1997, p. 69.

49. Linda Zerilli has a favorable evaluation of Kantian genius insofar as the genius has the "ability to present objects in new, unfamiliar ways." However, Zerilli emphasizes the "solitary" dimension of Kant's genius and turns to "reflective judgment" as the center of Kant's political insight in the Third Critique. There might be good reasons to view genius as a lonely creator or "lord of nature," since this is generally how the genius is perceived in the popular imagination. For Kant, however, the genius must be able to communicate with others and communication, by definition, cannot occur in isolation. Perhaps the genius is alone when she creates, but the act of creation connects to the past, present, and future. See Linda Zerilli, *Feminism and the Abyss of Freedom*, 2005, pp. 160-61. For Arendt, the originality of the artist depends on "making himself understood" (Arendt, *Lectures on Kant's Political Philosophy*, 1982, p. 63). Coles emphasizes the dialogical activity of

the genius. See Coles, *Rethinking Generosity: Critical Theory and the Politics of Caritas* (Ithaca, NY: Cornell University Press, 1997). For Deleuze, "genius is a summons sent out to another genius." See Gilles Deleuze, *Kant's Critical Philosophy: The Doctrine of the Faculties*, trans. Tomlinson & Habberjam (Minneapolis, MN: University of Minnesota Press, 1993), p. 57.

50. See Jacques Rancière for a defense of intellectual equality in *The Ignorant Schoolmaster: Five Lessons in Intellectual Emancipation*, trans. Ross (Stanford, CA: Stanford University Press, 1991).

51. Richard Herrnstein and Charles Murray, for example, argue poor people have low intelligence levels, whereas rich people are highly intelligent. This strikes me as an ideological justification for the current distribution of wealth parading as objective research. See *The Bell Curve: Intelligence and Class Structure in American Life* (New York: Free Press, 1994).

52. Kant, *Groundwork of the Metaphysics of Morals*, trans. Gregor (New York: Cambridge University Press, 1998), p. 38.

53. Kant, *Religion within the Boundaries of Mere Reason*, 1998, p. 67–68.

54. Kant, *Groundwork for the Metaphysics of Morals*, 1998, p. 47.

55. Kant, *Anthropology*, 1978, p. 129.

56. Kant, *Metaphysics of Morals*, 1991, p. 231.

57. Kant, "Answer to the Question: What Is Enlightenment?" 1991, p. 59.

58. Hans Reiss, "Kant and the Right of Rebellion," 1956, p. 192.

59. Kant, *Religion within the Boundaries of Mere Reason*, 1998, p. 68.

60. See John Rawls, "Justice as Fairness: Political Not Metaphysical"; *Philosophy and Public Affairs* 14 (1985): 223–51.

61. See Sheldon Wolin, "What Is Revolutionary Action Today," in *Dimensions of Radical Democracy: Pluralism, Citizenship, Community*, ed. Mouffe, (New York: Verso, 1992), p. 251.

62. See *Kant and the Concept of Race*, trans. and ed. Mikkelsen (Albany, NY: State University of New York, 2013). See also *Race and the Enlightenment: A Reader*, ed. Eze (Malden, MA: Wiley-Blackwell, 1997). For Kant's silence on race in Kant's late writings see Peter Fenves, *Late Kant: Towards Another Law of the Earth* (New York: Routledge, 2003), pp. 103–4. Finally, see *Feminist Interpretations of Immanuel Kant*, ed. Schott (University Park, PA: Pennsylvania University Press, 2007).

63. See John Rawls, "Justice as Fairness: Political Not Metaphysical" and Rawls, *Lectures on the History of Political Philosophy* (Cambridge, MA: Harvard University Press, 2007).

64. Kant, "Answer to the Question: What Is Enlightenment?" 1991, p. 59.

Chapter 3

1. John Rawls's ideal of reasonable citizens precludes a role for rage. See Rawls, *A Theory of Justice* (Cambridge, MA: Harvard University Press, 2003). Jürgen Habermas's conception of rational deliberation prevents him from according affect and rage a role in his theory of democracy. See Habermas, *Between Facts and Norms: Contributions to a Discourse Theory of Law and Democracy*, trans. Rehg (Cambridge, MA: Polity Press, 1996). Michael E. Morrell argues that the dialogic dimension of deliberative democracy could be improved if empathy was accorded a central place. This position risks obscuring political differences that call for anger and antagonism as opposed to empathetic communion. See Morrell, *Empathy and Democracy: Feeling, Thinking, and Deliberation* (University Park, PA: Pennsylvania State University Press, 2010).

2. For Aristotle, the ideal citizen is free of anger; see *Nicomachean Ethics*, trans. Roger Crisp (New York: Cambridge University Press, 2000). For Seneca, anger is "the most hideous and frenzied of all emotions"; it "refuses to be governed"; it "tears entire nations to pieces"; finally, "instead of moderating our anger, we should eliminate it altogether." See "On Anger," *Seneca: Moral and Political Essays*, ed. and trans. John Cooper (New York: Cambridge University Press, 1995), pp. 17, 37, 96, 114. For Thomas Hobbes, unrestrained appetite, desire, and passion guarantee mutual destruction. See *Leviathan*, ed. Edwin Curley (Indianapolis, IN: Hackett Press, 1994). For Immanuel Kant, virtue is based on inner freedom and commands man to bring his inclinations under reason's control; in *Metaphysics of Morals*, trans. Mary Gregor (New York: Cambridge University Press, 1991), p. 208. Kant claims "derangement accompanied by raging (rabies), that is, an affection of anger (toward a real or imaginary object) which renders one insensitive to all external stimuli, is only one variety of mental imbalance"; in *Anthropology from a Pragmatic Point of View*, trans. Victor Lyle Dowdell (Carbondale, IL: Southern Illinois University Press, 1978), p. 118.

3. W.E.B. Du Bois sought a "union of intelligence and sympathy" as a way to prevent "fierce hate and vindictiveness." See Du Bois,

The Souls of Black Folk (New York: Dover, 1994), pp. 80 and 113, esp. p. 80. For Martin Luther King Jr., black rage would not make life better for African Americans engaged in civil disobedience. Although rage may be justified, King feared it would wreak havoc on black America and lead to more explosive violence. King sought to find a middle course between "the 'do-nothingism' of the complacent" and "the hatred and despair of the black nationalist." Martin Luther King Jr., *Why We Can't Wait* (New York: Signet, 2000), p. 75. Echoing King's concern, James Baldwin believed that rage threatens the polity, inhibits understanding, and leads to self-destructive action. Baldwin describes the sickness of rage: "That year in New Jersey lives in my mind as though it were the year during which, having an unsuspected predilection for it, I first contracted some dread, chronic disease, the unfailing symptom of which is a kind of blind fever, a pounding in the skull and fire in the bowels. Once this disease is contracted, one can never be really carefree again, for the fever, without an instant's warning, can recur at any moment. It can wreck more important things than race relations. *There is not a Negro alive who does not have this rage in his blood*—one has the choice, merely, of living with it consciously or surrendering to it. As for me, this fever has recurred in me, and does, and will until the day I die" [emphasis added] in "Notes of a Native Son" (New York: Library of America, 1998), pp. 69–70. For Cornel West, rage is not politically productive but rather needs to be contained and culturally channeled through the black church and music in order to avert its self-destructive consequences. See West, *Race Matters* (New York: Vintage, 1994), pp. 135–51. Malcolm X goes in the opposite direction: "Douglass was great. I would rather have been taught about Toussaint L'Ouverture. We need to be taught about people who fought, who bled for freedom and made others bleed," in Malcolm X, *By Any Means Necessary* (New York: Pathfinder, 1992), p. 124.

4. *Compact Edition of the Oxford English Dictionary* (New York: Oxford University Press, 1971), p. 2405.

5. According to Simon Kemp and K. T. Strongman in "Anger Theory and Management: A Historical Analysis, "we find surprisingly few changes in our concepts about anger in more than 2,000 years," *American Journal of Psychology* 108, no. 3 (1995): 414.

6. bell hooks, *Killing Rage: Ending Racism* (New York: Henry Holt & Co., 1995). For a defense of rage as a source of political motivation

see Peter Sloterdijk: "The development of a culture of indignation through the methodically exercised excitation of rage becomes the most important psychopolitical task, a task first taken up in the French Revolution" in *Rage and Time: A Psychopolitical Investigation*, trans. Mario Wenning (New York: Colombia University Press, 2010), p. 119. Finally, for Terri A. Hasseler, "we can learn a great deal from the ways in which different groups respond to and articulate their rage"; see "Socially Responsible Rage: Postcolonial Feminism, Writing, and the Classroom," *Feminist Teacher* 12, no. 3 (1999): 220.

7. bell hooks, *Killing Rage*, pp. 12–26.

8. Audre Lorde, "The Uses of Anger," *Women's Studies Quarterly* 9, no. 3 (1981): 8–9. See also Valerie C. Lehr, "Redefining and Building Community: The Importance of Anger," *Women & Politics* 15, no. 1 (1995): 40. See, finally, David Ost, "Politics as the Mobilization of Anger: Emotions in Movements and in Power," *European Journal of Social Theory* 7, no. 2 (2004), where he argues political stability is "congealed anger," p. 230.

9. My paper builds on Nick Bromell's "Democratic Indignation: Black American Thought and the Politics of Dignity," *Political Theory* 41, no. 2 (2013), where he argues that indignation works in a dialectical fashion insofar as it "monitors and assesses one's response to insult," p. 287. Through the interaction between insult and reflection, anger is guided "toward productive political and social ends," p. 287. Margaret Kohn productively illustrates Douglass's fight with Covey via Hegelian dialectics. See Kohn, "Frederick Douglass's Master-Slave Dialectic" *Journal of Politics* 67, no. 2 (2005): 497–514.

10. See Frederick Douglass, *Narrative of the Life of Frederick Douglass: An American Slave, Written by Himself* (New York: Signet, 2005), hereafter NLFD. See Douglass, *My Bondage and My Freedom* (New York: Library of America, 1994), hereafter MBMF. See Douglass, *Life and Times of Frederick Douglass* (New York: Library of America, 1994), hereafter LTFD. See Philip S. Foner (ed.), *Frederick Douglass: Selected Speeches and Writings* (Chicago, IL: Lawrence Hill Books, 1999).

11. See Leonard Harris in "Honor and Insurrection or A Short Story about Why John Brown (with David Walker's Spirit) was Right and Frederick Douglass (with Benjamin Banneker's Spirit) was Wrong" in *Frederick Douglass: A Critical Reader*, eds. Bill Lawson and Frank Kirkland (New York: Basil Blackwell, 1999), p. 239. Angela Davis

argues that Douglass was not radical enough insofar as "Douglass failed to use his position to forcefully challenge the Republican Party's complicity with the repressive process of reestablishing control over southern black labor" in "From the Prison of Slavery to the Slavery of the Prison: Frederick Douglass and the Convict Lease System," in *Frederick Douglass: A Critical Reader*, p. 344. Charles W. Mills argues that "Douglass is a classic representative in the black American political tradition of the dominant assimilationist view" in *Blackness Visible: Essays on Philosophy and Race* (Ithaca, NY: Cornell University Press, 1998), p. 171.

12. John Brown (1800–59) was an American abolitionist who pursued armed insurrection as a political strategy to overthrow slavery. See Harris, 1999, p. 239. This position is challenged by William Gleason in "Volcanoes and Meteors: Douglass, Melville, and the Moral Economies of American Authorship" in Robert Levine and Samuel Otter (eds.), *Frederick Douglass and Herman Melville: Essays in Relation* (Chapel Hill, NC: University of North Carolina Press, 2008). "In 'The Tyrants' Jubilee,'" according to Gleason, "we can see Douglass exploring what it might mean not only to warn of insurrection but also actively, even intemperately, desire it, should the South refuse to recognize both the humanity of blacks and the insurrectionary hubris of its own ways. The final line of the poem—'And the wind whispers Death as over them sweeping'— is as close to a call for exterminatory violence as one will find in Douglass before the war," pp. 125–26.

13. Davis (1999), pp. 341, 351.

14. Mills (1998), pp. 167–200.

15. Leslie Friedman Goldstein, "Morality and Prudence in the Statesmanship of Frederick Douglass: Radical as Reformer," *Polity* 16, no.4 (1984): pp. 610, 619.

16. See Omedi Ochieng, "A Ruthless Critique of Everything Existing: Frederick Douglass and the Architectonic of African American Radicalism," *Western Journal of Communication* 75, no. 2 (2011): 169.

17. Gooding-Williams (2009), p. 167.

18. Even though he opposed capital punishment (see "Resolutions Proposed for Anti-Capital Punishment Meeting," 1858), in "A Terror to Kidnappers" (1853), Douglass states: "Everything must be dealt with according to its kind," (Foner, p. 271). In his speech "Is It Right and Wise to Kill a Kidnapper" (1854), which was a response

to the public outcry over the death of an individual attempting to implement the Fugitive Slave Act in Boston, Douglass claims: "We hold that he had forfeited his right to live, and that his death was necessary, as a warning, to others liable to pursue a like course" (Foner, p. 279). In the same speech, Douglass states: "Resistance is wise as well as just" (Foner, p. 279).

19. See Muneer I. Ahmad, "A Rage Shared by Law: Post-September 11 Racial Violence as Crimes of Passion," *California Law Review* 92, no. 5 (2004): 1259-330 for the reciprocally reinforcing character of law and popular rage.

20. See James Allen et al. for a photographic account of extra-legal violence against African Americans. In Allen et. al., *Without Sanctuary: Lynching Photography in America* (Santa Fe, NM: Twin Palms Publishers, 2000). Douglass interpreted the increasing use of lynching as follows: "The resistance met by the Negro is to me evidence that he is making progress. . . . The men lynched at Memphis were murdered because they were prosperous. . . . When he shakes off his rags and wretchedness and presumes to be a man, and a man among men, he contradicts this popular standard and becomes an offence to his surroundings" (Foner, 748).

21. Robert Gooding-Williams, *In the Shadow of Du Bois: Afro-Modern Political Thought in America* (Cambridge, MA: Harvard University Press, 2009), p. 176.

22. See Hester Blum, "Douglass's and Melville's 'Alphabets of the Blind,'" in Robert Levine and Samuel Otter (eds.) *Frederick Douglass and Herman Melville: Essays in Relation* (Chapel Hill, NC: The University of North Carolina Press, 2008), p. 262.

23. Foner, p. 752 (emphasis added).

24. Foner, p. 751 (emphasis added).

25. Runaway slaves were branded with an *R* on their face, had an ear cut off, were dismembered, tortured to death, or killed.

26. LTFD, p. 501.

27. See Douglass, "The Heroic Slave" (Foner, p. 226).

28. MBMF, p. 171.

29. Foner, p. 375.

30. Foner, p. 375.

31. Foner, p. 239. For Harris, Douglass was comfortable defending a literary version of mutiny rather than practicing it himself in "Honor and Insurrection," pp. 238-39.

32. Friedrich Nietzsche, *On the Genealogy of Morals*, trans. Walter Kaufmann and R. J. Hollingdale (New York: Vintage Books, 1989): "*Ressentiment* itself, if it should appear in the noble man, consummates and exhausts itself in an immediate reaction, and therefore does not *poison*" (p. 39).

33. Bromell (2013), p. 290.

34. NLFD, p. 54.

35. MBMF, p. 223.

36. NLFD, p. 55.

37. MBMF, p. 209.

38. NLFD, p. 89.

39. See Kohn (2005): "Literacy would undermine the system by strengthening slaves' recognition of their own humanity and desire to be free," p. 499.

40. MBMF, p. 230 (emphasis added).

41. Foner, p. 375.

42. See George Shulman, *American Prophecy: Race and Redemption in American Political Culture* (Minneapolis, MN: University of Minnesota Press, 2008), p. 19.

43. Foner, pp. 195–97.

44. Foner, pp. 200–3.

45. MBMF, p. 165.

46. MBMF, p. 182.

47. MBMF, p. 294.

48. For Foucault, the body is a target of power and rendered docile so that it can be "subjected, used, transformed and improved." See Michel Foucault, *Discipline and Punish: The Birth of the Prison*, trans. Alan Sheridan (New York: Vintage Books, 1979), p. 136.

49. MBMF, p. 277.

50. NLFD, p. 82.

51. Washington states: "In the cold passion that took possession of him, the slave-boy became utterly reckless of consequences, reasoning to himself that the limit of suffering at the hands of this relentless slave-breaker had already been reached," See Booker T. Washington, *Frederick Douglass* (Philadelphia, PA: George W. Jacobs & Co., 1906), pp. 39–40.

52. MBMF, p. 282.

53. MBMF, p. 283.

54. MBMF, p. 284.

55. MBMF, p. 285.
56. MBMF, p. 286.
57. See Kohn (2005), p. 503.
58. NLFD, p. 82.
59. MBMF, p. 287.
60. Washington (1906), pp. 39-40.
61. See Irving Howe, "Black Boys and Native Sons," *Dissent* (Autumn 1963), p. 12.
62. NLFD, p. 73.
63. NLFD, p. 72.
64. MBMF, pp. 263, 265.
65. MBMF, p. 310.
66. See Ian F. Haney López, *White by Law: The Legal Construction of Race* (New York: New York University Press, 1996).
67. MBMF, p. 291.
68. MBMF, pp. 291-92.
69. MBMF, p. 245.
70. As Douglass claims, "voting supplies for Slavery—perpetuation of Slavery in this land" (Foner, p. 78).
71. NLFD, p. 104.
72. MBMF, p. 197.
73. Houston A. Baker argues silence can be a gesture of political resistance. Silence can also signal the expectation that blacks must earn the right to speak or that someone else will speak for them; see Baker, "Scene . . . Not Heard" in Robert Gooding-Williams (ed.), *Reading Rodney King, Reading Urban Uprising* (New York: Routledge, 1993), pp. 38-48.
74. MBMF, p. 342.
75. See Douglass, "Capt. Brown Not Insane" (1859); Foner, p. 375.
76. Washington (1906), p. 47.
77. Foner, p. 193. See Michelle Alexander, *The New Jim Crow: Mass Incarceration in the Age of Colorblindness* (New York: The New Press, 2012) for the connections between slavery, Jim Crow, the doctrine of color blindness, and the War on Drugs.
78. See James A. Colaiaco, *Frederick Douglass and the Fourth of July* (New York: Palgrave, 2006) for Douglass as a pragmatist (p. 92).
79. Joel Olson, "The Freshness of Fanaticism: The Abolitionist Defense of Zealotry," *Perspectives on Politics* 5, no. 4 (2007): 690.

Chapter 4

1. For Martin Luther King, "wait means never"; in *Why We Can't Wait* (New York: Signet, 2000). The expression "with all deliberate speed" in the *Brown* decision is painfully ambiguous.

2. For a classic statement on the psychological and social sources of rebellion see Ted Robert Gurr, *Why Men Rebel* (Princeton, NJ: Princeton University Press, 1970). The view that race no longer matters and that we live in a color blind society can be found in the writings of U.S. Chief Justice John Roberts, Justice Antonin Scalia, and Justice Clarence Thomas. See, in particular, the dismantling of the Voting Rights Act 1965 in *Shelby County v. Holder* 2013. In contrast to the view that we have entered a postracial society, the following research demonstrates that race continues to be a major factor in American politics. See Michelle Alexander, *The New Jim Crow: Mass Incarceration in the Age of Colorblindness* (New York: The New Press, 2012); Katherine Beckett, *Making Crime Pay: Law and Order in Contemporary American Politics* (New York: Oxford University Press, 1997); Ian F. Haney López, *White by Law: The Legal Construction of Race* (New York: New York University Press, 1996); Becky Pettit, *Invisible Men: Mass Incarceration and the Myth of Black Progress* (New York: Russell Sage Foundation, 2012); Joel Olson, *The Abolition of White Democracy* (Minneapolis, MN: University of Minnesota Press, 2004); Charles W. Mills, *The Racial Contract* (Ithaca, NY: Cornell University Press, 1997). See also Clarence Luanne, *The Black History of the White House* (San Francisco, CA: City Lights Books, 2011).

3. References to the writings of Du Bois refer to the following editions: Du Bois, *The Philadelphia Negro: A Social Study* (Philadelphia, PA: University of Pennsylvania Press, 1996); Du Bois, *John Brown* (New York: Modern Library, 2001); Du Bois, *The Gift of Black Folk: Negroes in the Making of America* (Garden City Park: Square One Publishers, 2009); Du Bois, *Darkwater: Voices from within the Veil* (Mineola: Dover Publications, 1999); Du Bois, *The Autobiography of W.E.B. Du Bois: A Soliloquy on Viewing My Life from the Last Decade of Its First Century* (New York: International Publishers, 1991); Du Bois, *Black Reconstruction in America, 1860–1880* (New York: Free Press, 1992); Du Bois, *Writings: The Suppression of the African Slave-Trade, The Souls of Black Folk, Dusk of Dawn, Essays*

and Articles (New York: Library of America, 1986); Du Bois, *The Souls of Black Folk* (New York: Dover, 1994).

4. Du Bois, "Essays" in *Writings*, 1986, p. 725.

5. Du Bois, "Methods of Attack," *Writings*, 1986, p. 1259 (emphasis added). See also Michael Hardt, "Militant Life," *New Left Review* 64 (July–August 2010). See Michel Foucault, *The Courage of Truth: The Government of Self and Others II*, trans. Burchell (New York: Palgrave, 2011).

6. The charge could be made that this inflates revolt to include everything which in turn makes it meaningless. I disagree. It is interesting to note that the standard definition of revolt in the *Merriam-Webster Collegiate Dictionary, Tenth Edition* as "to renounce allegiance or subjection" (p. 1003) includes a wide range of practices. To limit the meaning of the word *revolt* risks distorting Du Bois's historical significance and contemporary relevance. Political concepts are not prisons but are open to resignification when inherited meanings no longer illuminate the contemporary political moment.

7. See Nancy L. Rosenblum, "Thoreau's Militant Conscience," *Political Theory* 9 (1981), pp. 81–110. For the purposes of this chapter, I am interested in Rosenblum's critique of the concept of the militant, not her critique of Thoreau. See also Heinz Eulau, "Wayside Challenger: Some Remarks on the Politics of Henry David Thoreau," *Antioch Review* 9 (1949): 509–22.

8. See Nancy L. Rosenblum, "Romantic Militarism," *Journal of the History of Ideas* 43 (1982): 249–68. She states: "Anger, challenge, and insistence on change accompany militancy, but so, very often, a feeling of impotence and actual powerlessness." For her, the militant "typically wages a personal war against the world" (268).

9. Rosenblum claims that "parties are the most important agenda-setting institution for the public interests of democratic society as a whole" in "Religious Parties, Religious Political Identity, and the Cold Shoulder of Liberal Democratic Thought," *Ethical Theory and Moral Practice* 6 (2003): 50.

10. For Nancy L. Rosenblum, "American parties draw support from every socioeconomic group"; "Political Parties as Membership Groups," *Columbia Law Review* 100 (2000): 824.

11. Today, race continues to be a significant problem evident in disparities in rates of incarceration and sentencing for the same crime

for whites and blacks, police brutality against people of color, black poverty rates, higher unemployment, higher infant mortality rates, and lower life-expectancy for people of color. See Michelle Alexander, *The New Jim Crow: Mass Incarceration in an Age of Color Blindness*, 2012. According to Balfour, Americans routinely deny the significance of racial injustice and are plagued "by the inability to talk constructively about race." See Lawrie Balfour, *The Evidence of Things Not Said: James Baldwin and the Promise of American Democracy* (Ithaca, NY: Cornell University Press, 2001), pp. 2-3.

12. See Julia Kristeva, *Revolt, She Said*, trans. O'Keeffe, ed. Lotringer (New York: Semiotext(e), 2002).

13. Friedrich Nietzsche, *On the Genealogy of Morals*, trans. Kaufman and Hollingdale (New York: Vintage Books, 1989).

14. Manning Marable, *W.E.B. Du Bois: Black Radical Democrat* (Boston, MA: Dwayne Publishers, 1986), p. 108.

15. See Andrew L. Barlow, *Between Fear and Hope: Globalization and Race in the United States* (New York: Rowman & Littlefield, 2003).

16. In "An Address to the Slaves of the United States of America" in 1843 by Henry Highland Garnet, he states: "You had far better all die—*die immediately*—than live as slaves and entail your wretchedness upon your posterity." He continues: "Let your motto by Resistance! *Resistance!* RESISTANCE! No oppressed people have ever secured their Liberty without resistance"; in *Great Speeches by African Americans: Frederick Douglass, Sojourner Truth, Dr. Martin Luther King, Jr., Barack Obama, and Others*, ed. Daley (Mineola, NY: Dover, 2006), pp. 5, 7.

17. See Michael Hardt and Antonio Negri, *Commonwealth* (Cambridge, MA: Harvard University Press, 2009).

18. See Herbert Aptheker, *American Negro Slave Revolts* (New York: International Publishers, 1993). See also C. L. R. James, *A History of Pan-African Revolts* (Oakland, CA: PM Press, 2012).

19. Du Bois, *Darkwater*, 1999, p. 79.

20. Autobiography in the form of slave narratives is arguably a practice of resistance that reclaims one's dignity and agency and creates a productive outlet for one's voice.

21. Lawrie Balfour, *The Evidence of Things Not Said*, 2001, p. 44.

22. Du Bois, *Black Reconstruction*, 1992, pp. 367-67. Because of this, Du Bois claims, "the development of the Negro is followed with great difficulty" (*Black Reconstruction*, 1992, p. 562).

23. See Du Bois, *Black Reconstruction*, 1992, p. 562. See also Lawrie Balfour for her contention that there is a "tradition of representing black subjects as will-less" in Balfour, *Democracy's Reconstruction: Thinking Politically with W.E.B. Du Bois* (New York: Oxford University Press, 2011), p. 13. Du Bois retells the history of black Americans that highlights their agency. One of the most dramatic moments of the black spirit of revolt can be found in Frederick Douglass's fight with the slave-breaker Edward Covey as depicted in Douglass's narrative of his life as a slave. After suffering under the whip and nearly being worked to death for months, Douglass had had enough. Douglass was not restrained and patient. He refused to be abused and fought Covey. This was a revolutionary moment insofar as Douglass challenged slave plantation power politics. As a result of his willingness to fight, Douglass earned his dignity which ultimately gave him the confidence to escape. See Frederick Douglass, *Narrative of the Life of Frederick Douglass, an American Slave* (New York: Signet, 2005), p. 82. Other black leaders made an incredible impact on the living conditions for African Americans and did so through radical action including Harriet Tubman, Ida B. Wells-Barnett, Sojourner Truth, Martin Luther King Jr., Malcolm X, Ella Baker, and others. Revolt, albeit practiced in different ways, was the answer. Acquiescence meant death. For helpful discussions of these individuals, see Cornel West, *Black Prophetic Fire*, edited by Christa Buschendorf (Boston, MA: Beacon Press, 2014).
24. Du Bois, *Souls*, 1994, p. 113.
25. Du Bois, *Philadelphia Negro*, 1996, p. 393. See Du Bois, *John Brown*, 2001. For Du Bois, "violence is not an effective or necessary step to reform the American state" (Du Bois, *Dusk*, 1986, p. 763).
26. Du Bois, *Dusk*, 1986, pp. 612, 763, 696, 715. See also Du Bois, "Protest" in *Writings*, 1986, p. 1257.
27. See Du Bois, *Autobiography*, 1991, p. 222.
28. See Leo Strauss, *Persecution and the Art of Writing* (Chicago, IL: University of Chicago Press, 1988) for a discussion of the relationship between political context and the various ways authors craft arguments in response to it.
29. See Adolph L. Reed Jr., *W.E.B. Du Bois and American Political Thought: Fabianism and the Color Line* (New York: Oxford University Press, 1997). For Reed, Du Bois was an elitist.

30. For Robert Gooding-Williams, Du Bois advocates a "politics of expressive self-realization;" see Gooding-Williams, *In the Shadow of Du Bois: Afro-Modern Political Thought in America* (Cambridge, MA: Harvard University Press, 2009). Arnold Rampersad calls Du Bois a poet in *The Art and Imagination of W.E.B. Du Bois* (New York: Schocken Books, 1990). For Kenneth Barkin, Du Bois was an aesthete. See Barkin, "W.E.B. Du Bois' Love Affair with Imperial Germany," *German Studies Review* 28, no. 2 (May 2005): 285–302. Melvin L. Rogers focuses on Du Bois's rhetoric in "The People, Rhetoric, and Affect: On the Political Force of Du Bois' *The Souls of Black Folk*," *American Political Science Review* 106, no. 1 (February 2012): 188–203. For Eugene Victor Wolfenstein, Du Bois sought to create a common pathos. See *A Gift of the Spirit: Reading The Souls of Black Folk* (Ithaca, NY: Cornell University Press, 2007). For Shamoon Zamir, Du Bois was a scholar with "complex and multiple models of agency"; see Zamir, *Dark Voices: W.E.B. Du Bois and American Thought, 1888–1903* (Chicago, IL: University of Chicago Press, 1995). See also Manning Marable, *W.E.B. Du Bois: Black Radical Democrat* (Boston, MA: Twayne Publishers, 1986). See Nick Bromell, "W.E.B. Du Bois and the Enlargement of Democratic Theory," *Raritan* 30, no. 4 (2014): 140–61. For Lawrie Balfour, Du Bois forces Americans to acknowledge the legacies of slavery and colonialism in order to fight racism in the present. See Balfour, *Democracy's Reconstruction: Thinking Politically with W.E.B. Du Bois* (New York: Oxford University Press, 2011). Both Rogers and Wolfenstein have organized their interpretations around *The Souls of Black Folk* and this has arguably clouded the more radical dimensions of Du Bois's thinking. Rampersad's poetic rendering of Du Bois leads him to the conclusion that Du Bois never gave expression to prophetic rage as a result of his "humbleness in relation to the universe" (p. 284).

31. According to Marable, "Du Bois's major weakness as a black leader was his severe reluctance to mobilize political groups and to engage in tactical warfare against his opponents"; see Marable, 1986, p. 52. According to Gooding-Williams, "Du Bois' notion of black politics is too narrow," 2009, p. 36.

32. Wolfenstein claims Du Bois "renounced the path of revolt and revenge along with that of accommodation and acquiescence" (p. 74). Wolfenstein, however, does not develop this claim in his

provocative treatment of Du Bois. See Wolfenstein, *A Gift of the Spirit*, 2007.

33. Du Bois, *The Gift of Black Folk*, 2009, p. 65.

34. See Rogers, "The People, Rhetoric, and Affect," 2012; see also Wolfenstein, *A Gift of the Spirit*, 2007.

35. See Rampersad, *The Art and Imagination of W.E.B. Du Bois*, 1990, p. 205.

36. For a study of the role slavery played in the Industrial Revolution, see Eric Williams, *Capitalism and Slavery* (Chapel Hill, NC: University of North Carolina Press, 1994).

37. Du Bois, *Souls* in *Writings*, 1986, p. 463.

38. Du Bois, *Black Reconstruction*, 1992, p. 7.

39. Du Bois, *Black Reconstruction*, 1992, p. 347.

40. Du Bois, *Gift*, 2009, p. 59.

41. Du Bois, *Gift*, 2009, p. 80.

42. Du Bois, *Gift*, 2009, p. 117.

43. Du Bois, "Souls," in *Writings*, 1986, p. 395.

44. Du Bois, *Autobiography*, 1991, p. 354.

45. See Frantz Fanon, *The Wretched of the Earth*, trans. Philcox (New York: Grove Press, 2004).

46. Du Bois, "Souls" in *Writings*, 1986, p. 502 (italics added).

47. See Du Bois, *Black Reconstruction*, 1992, pp. 711-29.

48. Du Bois, *Autobiography*, 1991, p. 295.

49. Du Bois, as quoted in Rampersad, *The Art and Imagination of W.E.B. Du Bois*, 1990, p. 96.

50. Du Bois, *Darkwater*, 1999, p. 56.

51. Du Bois, *Darkwater*, 1999, p. 114.

52. Since this debate is well known and treated throughout the scholarly literature, I do not plumb the differences between the two authors on this issue here. See, for example, Manning Marable, *W.E.B. Du Bois: Black Radical Democrat*, 1986.

53. See Du Bois, *The Education of Black People: Ten Critiques, 1906-1960*, ed. Aptheker (New York: Monthly Review Press, 2001), p. 81.

54. See Aptheker, "Introduction," in *The Education of Black People*, 2001, xiii.

55. Du Bois, "Souls" in *Writings*, 1986, p. 385.

56. For Du Bois, "the world regards and always has regarded education first as a means of buttressing the established order of things rather than improving it" (Du Bois, *Darkwater*, 1999, p. 121).

57. In order to fight this, Du Bois highlighted the "extraordinary record of accomplishment" of the Negro in *Black Reconstruction*, 1992, p. 702.

58. For Du Bois, "everything Negroes did was wrong. If they fought for freedom, they were beasts; if they did not fight, they were born slaves. If they cowered on plantations, they loved slavery; if they ran away, they were lazy loafers. If they sang, they were silly, if they scowled, they were impudent," in Du Bois, *Black Reconstruction*, 1992, p. 125. See also bell hooks, *Black Looks: Race and Representation* (Boston, MA: South End Press, 1992). Finally, for the argument that poor people have lower intelligence levels see Richard J. Herrnstein and Charles Murray, *The Bell Curve: Intelligence and Class Structure in American Life* (New York: Free Press, 1996).

59. Du Bois, *Autobiography*, 1991, p. 34.

60. Du Bois, *Black Reconstruction*, 1992, p. 383. Elsewhere, he states: "The whole history of the American Negro and other black folk . . . has never been written," in Du Bois, *Darkwater*, 1999, p. 746. Du Bois also states white Americans "obliterated the history of the Negro in America" in *Black Reconstruction*, 1992, p. 723. Hence, "the development of the Negro is followed with great difficulty" in *Black Reconstruction*, 1992, p. 562.

61. See also Du Bois, *Autobiography*, 1991, p. 420.

62. Du Bois, *Darkwater*, 1999, p. 18.

63. See Cheryl Harris, "Whiteness as Property," *Harvard Law Review* 106, no. 8 (1993): 1718. See also López, *White by Law*, 1996.

64. Du Bois, *Black Reconstruction*, 1992, p. 633.

65. Du Bois, *Black Reconstruction*, 1992, p. 14.

66. Du Bois, *Black Reconstruction*, 1992, p. 241. See Martin Luther King Jr. on the "white moderate" in "Letter from a Birmingham Jail" in *Why We Can't Wait*, 2000, p. 73.

67. Du Bois, *Black Reconstruction*, 1992, p. 678.

68. Du Bois, *Black Reconstruction*, 1992, p. 53.

69. See *Race and the Enlightenment: A Reader*, ed. Emmanuel Chukwudi Eze (Malden, MA: Blackwell, 2001). See also Clarence Lusane, *The Black History of the White House* (San Francisco, CA: City Lights, 2011).

70. Du Bois, *Black Reconstruction*, 1992, p. 239.

71. Du Bois, *Black Reconstruction*, 1992, p. 187.

72. Du Bois, *Black Reconstruction*, 1992, pp. 320, 346.

73. Du Bois, *Black Reconstruction*, 1992, p. 165.

74. See Catherine A. Holland for an insightful analysis of the slave revolt in Haiti and how Thomas Jefferson responded to it in *The Body Politic: Foundings, Citizenship, and Difference in the American Political Imagination* (New York: Routledge, 2001), pp. 35-37. See also Raphael Hoermann, "Thinking the 'Unthinkable'? Representations of the Haitian Revolution in British Discourse, 1790 to 1805" in Gesa Mackenthun and Raphael Hoermann (eds.), *Human Bondage in the Cultural Contact Zone: Transdisciplinary Perspectives on Slavery and Its Discourses* (New York: Waxman, 2010).

75. See Du Bois, *John Brown*, 2001, p. 231. See also Stokely Carmichael [Kwame Ture], *Stokely Speaks: From Black Power to Pan-Africanism* (Chicago, IL: Chicago Review Press, 2007).

76. Du Bois, *Black Reconstruction*, 1992, p. 238.

77. Du Bois, *John Brown*, 2001, p. 44.

78. Du Bois, "Souls" in *Writings*, 1986, p. 435.

79. Du Bois, "Souls" in *Writings*, 1986, p. 452.

80. Du Bois, *Darkwater*, 1999, p. 138.

81. Du Bois, "The Talented Tenth" in *Writings*, 1986, p. 855.

82. Du Bois, *Black Reconstruction*, 1992, p. 66.

83. Du Bois, "Suppression" in *Writings*, 1986, p. 146.

84. Du Bois, "Suppression" in *Writings*, 1986, p. 129. Du Bois also states: "American slavers cleared for foreign ports, there took a foreign flag and papers, and then sailed boldly past American cruisers, although their real character was often well known" in "Suppression" in *Writings*, 1986, pp. 129, 144, 146.

85. See Du Bois, "Suppression," in *Writings*, 1986, p. 61.

86. C. L. R. James, *The Black Jacobins: Toussaint L'Ouverture and the San Domingo Revolution* (New York: Vintage, 1989).

87. James, *The Black Jacobins*, 1989. See also C. L. R. James, *A History of Pan-African Revolt* (Chicago, IL: PM Press, 2012).

88. Du Bois, *Autobiography*, 1991, p. 352.

89. Du Bois, *John Brown*, 2001, p. 43.

90. See Leslie M. Alexander, "The Black Republic: The Influence of the Haitian Revolution on Northern Black Political Consciousness, 1816-1862" in *African Americans and the Haitian Revolution: Selected Essays and Historical Documents*, ed. Maurice Jackson and Jacqueline Bacon (New York: Routledge, 2010), pp. 76-77.

91. See Amy E. Earhart, "Representative Men, Slave Revolt, and Emerson's 'Conversion' to Abolitionism, *ATQ* (1999): p. 295.

92. Du Bois, "Souls," in *Writings*, 1986, p. 436-37.

93. Du Bois, "Essays," in *Writings*, 1986, p. 861.

94. Du Bois, *Black Reconstruction*, 1992, p. 618.

95. Du Bois, *John Brown*, 2001, p. 44.

96. Du Bois, "On Being Ashamed of Oneself" in *Writings*, 1986, p. 1025.

97. Du Bois, *Black Reconstruction*, 1992, p. 703 (emphasis added). For Martin Luther King Jr., "If repressed emotions are not released in nonviolent ways, they will seek expression through violence; this is not a threat but a fact of history"; *Why We Can't Wait*, 2000, p. 76.

98. See Rogers, "The People, Rhetoric, and Affect," 2012, p. 201.

99. Du Bois, "Souls" in *Writings*, 1986, p. 426.

100. See Ted Robert Gurr, *Why Men Rebel*, 1970.

101. As quoted in Rampersad, *The Art and Imagination of W.E.B. Du Bois*, 1990, p. 106.

102. Du Bois, "Dusk," *Writings*, 1986, p. 696. The recent police shootings of young African Americans is a relevant reminder of the unspoken but visible character of the presence of violent racial dictatorship in the United States.

103. See Andrew L. Barlow, *Between Fear and Hope: Globalization and Race in the United States* (New York: Rowman & Littlefield, 2003).

104. Du Bois, *Darkwater*, 1999, p. 696.

105. Du Bois, "Essays" in *Writings*, 1986, p. 1257.

106. Du Bois, *Autobiography*, 1991. Du Bois, "Souls" in *Writings*, 1986, p. 503. Ida B. Wells-Barnett also argued that African Americans would be well advised to purchase shotguns for self-defense. See Ida B. Wells-Barnett, *On Lynchings* (Amherst, NY: Humanity Books, 2002).

107. Du Bois, "Essays," *Writings*, 1986, p. 1259 (emphasis added).

108. Du Bois, *Autobiography*, 1991, p. 414.

109. Du Bois, *Black Reconstruction*, 1992, p. 703.

110. See Heinz Eulau, "Wayside Challenger: Some Remarks on the Politics of Henry David Thoreau," *Antioch Review* 9 (1949), pp. 509-22. I am not interested in Eulau's specific critique of Thoreau as I am in Eulau's critique of the concept of the political militant.

111. Eulau, 1949, p. 519.

112. Eulau, 1949, p. 514.

113. Eulau, 1949, 518.

114. See Nancy L. Rosenblum, "Thoreau's Militant Conscience," *Political Theory* 9 (1981).

115. Nancy L. Rosenblum, "Thoreau's Militant Conscience," *Political Theory* 9 (1981), p. 93.

116. Rosenblum, 1981, p. 90.

117. Rosenblum seems to have put Thoreau to good use since he appears as the negative foil for Rosenblum's defense of liberalism in "Strange Attractors: How Individualists Connect to Form Democratic Unity," *Political Theory* 18 (1990): 583 in "Democratic Education at Home: Residential Community Associations and 'Our Localism,'" *The Good Society* 7 (1997): 12. See also Rosenblum, "The Moral Uses of Civil Society: Three Views," *The Newsletter of PEGS* 3 (1993): 6.

118. See Heinz Eulau, "Skill Revolution and Consultative Commonwealth"; *American Political Science Review* 67 (1973): 189.

119. See Thomas Hobbes, *Leviathan*, ed. Curley (Indianapolis, IN: Hackett Press, 1994), p. 95. See also Nancy L. Rosenblum, *On the Side of the Angels: An Appreciation of Parties and Partisanship* (Princeton, NJ: Princeton University Press, 2008). See, in particular, the chapter titled "Militant Democracy: Banning Parties," pp. 412–455. Parties should be banned, according to Rosenblum, if they promote violence, incite hate, represent an existential challenge to national identity, and/or undermine democratic attitudes and dispositions; p. 435–36. These criteria are vague and could be applied to Abolitionists, Civil Rights Movement activists, Occupy protestors, and members of Black Lives Matter. For a defense of the productive deployment of hatred and how proclaimed existential threats to national identity shore up hierarchical state power and lead to militarism, see William W. Sokoloff, "In Defense of Hatred," *New Political Science* 37 (2015): 163–80.

120. Rosenblum, 1981, p. 100.

121. Rosenblum, 1981, p. 104.

122. Rosenblum, "Anything but Partisanship: Anti-Partyism, Bipartisanship, and the Luster of Independence," *Dissent*, October 15, 2009.

123. See Carl Boggs, *Imperial Delusions: American Militarism and Endless War* (New York: Rowman & Littlefield, 2005).

124. Eulau, 1949, p. 522.
125. See Rosenblum, "Thoreau's Militant Conscience," pp. 101, 102, 106. See also Rosenblum, "Romantic Militarism" *Journal of the History of Ideas* 43 (1982): 249-68. For a critique of the romantic that focuses on his/her passivity see Carl Schmitt, *Political Romanticism*, trans. Guy Oakes (Cambridge, MA: MIT Press, 1986). In a different article, Rosenblum defends American political parties because they "draw support from every socioeconomic group" (p. 824). Barriers to voting, for her, "have not turned out to be legal and bureaucratic (registration methods, for example) but attitudinal" (p. 842). See Nancy L. Rosenblum, "Political Parties as Membership Groups," *Columbia Law Review* 100 (2000): 813-44. For a sociological and historical analysis of restrictions on voting that challenge Rosenblum's claim, see Frances Fox Piven and Richard A. Cloward, *Why Americans Still Don't Vote and Why Politicians Want It That Way* (Boston, MA: Beacon, 2000).
126. See Alexander, *The New Jim Crow*.
127. See Charles E. Cobb Jr., *This Nonviolent Stuff'll Get You Killed: How Guns Made the Civil Rights Movement Possible* (New York: Basic Books, 2014). Cobb states: "Nonviolence was crucial to the gains made by the freedom struggle of the 1950s and '60s, but those gains could not have been achieved without the complementary and still underappreciated practice of armed self-defense" (p. 1). Cobb continues: "Armed self-defense as part of black struggle began not in the 1960s with angry "militant" and "radical" young Afro-Americans, but in the earliest years of the United States as one of African people's responses to oppression" (pp. 1-2).
128. See Supreme Court Justice Antonin Scalia's views on race relations in *City of Richmond v. J.A. Croson Co.*, 1989, *Adarand Constructors, Inc. v. Peña*, 1995 and *Grutter v. Bollinger*, 2003.
129. See Michelle Alexander, *The New Jim Crow: Mass Incarceration in the Age of Colorblindness*, 2012.
130. See Angela Y. Davis, *Are Prisons Obsolete?* (New York: Seven Stories Press, 2003).
131. Du Bois, *John Brown*, 2001, p. 202.
132. Du Bois, *The Philadelphia Negro*, 1996, p. 393.
133. Martin Luther King Jr., *Why We Can't Wait*, 2000, p. 19.
134. Du Bois, *Education of Black People*, 2001, p. 51.

135. Du Bois, "Souls," *Writings*, 1986, p. 448.

136. Du Bois, "Essays," *Writings*, 1986, p. 725.

137. Du Bois, *Autobiography*, 1991, p. 405.

138. Du Bois, "Dusk," *Writings*, 1986, p. 653.

139. Du Bois, "Dusk," *Writings*, 1986, p. 653.

140. Du Bois, *Darkwater*, 1999, p. 86.

141. Charles W. Mills, *The Racial Contract* (Ithaca, NY: Cornell University Press, 1997), p. 1.

142. Du Bois, *Education of Black People*, 2001, p. 132.

Chapter 5

1. See Seyla Benhabib, *The Reluctant Modernism of Hannah Arendt* (New York: Rowman & Littlefield, 2003); Bonnie Honig, *Political Theory and the Displacement of Politics* (Ithaca, NY: Cornell University Press, 1993); see also Bonnie Honig, "Toward an Agonistic Feminism: Hannah Arendt and the Politics of Identity" in *Feminists Theorize the Political*, eds. Judith Butler and Joan Scott (New York: Routledge, 1992); George Kateb, *Hannah Arendt: Politics, Conscience, Evil* (Totowa, NJ: Rowman & Allanheld, 1983); Dana Villa, *Arendt and Heidegger: The Fate of the Political* (Princeton, NJ: Princeton University Press, 1995). See also Sheldon Wolin, "Hannah Arendt: Democracy and the Political," *Salmagundi* 60 (1983): 3-19.

2. See Jeffrey Isaac, *Arendt, Camus, and Modern Rebellion* (New Haven, CT: Yale University Press, 1992).

3. See John Rawls, *A Theory of Justice* (Cambridge, MA: Harvard University Press, 1971) and *Political Liberalism* (New York: Columbia University Press, 1993).

4. See Michel Foucault, *A History of Sexuality*, trans. Hurley (New York: Vintage Books, 1990). See also Wendy Brown, *Undoing the Demos: Neoliberalism's Stealth Revolution* (New York: Zone Books, 2015).

5. Hannah Arendt, *Between Past and Future: Eight Exercises in Political Thought* (New York: Penguin Books, 1968), viii.

6. Arendt, *The Human Condition* (Chicago, IL: University of Chicago Press, 1958), p. 176; Arendt, "Socrates" in *The Promise of Politics*, ed. Kohn (New York: Schocken Books, 2005), p. 21.

7. See Arendt, *Between Past and Future*, pp. 3-4; Arendt, *Eichmann in Jerusalem: A Report on the Banality of Evil* (New York: Penguin, 1977), pp. 171-72; Arendt, *Crises of the Republic* (New York: Harcourt Press, 1972), p. 76; Arendt, *On Revolution* (New York: Penguin, 1965), p. 112, 271; and Arendt, *The Human Condition*, 1958, p. 190.

8. Arendt, *The Origins of Totalitarianism* (New York: Harcourt Press, 1968), ix.

9. Arendt, *The Origins of Totalitarianism*, 1968, p. 296.

10. See also Martin Heidegger, "The Question Concerning Technology," trans. Lovitt in *Martin Heidegger: Basic Writings*, ed. Krell (New York: Harper & Row, 1977).

11. Arendt, *Between Past and Future*, 1968, p. 91.

12. Arendt, *Between Past and Future*, 1968, p. 92.

13. Arendt, *Between Past and Future*, 1968, pp. 92-93.

14. Arendt, *Between Past and Future*, 1968, p. 97.

15. Arendt, *Between Past and Future*, 1968, p. 104.

16. Arendt, *Between Past and Future*, 1968, p. 136.

17. Arendt, *On Revolution*, 1965, p. 37.

18. Arendt, *On Revolution*, 1965, p. 202.

19. Arendt, *Between Past and Future*, 1968, p. 95.

20. Arendt, *Between Past and Future*, 1968, pp. 120-23.

21. Arendt, *Between Past and Future*, 1968, p. 91.

22. Arendt, *On Revolution*, 1965, p. 260.

23. Arendt, *Between Past and Future*, 1968, p. 92.

24. Arendt, *On Revolution*, 1965, p. 146.

25. Arendt, *Between Past and Future*, 1968, p. 141.

26. Arendt, *Between Past and Future*, 1968, p. 174.

27. Arendt, *Men in Dark Times* (New York: Harcourt Press, 1968), p. 134.

28. Arendt, *The Origins of Totalitarianism*, 1968, p. 473.

29. Arendt, *Between Past and Future*, 1968, p. 25. This is an arguably Heideggerian dimension to Arendt's political theorizing where a concept is interrogated to reactivate the force contained in it.

30. Arendt, *Between Past and Future*, 1968, p. 106.

31. Arendt, *Between Past and Future*, 1968, p. 146.

32. Arendt, "Personal Responsibility under Dictatorship" in *Responsibility and Judgment*, ed. Kohn (New York: Schocken Books, 2003), p. 46.

33. Arendt, *Eichmann in Jerusalem*, 1977, p. 289.

34. Arendt, *On Revolution*, 1965, pp. 223–24.

35. Arendt, *On Revolution*, 1965, p. 223.

36. Arendt, *On Revolution*, 1965, p. 223.

37. Arendt, *Crises of the Republic*, 1972, p. 88.

38. Arendt, *The Origins of Totalitarianism*, 1968, pp. 234, 306, 466.

39. Arendt, "The Moral of History," in *The Jew as Pariah: Jewish Identity and Politics in the Modern Age*, ed. Feldman (New York: Grove Press, 1978), p. 110.

40. Arendt, "Europe and the Atom Bomb" in *Essays in Understanding*, ed. Kohn (New York: Harcourt, 1994), p. 420.

41. Arendt, *Crises of the Republic*, 1972, p. 80.

42. Arendt, "Europe and the Atom Bomb" in *Essays in Understanding*, 1994, p. 420.

43. Arendt, *On Revolution*, 1965, pp. 183–84.

44. See William W. Sokoloff, "Between Justice and Legality: Derrida on Decision," *Political Research Quarterly* 58 (2005): 341–52.

45. Arendt, *Crises of the Republic*, 1972, p. 230.

46. Arendt, *On Revolution*, 1965, p. 228.

47. See Carl Schmitt, *Political Theology: Four Chapters on the Concept of Sovereignty*, trans. Schwab (Cambridge, MA: MIT Press, 1988).

48. Arendt, *The Human Condition*, 1958, p. 33.

49. Arendt, *Between Past and Future*, 1968, p. 165.

50. Arendt, *Eichmann in Jerusalem*, 1977, p. 101.

51. See John Rawls, *A Theory of Justice*, 1971; Rawls, *Political Liberalism*, 1996.

52. Rawls, *A Theory of Justice*, 1971, p. 232.

53. Rawls, *A Theory of Justice*, 1971, p. 429.

54. Rawls, *A Theory of Justice*, 1971, p. 308.

55. Rawls, *A Theory of Justice*, 1971, p. 312.

56. See Michel Foucault, "Technologies of the Self" in *Technologies of the Self: A Seminar with Michel Foucault*, ed. Martin et. al. (London, UK: Tavistock, 1988).

57. Michel Foucault, *The History of Sexuality*, 1990, pp. 95, 93.

58. Michel Foucault, "On Popular Justice: A Discussion with Maoists" in *Power/Knowledge: Selected Interviews & Other Writings, 1972–1977*, ed. Gordon. Trans. Gordon et. al. (New York: Pantheon Books, 1980), p. 16.

59. Michel Foucault, "Revolutionary Action 'Until Now'" in *Language, Counter-Memory, Practice: Selected Essays and Interviews by Michel*

Foucault, ed. Bouchard, trans. Bouchard et. al. (Ithaca, NY: Cornell University Press, 1977), p. 230.

60. See Michel Foucault, *The History of Sexuality: An Introduction*, vol. 1, trans. Hurley (New York: Vintage, 1990).

61. Of course, Arendt can be faulted for a rigid public/private distinction that perpetuates a masculine notion of politics that blinds her to the political dimensions of gender, racial, and economic domination. Also, she exhibits a neorepublican elitism that arguably restricts political activity to the few. For these and related themes, see *Feminist Interpretations of Hannah Arendt*, ed. Honig, (University Park, PA: Pennsylvania University Press, 1995).

Chapter 6

1. See Ian Haney López, *White by Law*, 2006.

2. Arthur Schlesinger Jr., *The Disuniting of America: Reflections on a Multicultural Society* (New York: W. W. Norton, 1998); Samuel P. Huntington, *Who Are We? The Challenges to America's National Identity* (New York: Simon & Schuster, 2004); Allan Bloom, *The Closing of the American Mind* (New York: Simon & Schuster, 1987).

3. See John Rawls, "Justice as Fairness: Political Not Metaphysical" (1985); Wendy Brown, *States of Injury: Power and Freedom in Late Modernity* (1995); Sheldon Wolin, "Democracy, Difference, and Re-Cognition" in *Fugitive Democracy and Other Essays*, 2016.

4. See Susan Bickford, "Anti-Anti-Identity Politics: Feminism, Democracy, and the Complexities of Citizenship"; *Hypatia* (2001): 119-20.

5. The border is an intersection between two states, two nations, two histories, two cultures, two economies, two "worlds"—first and third. This "twoness" has been intersecting and intertwined for nearly two hundred years (longer if Native Americans are included).

6. Anzaldúa, *Borderlands/La Frontera*, "Preface," 2007.

7. No reference to Anzaldúa is in Lisa García Bedolla, *Latino Politics*, 2nd ed. (Cambridge: UK: Polity Press, 2014). Exceptions in political science include Cristina Beltrán "Patrolling Borders: Hybrids, Hierarchies and the Challenge of Mestizaje" *Political Research Quarterly* 57 (2004): 595-607; Susan Bickford "Anti-Anti-Identity Politics: Feminism, Democracy, and the Complexities of Citizenship";

Hypatia (2001): 111-31; Romand Coles "*Traditio*: Feminists of Color and the Torn Virtues of Democratic Engagment"; *Political Theory* 29 (2001): 488-516. Even in the face of this research, Anzaldúa has not received the attention she deserves. This is unfortunate because as Coles (2001) puts it, Anzaldúa "articulates a vibrant ethos for learning to live in the midst of and from our differences." Coles continues: a "new identity; a new way of perception, thought, and relationship; a new way of passing on (in the senses of carrying forth, letting pass, living, dying) tradition," pp. 491, 495.

8. See Marcos Pizarro, *Chicanas and Chicanos in School: Racial Profiling, Identity Battles, and Empowerment* (Austin, TX: University of Texas Press, 2005).

9. See Kelly Lytle Hernández, *Migra! A History of the U.S. Border Patrol* (Berkeley, CA: University of California Press 2010; Ian Haney López, *Racism on Trial: The Chicano Fight for Justice* (Cambridge, MA: Harvard University Press, 2003); Joseph Nevins, *Operation Gatekeeper: The Rise of the "Illegal Alien" and the Making of the U.S.-Mexico Boundary* (New York: Routledge, 2002); Mae M. Ngai, *Impossible Subjects: Illegal Aliens and the Making of Modern America* (Princeton, NJ: Princeton University Press, 2004); Ricardo Romo, *East Los Angeles: History of a Barrio* (Austin, TX: University of Texas Press, 1983). *Colonias* are isolated unincorporated communities in deep south Texas prone to flooding with concentrated poverty and minimal public services. See, finally, William D. Carrigan and Clive Webb "The Lynching of Persons of Mexican Origin or Descent in the United States, 1848-1928"; *Journal of Social History* 37 (2003): 411-38 for data on the lynching of Mexican-Americans in the United States.

10. See Otto Santa Ana, *Brown Tide Rising: Metaphors of Latinos in Contemporary American Public Discourse* (Austin, TX: University of Texas Press, 2002).

11. Anzaldúa, *Borderlands/La Frontera*, 2007, "Preface," p. 60.

12. *The Gloria Anzaldúa Reader*, ed. AnaLouise Keating (Durham, NC: Duke University Press, 2009, p. 184.

13. Anzaldúa, *Borderlands/La Frontera*, 2007, p. 25.

14. Anzaldúa, *Borderlands/La Frontera*, 2007, 25.

15. Anzaldúa, *Borderlands/La Frontera*, 2007, p. 25.

16. "Making soul" refers to the need to fashion oneself on the inside as well. See also Susan Bickford, "Anti-Anti-Identity Politics," 2001.

17. Anzaldúa, *Borderlands/La Frontera*, 2007, p. 44.
18. See *Gloria Anzaldúa Reader*, ed. Keating, 2009, p. 147. Racial meanings are ascribed to faces. See Ian Haney López, *White by Law: The Legal Construction of Race* (New York: New York University Press, 1996), p. 14. Racial aesthetics and the accompanying privileges that go along with being white exert a powerful pressure to conform for those with brown or black skin color. In 1990, for example, "44 million was spent on chemical treatments to lighten and whiten skin"; p. 192.
19. See *Making Face Making Soul Haciendo Caras: Creative and Critical Perspectives by Feminists of Color*, ed. Gloria Anzaldúa (San Francisco, CA: Aunt Lute Books, 1990), xv.
20. Anzaldúa, *Borderlands/La Frontera*, 2007, p. 38.
21. Anzaldúa, *Borderlands/La Frontera*, 2007, p. 106. *Puta* is the Spanish word for whore.
22. Anzaldúa, *Borderlands/La Frontera*, 2007, p. 106. She continues: "We Need a New Masculinity and the New Man Needs a Movement" in *Borderlands/La Frontera*, p. 106.
23. Anzaldúa, *Borderlands/La Frontera*, 2007, p. 38.
24. Anzaldúa, *Borderlands/La Frontera*, 2007, p. 64.
25. Anzaldúa, *Borderlands/La Frontera*, 2007, p. 64; Anzaldúa, *Borderlands/La Frontera*, 2007, "Interview" p. 238; Anzaldúa, *Borderlands/La Frontera*, 2007, "Preface"; Anzaldúa, *Borderlands/La Frontera*, 2007, p. 38.
26. Anzaldúa, *Borderlands/La Frontera*, 2007, p. 43.
27. See Barbara Ehrenreich, *Nickel and Dimed: On (Not) Getting by in America* (New York: Holt, 2001).
28. Sonia Saldivar-Hull, "Introduction to the Second Edition," in Anzaldúa, *Borderlands/La Frontera*, 2007.
29. Anzaldúa, *Borderlands/La Frontera*, 2007, p. 38.
30. See "Interview by Karin Ikas," in Anzaldúa, *Borderlands/La Frontera*, 2007, p. 233.
31. Anzaldúa, *Borderlands/La Frontera*, 2007, p. 42.
32. Anzaldúa, *Borderlands/La Frontera*, 2007, p. 43.
33. Keating, *Gloria Anzaldúa Reader*, 2009, p. 245.
34. Anzaldúa, *Borderlands/La Frontera*, 2007, pp. 242, 73.
35. Anzaldúa, *Borderlands/La Frontera*, 2007, p. 229.
36. Anzaldúa, *Borderlands/La Frontera*, 2007, pp. 196, 100.

37. Anzaldúa, "Foreword to the Second Edition," *This Bridge Called My Back: Writings by Radical Women of Color*, eds. Cherríe Moraga and Gloria Anzaldúa (New York: Kitchen Table: Women of Color Press, 1983).

38. Anzaldúa, *Borderlands/La Frontera*, 2007, p. 67.

39. *The Gloria Anzaldúa Reader*, ed. Keating, 2009, p. 164. Cf. Isabella Baumfree, who became Sojourner Truth, the name she gave herself as a way to redefine herself spiritually and reclaim herself from slavery. See Sojourner Truth, *Narrative of Sojourner Truth* (New York: Dover Press, 1997). See also Audre Lorde, *Sister Outsider: Essays and Speeches by Audre Lorde* (Berkeley, CA: Crossing Press, 2007): "If I didn't define myself for myself, I would be crunched into other people's fantasies for me and eaten alive"; p. 137.

40. Moraga and Anzaldúa, *This Bridge Called My Back*, 1983, p. 172.

41. Anzaldúa, *Borderlands/La Frontera*, 2007, pp. 72, 196.

42. *The Gloria Anzaldúa Reader*, ed. Keating, 2009, p. 122. The imposition of a foreign language on a conquered population is an often overlooked aspect of colonial rule.

43. Anzaldúa, *Borderlands/La Frontera*, 2007, p. 76.

44. *The Gloria Anzaldúa Reader*, ed. Keating, 2009, p. 187.

45. *The Gloria Anzaldúa Reader*, ed. Keating, 2009, p. 89; Anzaldúa, *Borderlands/La Frontera*, 2007, p. 78. Mohammad H. Tamdigidi argues: "Writing is not just a call for developing and implementing a future liberatory vision; it is both, and simultaneously, a process of knowing and transforming the self and world in the here-and-now"; Mohammad H. Tamdgidi, "'I Change Myself, I Change the World': Gloria Anzaldúa's Sociological Imagination in *Borderlands/La Frontera: The New Mestiza*"; *Humanity & Society* 32 (Nov. 2008): 319.

46. Marraga and Anzaldúa, *This Bridge Called My Back*, 1983, p. 169.

47. Anzaldúa, *Making Face, Making Soul, Haciendo Caras*, 1990, xxiv.

48. Anzaldúa, *Borderlands/La Frontera*, 2007, p. 86.

49. Anzaldúa, *Borderlands/La Frontera*, 2007, p. 104.

50. I disagree with Nikolas Kompridis who argues that "hybridity turns into a difference erasing concept, negating the foreignness of the foreigner, the otherness of the other" in "Normativizing Hybridity/Neutralizing Culture"; *Political Theory* 33 (2005): 322. The type of hybridity conceptualized by Anzaldúa exceeds the

opposition between essentialism and anti-essentialism that frames Kompridis's argument.

51. *The Gloria Anzaldúa Reader*, ed. Keating, 2009, p. 209.
52. Anzaldúa, *Borderlands/La Frontera*, 2007, p. 236; *The Gloria Anzaldúa Reader*, ed. Keating, 2009, p. 180.
53. Anzaldúa, *Borderlands/La Frontera*, 2007, p. 107.
54. "Interview with Karin Ikas" in Anzaldúa, *Borderlands/La Frontera*, 2007, p. 234.
55. Anzaldúa, *Borderlands/La Frontera*, 2007, pp. 102–3.
56. Anzaldúa, *Borderlands/La Frontera*, 2007, p. 101.
57. Maria Lugones, "On *Borderlands/La Frontera*: An Interpretive Essay, *Hypatia* 7 (1992): 36.
58. *The Gloria Anzaldúa Reader*, ed. Keating, 2009, p. 143.
59. *The Gloria Anzaldúa Reader*, ed. Keating, 2009, p. 152.
60. Anzaldúa, *Borderlands/La Frontera*, 2007, p. 108.
61. But she would have to leave this behind if she wanted to enter the Rawlsian "original position." See John Rawls, *Political Liberalism* (New York: Columbia University Press, 1996).
62. *Making Face Making Soul*, ed. Anzaldúa, 1990, xxiv.
63. See López, *White by Law*, for an analysis of "color blindness" (e.g., the discourse of neutrality and universality) as a way to perpetuate white racial privilege.
64. Anzaldúa, *Borderlands/La Frontera*, 2007, p. 41.
65. Anzaldúa, *Borderlands/La Frontera*, 2007, p. 44.
66. For an analysis and critique of "new girl" toughness, see Mary Caputi, *Feminism and Power: The Need for Critical Theory* (Lanham, MD: Lexington Books, 2013).
67. For an explanation and critique of sovereign subjectivity, see Romand Coles, *Rethinking Generosity: Critical Theory and the Politics of Caritas*, 1997, pp. 24–74.
68. The origin of all violence, she claims, was based on the subject/object duality. See Anzaldúa, *Borderlands/La Frontera*, 2007, p. 59.
69. See José Angel Gutiérrez, *The Making of a Chicano Militant* (Madison, WI: University of Wisconsin Press, 1998) for a classic statement of Chicano politics. While it may be appropriate to discuss the color line that prevents contact between members of different cultures living in the same society, Gutiérrez may want to rethink the assumptions that lead him to include references to

his dating practices and to women based on how they look in his book (pp. 59–60).

70. Anzaldúa, *Borderlands/La Frontera*, 2007, p. 88.
71. This wasn't always the case. Anzaldúa explains: "I have used rage to drive others away and to insulate myself against exposure" in *Borderlands/La Frontera*, 2007, p. 67.
72. Anzaldúa, *Borderlands/La Frontera*, 2007, p. 72.
73. Anzaldúa, *Borderlands/La Frontera*, 2007, p. 104.
74. Anzaldúa, *Borderlands/La Frontera*, 2007, p. 110.
75. Anzaldúa, *Borderlands/La Frontera*, 2007, p. 92.
76. See Wendy Brown's critique of identity claims as reactive resentment stemming from the "moralizing revenge of the powerless" in *States of Injury*, 1995, p. 66.
77. Moraga and Anzaldúa, *This Bridge Called My Back*, 1983, p. 171.
78. Anzaldúa, *Borderlands/La Frontera*, 2007, p. 97.
79. Romand Coles, "*Traditio*: Feminists of Color and the Torn Virtues of Democratic Engagement," *Political Theory* 29 (2001): 495.
80. Maria Lugones, "On *Borderlands/La Frontera*," *Hypatia* 7 (1992), p. 31.
81. *The Gloria Anzaldúa Reader*, ed. Keating, 2008, p. 49.
82. Jacques Derrida, *The Other Heading: Reflections on Today's Europe*, trans. Brault and Nass (Bloomington, IN: Indiana University Press, 1992), pp. 9–10 (italics in original).
83. Cristina Beltrán, "Patrolling Borders: Hybrids, Hierarchies and the Challenge of Mestizaje" *Political Research Quarterly* 57 (2004): 596.
84. See also Juliet Hooker, "Hybrid Subjectivities, Latin American Mestizaje, and Latino Political Thought on Race"; *Politics, Groups, Identities* 2 (2014): 606.
85. Beltrán, 2004, p. 595.
86. Beltrán, 2004, p. 600.
87. Beltrán, 2004, pp. 604–606.
88. Beltrán, 2004, p. 605.
89. Beltrán, 2004, p. 600.
90. Beltrán, 2004, p. 604.
91. Beltrán, 2004, p. 596.
92. Yvonne Yarbro-Bejarano, "Gloria Anzaldúa's *Borderlands/La Frontera*: Cultural Studies, 'Difference,' and the Non-Unitary Subject"; *Culture Critique* 28 (1994): 12.

93. Beltrán's appeal to contestation risks becoming an elusive end-in-itself. Permanently perpetuating contestation becomes the main goal. Contesting everything could become politically discouraging and possibly alien to individuals fighting for basic survival on the margins and borders of the new global order. See Beltrán, *The Trouble with Unity: Latino Politics and the Creation of Identity* (New York: Oxford University Press, 2010).

94. Anzaldúa states: "I hate Protestantism, I hate Christianity, I hate Judaism"; see *The Gloria Anzaldúa Reader*, ed. Keating, 2008, p. 94. For Anzaldúa, the Catholic Church impoverishes "all life, beauty, pleasure" in Anzaldúa, *Borderlands/La Frontera*, 2007, p. 59.

95. Anzaldúa, *Borderlands/La Frontera*, 2007, p. 77; Anzaldúa, *Borderlands/La Frontera*, 'Preface'; Anzaldúa, *Borderlands/La Frontera*, 2007, p. 81.

96. Anzaldúa, *Borderlands/La Frontera*, 2007, p. 80.

97. See Rodolfo Gonzales, *I Am Joaquín/Yo Soy Joaquín* (New York: Bantam Press, 1967/1972) for a classic statement of nationalist Chicano politics.

98. References to these authors are included in the notes in *Borderlands/La Frontera*, 2007, pp. 114-20. Anzaldúa's complex understanding of identity, rejection of oppositional thinking, and spiritual activism support this claim.

99. Anzaldúa's work represents continuity as well as break with Chicano nationalist politics. Anzaldúa shares a belief in the importance of knowledge of historical oppression and ethnic pride with radical Chicano politics. However, Anzaldúa moves beyond their "us versus them" identity formation, theorizes the intersections between ethnic, class, gender, and sexual oppression, and puts forward a new self that is plural and capable of forging connections with a larger variety of oppressed groups. Hence, Anzaldúa opens new horizons for Latina/o politics.

100. Anzaldúa, *Borderlands/La Frontera*, 2007, p. 107.

101. Beltrán, "Patrolling Borders," *Political Research Quarterly* (2004), p. 603.

102. Beltrán's notion of contestation resembles Rawls's (1971) "original position." Both require citizens to forget about identity attributes as a precondition for admission to the realm of politics. See John Rawls, *A Theory of Justice* (Cambridge, MA: Harvard University Press, 1971).

103. Anzaldúa, *Borderlands/La Frontera*, 2007, p. 234.

104. Andrew Barlow, *Between Hope and Fear*, 2004, p. 156.

105. See Étienne Balibar, *We, the People of Europe? Reflections on Transnational Citizenship*, trans. Swenson (Princeton, NJ: Princeton University Press, 2004).

106. Today, the entire globe is arguably becoming a borderland, that is, a zone of militarization and permanent police presence. The populations subject to these conditions manifest both desperation and resilience. What may seem at face value to be marginal books written by a lesbian Chicana feminist are actually central to the lived experiences of a growing number of people.

107. See, for example, Ian Haney López, *Dog Whistle Politics: How Coded Racial Appeals Have Reinvented Racism and Wrecked the Middle Class* (New York: Oxford University Press, 2014); Beckett, *Making Crime Pay*, 1997; Barlow, *Between Fear and Hope*, 2003; Hancock, *The Politics of Disgust*, 2004; Alexander, *The New Jim Crow*, 2010; and Pizarro, *Chicanas and Chicanos in School*, 2005. The claim that the United States is a postracial society is out of alignment with data on the educational and economic achievement of racial and ethnic minorities. Also, repeated occurrences (on nearly a daily basis) of excessive police force against people of color persist.

108. For a critique of racist aspects in Marx see Mary Hawkesworth, "From Constitutive Outside to the Politics of Extinction: Critical Race Theory, Feminist Theory, and Political Theory," *Political Research Quarterly* 63 (2010): 686–96.

109. For Michael Hardt and Antonio Negri, the term *people* "reduces diversity to a unity and makes of the population a single identity. The multitude is composed of innumerable internal differences that can never be reduced to a unity or single identity." See Hardt and Negri, *Multitude: War and Democracy in an Age of Empire* (New York: Penguin, 2004), xiv.

110. See Yarboro-Bejarano, 1994, p. 11.

111. See Juliana Menasce Horowitz and Gretchen Livingston, "How Americans View the Black Lives Matter Movement"; July 8, 2016, http://pewresearch.org.

112. See Tyler Cherry, "Native Water Protectors, Veterans, Activists at Standing Rock Got Zero Attention on Major Sunday Shows Again"; December 4, 2016, http://mediamatters.org.

Chapter 7

1. For Piven and Cloward, "so long as lower-class groups abided by the norms governing the electoral-representative system, they would have little influence," See Frances Fox Piven and Richard Cloward, *Poor People's Movements: Why They Succeed, How They Fail* (New York: Vintage Books, 1979), p. 3.

2. See Patricia Hill Collins, *Fighting Words: Black Women and the Search for Justice* (Minneapolis, MN: University of Minnesota Press, 1988), pp. 193-195 for a discussion of standpoint theory.

3. See Plato, *Republic*, trans. Grube and Reeve (Indianapolis: Hackett Press, 1992).

4. Thomas Hobbes argued that educational institutions serve a valuable function insofar as they can partially domesticate the passions and perpetuate monarchical rule. See Thomas Hobbes, *Leviathan*, ed. Curley (Indianapolis, IN: Hackett Press, 1994). Throughout the modern era, schools operate according to liberal (enlighten the general public), Marxist (create a qualified reserve army of labor for the capitalist class), Weberian (professionalize the workforce via credentials), and Foucaultian (employ microtactics of domination in order to control and manage unruly populations) paradigms. See Roger Duncan, "Michel Foucault on Education: A Preliminary Theoretical Overview," *South African Journal of Education* 26(2) 2006: 177-87.

5. For Richard Ashcraft, "political scientists have accepted not only a modified market economy as a general model but an 'ethos of technology.' The objectives to be achieved through theorizing have been drastically narrowed"; Richard Ashcraft, "Economic Metaphors, Behavioralism, and Political Theory: Some Observations on the Ideological Uses of Language" in *The Western Political Quarterly* 30, no. 3 (September, 1997): 323.

6. For the "iron law of oligarchy" see Robert Michels, *Political Parties: A Sociological Study of the Tendencies of Modern Democracy*, trans. by Eden Paul and Cedar Paul (New York: Free Press, 1962), p. 342.

7. There have been many good studies of Freire's work by scholars outside of the field of political science. See Sandra Smidt, *Introducing Freire: A Guide for Students, Teachers, and Practitioners* (New York: Routledge, 2014); Antonia Darder, *Freire and Education*, (New York: Routledge, 2014). See also Henry Giroux, *On Critical*

Pedagogy (New York: Bloomsbury, 2011); bell hooks, *Teaching to Transgress: Education as the Practice of Freedom* (New York: Routledge, 2014); Peter McLaren, *Che Guevara, Paulo Freire and the Pedagogy of Revolution* (New York: Rowman and Littlefield, 1999); Donald Macedo, *Literacies of Power: What Americans Are Not Allowed to Know* (Boulder, CO: Westview Press, 1994).

8. See Wendy Brown, *Undoing the Demos: Neoliberalism's Stealth Revolution* (New York: Zone Books, 2015).

9. The American Political Science Association defines itself as an organization that is "nonpartisan." See "The Constitution of the American Political Science Association," Article II: Purpose, November 3, 2011. Given that many political scientists are trained as behavioralists, it is far from clear whether this methodological choice is a neutral or nonpartisan one. As we shall see, Freire argues that methodological choices are inescapably political. As Christian Bay puts it, "much of the current work on political behavior generally fails to articulate its very real value biases"; see Christian Bay "Politics and Pseudopolitics: A Critical Evaluation of Some Behavioral Literature"; *American Political Science Review* 59 (1965): 39.

10. Freire states: "The dream of a better world is born from the depths of the bowels of its opposite" in *Pedagogy of Indignation* (Boulder, CO: Paradigm Publishers, 2004), p. 121.

11. The expression "Third World" is used by Freire.

12. Kant attributes intellectual immaturity to a lack of resolution and courage to use one's own understanding. Although Freire shares Kant's defense of intellectual autonomy, dignity of the human person, and self-liberation, Freire views intellectual immaturity as a consequence of political oppression and the material conditions of everyday life, not as something that is self-incurred. See Immanuel Kant, "An Answer to the Question: 'What Is Englightenment?'" in *Kant: Political Writings*, ed. Reiss, trans. Nisbet (New York: Cambridge University Press, 1991).

13. Freire, *Pedagogy of Freedom*, 1998, p. 74.

14. Cornel West in *Paulo Freire, A Critical Encounter*, Eds. McLaren and Leonard (New York: Routledge, 1993), xiii. For bell hooks, "Freire's work affirmed my right as a subject in resistance to define my reality." See bell hooks, *Teaching to Transgress: Education as the Practice of Freedom*, 1994, p. 53.

15. For research on the corporatization and corruption of higher education see Kevin B. Smith, *The Ideology of Education: The Commonwealth, the Market, and America's Schools* (Albany, NY: State University of New York Press, 2003); James McKeen Cattell, *University Control* (New York: Science Press, 1913); Thorstein Veblen, *The Higher Learning in America: A Memorandum on the Conduct of Universities by Businessmen* (New York: Sagamore Press, 1957); Upton Sinclair, *The Goose-Step: A Study of American Education*, rev. ed. (Pasadena, CA: Privately Printed, 1923); Earl J. McGrath, "The Control of Higher Education in America," *Educational Record* 17 (April 1936): 259-72; Hubert Park Beck, *Men Who Control Our Universities* (New York: King's Crown Press, 1947). David N. Smith, *Who Rules the Universities? An Essay in Class Analysis* (New York: Monthly Review Press, 1974); Barbara Ann Scott, *Crisis Management in American Higher Education* (Westport, CT: Praeger Press, 1983); Clyde W. Barrow, *Universities and the Capitalist State: Corporate Liberalism and the Reconstruction of American Higher Education, 1894-1928* (Madison, WI: University of Wisconsin Press, 1990); Sheila Slaughter, *The Higher Learning and High Technology: Dynamics of Higher Education Policy Formation* (Albany, NY: State University of New York Press, 1990); Wesley Shumar, *College for Sale: A Critique of the Commodification of Higher Education* (Oxfordshire, UK: Routledge Falmer Press, 1997); Sheila Slaughter and Larry L. Leslie, *Academic Capitalism: Politics, Policies and the Entrepreneurial University* (Baltimore, MD: Johns Hopkins University Press, 1997); Gary Rhodes, *Managed Professionals: Unionized Faculty and Restructuring Academic Labor* (Albany, NY: State University of New York Press, 1998); Geoffrey White, ed., *Campus, Inc.* (Amherst, NY: Prometheus Books, 2000); Stanley Aronowitz, *The Knowledge Factory* (Boston, MA: Beacon Press, 2001); Clyde W. Barrow, Sylvie Didou-Aupetit, and John Mallea, *Globalisation, Trade Liberalisation, and Higher Education in North America: The Emergence of a New Market Under NAFTA?* (Dordrecht, The Netherlands: Kluwer Academic Publishers, 2003); Sheila Slaughter and Gary Rhoades, *Academic Capitalism and the New Economy: Markets, State, and Higher Education* (Baltimore, MD: Johns Hopkins University Press, 2004); Jennifer Washburn, *University Inc.: The Corporate Corruption of Higher Education* (New York: Basic Books, 2005); Frank Donoghue, *The Last Professors:*

The Corporate University and the Fate of the Humanities (New York: Fordham University Press, 2008); Benjamin Ginsberg, *The Fall of the Faculty: The Rise of the All-Administrative University and Why It Matters* (New York: Oxford University Press, 2011).

16. See Greg Grandin, "Interview with Noam Chomsky on the Crisis in Central America and Mexico," *The Nation*, October 31, 2014.

17. Freire, *Politics of Education: Culture, Power, and Liberation*, trans. Macedo (Westport, CT: Bergin & Garvey, 1985), p. 39.

18. Freire, *Cultural Action for Freedom* (Cambridge, MA: Harvard Educational Review, 2000), p. 13.

19. See Peter McLaren, *Che Guevara, Paulo Freire, and the Pedagogy of Revolution*, 2000.

20. By claiming to be scientific, above politics, and nonideological, behavioralism was in fact a political stance and a form of establishment ideology as a result of its noncritical orientation to the political status quo. I disagree with Timothy V. Kaufman Osborn's claim that "the threat of behavioralism subsided in the late 1960s and early 1970s" in "Political Theory as Profession and as Subfield?" *Political Research Quarterly* 63 (2010): 657. According to John Gunnell, a lot of political theory "manifests an elitist, antidemocratic bias that echoes its origins in the moralism of nineteenth-century political science and in the scientism of its early twentieth-century successors" in "Professing Political Theory"; *Political Research Quarterly* 63 (2010): 678.

21. Freire, *Pedagogy of Freedom*, 1998, p. 129. For a compelling example of the yearning for a scientific understanding of political life, see David Easton, *The Political System: An Enquiry into the State of Political Science* (New York: Alfred A. Knopf, 1953). For a recent example of this scientific orientation and yearning, see "An Interview with Lynn Vavreck," in *PS: Political Science and Politics* 48, Supplement S1, 2015: 43–46. In this interview, Vavreck states: "We need our young scholars doing science" (p. 44). She continues: "The average person is not going to read a scientific publication and understand or track what the finding is. . . . That's okay"; (p. 43).

22. Freire, *Pedagogy of Indignation*, 2004, p. 7.

23. See John G. Gunnell, "The Reconstitution of Political Theory: David Easton, Behavioralism, and the Long Road to System," *Journal of the History of the Behavioral Sciences* 49, no. 2 (2013): 190–210 for a historical account of the rise of behavioralism.

24. See Richard Ashcraft, "Political Theory and the Problem of Ideology," *Journal of Politics* 42, no. 3 (1980): 687–705.

25. Freire, *Politics of Education*, 1985, p. 12.

26. Freire, *Politics of Education*, 1985, p. 157.

27. See Bertell Ollman, "What Is Political Science? What Should It Be?" *New Political Science* 22. no. 4 (2000): 553–62 for an interesting discussion of these issues.

28. See the *New York Times* bestseller by Richard J. Herrnstein and Charles Murray who argue "success and failure in the American economy are increasingly a matter of the genes that people inherit" in *The Bell Curve: Intelligence and Class Structure in American Life* (New York: The Free Press, 1996), p. 91. On the back cover, Milton Friedman states *The Bell Curve* is "brilliant, original, and objective." For an excellent analysis of the relationship between education and capitalism, see Samuel Bowles and Herbert Gintis, *Schooling in Capitalist America: Educational Reform and the Contradictions of Economic Life* (New York: Basic Books, 1976).

29. Freire, *Pedagogy of Hope*, 2009, p. 1.

30. For an account of the complicity of the scientific medical establishment with racial dictatorship in the United States see Harriet A. Washington, *Medical Apartheid: The Dark History of Medical Experimentation on Black Americans from Colonial Times to the Present* (New York: Doubleday, 2006).

31. See John Stuart Mill, *On Liberty*, for a discussion of uninformed versus informed discussion in *On Liberty and Other Writings*, ed. Stefan Collini (New York: Cambridge University Press, 2005).

32. Freire, *Pedagogy of Indignation*, 2004, p. 5.

33. Paulo Freire and Antonio Faundez, *Learning to Question: A Pedagogy of Liberation* (Geneva, Switzwerland: WCC Publications, 1989), p. 48.

34. Freire, *Pedagogy of the Oppressed*, 2010, p. 169.

35. Freire, *Pedagogy of the Oppressed*, 2010, p. 65.

36. This claim is based on my experience as Chair of the US Government "Textbook Committee" at my university. During the 2011 to 2012 and 2012 to 2013 academic years, I reviewed many of the dominant textbooks for introductory American government courses. Not a single book I reviewed had a sustained analysis of the relationship between capitalism and the political state.

37. See Herrnstein and Murray's *The Bell Curve* for a justification for the status quo masked as objective research. See also Charles Murray, *Losing Ground: American Social Policy, 1950-1980* (New York: Basic Books, 1984); Charles Murray, *Coming Apart: The State of White America, 1960-2010* (New York: Crown Forum, 2012). See also Thomas Sowell, *Black Rednecks and White Liberals* (New York: Encounter Books, 2006).

38. Freire, *The Politics of Education*, 1985, p. 102.

39. See "An Interview with Lynn Vavreck," *PS: Political Science and Politics, Supplement,* (2015), p. 43.

40. See John Dewey, *Democracy and Education: An Introduction to the Philosophy of Education* (New York: The Free Press, 1916).

41. Freire, *Education for Critical Consciousness* (New York: Bloomsbury Publishing, 2013), p. 13.

42. Freire, *Politics of Education*, 1985, p. 180.

43. Freire, *Teachers as Cultural Workers: Letters to Those Who Dare Teach*, trans. Macedo et al. (Boulder, CO: Westview Press, 2005), p. 17.

44. Freire, *Pedagogy of Hope*, 2009, p. 96.

45. Freire, *Teachers as Cultural Workers*, 2005, p. 26.

46. Freire, *Pedagogy of Hope*, 2009, p. 82. Freire is not specific about which Marxists he is addressing. Peter McLaren in *Che Guevara, Paulo Freire, and the Pedagogy of Revolution*, 2000, claims that Hayek is an "economist from hell" and Milton Friedman is a "fellow demon" (pp. 22-23).

47. Freire, *Teachers as Cultural Workers*, 2005, p. 66.

48. Freire, *Pedagogy of the Oppressed*, 2010, p. 60.

49. The political education of the people was of major concern for Thomas Jefferson. For an insightful commentary on this, see *Michael Hardt Presents Thomas Jefferson* (New York: Verso, 2007).

50. For literacy and other restrictions on voting in the US context see Frances Fox Piven and Richard Cloward, *Why Americans Still Don't Vote and Why Politicians Want It That Way* (Boston, MA: Beacon Press, 2000). For Piven and Cloward, "the United States is the only major democratic nation in which the less-well-off, as well as the young and minorities, are substantially underrepresented in the electorate" (p. 3).

51. See chapter 5 in Freire, *Pedagogy of Indignation*, 2004.

52. See Murray Edelman, *Constructing the Political Spectacle* (Chicago, IL: University of Chicago Press, 1988).

53. See Jodi Dean, *Democracy and Other Neoliberal Fantasies: Communicative Capitalism and Left Politics* (Durham, NC: Duke University Press, 2009).

54. See, for example, Martin Gilens, "Political Ignorance and Collective Policy Preferences," *American Political Science Review 95* no. 2 (2001): 379-96. See also Brendan Nyhan and Jason Reifler, "When Corrections Fail: The Persistence of Political Misperceptions," *Political Behavior* 32 (2010): 303-30.

55. Hannah Arendt diagnosed how totalitarian regimes create widespread cynicism to perpetuate their rule in *Origins of Totalitarianism* (New York: Harcourt, 1968).

56. Freire, *Teachers as Cultural Workers*, 2005, p. 132.

57. Freire, *Politics of Education*, 1985, p. 10.

58. Freire, *Pedagogy of Hope*, 2009, p. 30.

59. For these questions see Richard Arum and Josipa Roksa, *Academically Adrift: Limited Learning on College Campuses* (Chicago, IL: University of Chicago Press, 2011). For a critique of the discourse and ideology of "best practices" see Wendy Brown, *Undoing the Demos: Neoliberalism's Stealth Revolution*, 2015. For Brown, "best practices are intended to displace and replace politics" with "value free technical knowledge" (p. 139).

60. Stanley Aronowitz, *Against Orthodoxy: Social Theory and Its Discontents*, (New York: Palgrave MacMillan, 2015), p. 114.

61. Freire, *Pedagogy of Hope*, 2009, p. 47.

62. Freire, *Pedagogy of Hope*, 2009, p. 16.

63. Freire and Faundez, *Learning to Question*, 1989, p. 94.

64. Freire, *Education for Critical Consciousness*, 2013, p. 45.

65. Freire, *Education for Critical Consciousness*, 2013, p. 15.

66. Freire, *Pedagogy of Hope*, 2009, p. 91.

67. For Freire, "nobody is superior to anyone else"; *Pedagogy of Freedom*, 1998, p. 108.

68. Freire, *Education for Critical Consciousness*, 2013, p. 108.

69. Freire, *The Politics of Education*, 1985, p. 55.

70. Freire, *Pedagogy of Freedom*, 1998, p. 67.

71. Freire, *Education for Critical Consciousness*, 2013, p. 13.

72. Freire, *Pedagogy of Hope*, 2009, p. 19.

73. Freire, *Teachers as Cultural Workers*, 2005, p. 28.

74. Freire, *The Politics of Education*, 1985, p. 105.
75. See Michel Foucault, *Discipline and Punish: The Birth of the Prison*, trans. Sheridan (New York: Vintage Books, 1995).
76. See Roger Deacon, "Michel Foucault on Education: A Preliminary Theoretical Overview," *South African Journal of Education* 26, no. 2 (2006): 177–87.
77. Freire, *Teachers as Cultural Workers*, 2005, p. 13.
78. Freire, *Pedagogy of Indignation*, 2004, p. 58.
79. Eduardo Galeano, *Open Veins of Latin America: Five Centuries of the Pillage of a Continent*, trans. Belfrage (New York: Monthly Review Press, 1997).
80. Fanon, *The Wretched of the Earth*, trans. Philcox (New York: Grove Press, 2004), p. 81.
81. See Augusto Boal, *Theatre of the Oppressed*, trans. McBride and McBride (New York: Theatre Communications Group, 1985).
82. Freire, *The Politics of Education*, 1985, p. 178.
83. Freire, *Learning to Question*, 1989, p. 62.
84. Freire, *Cultural Action for Freedom*, p. 64. See also Leon Trotsky, *The Permanent Revolution*, ed. Jonson (New York: Create Space Independent Publishing Platform, 2014).
85. Freire, *Politics of Education*, 1985, p. 179.
86. Freire, *Pedagogy of Freedom*, 1998, p. 103.
87. Freire, *Pedagogy of Indignation*, 2004, p. 61.
88. Freire, *The Politics of Education*, 1985, p. 186.
89. Freire, *The Politics of Education*, 1985, p. 102.
90. See House Bill 2281, state of Arizona, 2010.
91. For the linkage between individualism, neoliberalism, and "Americanism" see Milton Friedman, *Capitalism and Freedom* (Chicago, IL: University of Chicago Press, 2002). The Straussian definition of the canon of political theory as essentially white, European, and male is also a form of curriculum control designed to perpetuate nostalgia for the past. See Leo Strauss and Joseph Cropsey, *History of Political Philosophy* (Chicago, IL: Rand McNally & Co., 1963).
92. In addition to laws that control the curriculum, the internal and often unspoken political concerns of educational institutions determine the types of individuals who are hired to teach, promoted, granted tenure, and then occupy positions of power in the administrative hierarchy. External political controls are also paramount.

The imposition of fiscal austerity, the attack on unionized teachers, external control of research agendas by grant awarding organizations, recognition and awards for particular types of scholarship by status granting institutions, and state control of the curriculum are all signs of the political significance (and vulnerability) of the sphere of education. See Clyde Barrow, "The Coming of the Corporate-Fascist University?" *New Political Science* 36, no. 4 (2014): 640–46.

93. See, for example, Wendy Brown *Manhood and Politics: A Feminist Reading in Political Theory* (New York: Rowman and Littlefield, 2002), *States of Injury: Power and Freedom in Late Modernity* (Princeton, NJ: Princeton University Press, 1995), *Regulating Aversion: Tolerance in the Age of Identity and Empire* (Princeton, NJ: Princeton University Press, 2006), *Politics Out of History* (Princeton, NJ: Princeton University Press, 2001); *Walled States and Waning Sovereignty* (New York: Zone Books, 2010); and *Undoing the Demos: Neoliberalism's Stealth Revolution* (New York: Zone Books, 2015).

94. See Wendy Brown, "American Nightmare: Neoliberalism, Neoconservatism, and De-Democratization," *Political Theory* 34 no. 6 (2006): 690–714. Similar themes are also articulated by Sheldon Wolin in *Politics and Vision: Continuity and Change in Western Political Thought* (Princeton, NJ: Princeton University Press, 1960/2004) and *Democracy Incorporated: Managed Democracy and the Specter of Totalitarianism* (Princeton, NJ: Princeton University Press, 2008).

95. Brown, *Undoing the Demos*, 2015, p. 176.

96. Brown, *Undoing the Demos*, 2015, pp. 221–22.

97. Brown, *Undoing the Demos*, 2015, p. 208. See also Sheldon Wolin, *Democracy Incorporated: Managed Democracy and the Specter of Inverted Totalitarianism* (Princeton, NJ: Princeton University Press, 2010).

98. Brown, *Undoing the Demos*, 2015, p. 188.

99. See Sheldon Wolin, *Politics and Vision*, 2004, p. 316; Sheldon Wolin, *Tocqueville between Two Worlds: The Making of a Political and Theoretical Life* (Princeton, NJ: Princeton University Press, 2001), p. 572; Sheldon Wolin, *Presence of the Past: Essays on the State and the Constitution* (Baltimore, MD: Johns Hopkins University Press, 1989), pp. 192–207. See Leo Strauss, *What Is Political Philosophy?*

(Glencoe, IL: Free Press, 1959). For Nietzsche, the aristocratic ideal has been eclipsed by slave morality in modernity. For Leo Strauss, the political-philosophical realm as a distinct area of study of the eternal forms has been displaced in modernity. For Heidegger, modern technology rules the day and has displaced concern for the question of Being. For Arendt, the political has been displaced by the social. For Wolin, concern for the political has been displaced by the economic sphere.

100. Wolin, *Politics and Vision*, 2004, pp. 352–434.

101. Wolin, *Politics and Vision*, 2004, p. 21. In *Undoing the Demos* (2015), Brown's nostalgia is apparent in the references she makes to the loss of quality universities as a result of online learning, the loss of college town ambience of coffee shops, bookstores, pubs, and thrift stores (p. 198), her claim that the North American twentieth century was a "golden age" for public higher education (p. 180). Her nostalgia turns into despair in the claim that we are reduced to reform and resistance, action as reaction (p. 220), as humanity enters its "darkest chapter" (p. 188). Wolin's *Tocqueville Between Two Worlds: The Making of a Political and Theoretical Life* (Princeton, NJ: Princeton University Press, 2001) refracts nostalgia for the French aristocrat Tocqueville who Wolin argues is the "first political theorist to treat democracy as a theoretical subject in its own right"; p. 59. Wolin's understanding of political theory as one where the theorist participates in a debate "the terms of which have largely been set beforehand" seems to foreclose the possibility of someone like Freire ever being a participant in this conversation; Wolin, *Politics and Vision*, 2004, p. 21. If the terms of political theory have been set beforehand, this radically narrows the range of possibilities for the practice of political theory. If, as Wolin states, the inquiry into the development of the analysis and understanding of politics is a form of "political education" (p. 26), this education is based on the transmission of a particular tradition. If one combines Wolin's view of "political theory as a vocation" with this, the type of education Wolin has in mind emerges as a priestly sort. For a critique of Wolin's priestly stance, see Linda M. G. Zerilli, "Machiavelli's Sisters: Women and 'The Conversation' of Political Theory," *Political Theory* 19, no. 2 (May 1991): 252–76.

102. Brown, *Undoing the Demos*, 2015, p. 52.

103. See Herbert Marcuse, *One-Dimensional Man: Studies in the Ideology of Advanced Industrial Society* (Boston, MA: Beacon Press, 1964).

104. See Étienne Balibar, *Equaliberty: Political Essays,* trans. Ingram (Durham, NC: Duke University Press, 2014), pp. 20–25 and Étienne Balibar, *Citizenship,* trans. Scott-Railton (Malden, MA: Polity Press, 2015), pp. 102–18. For the end of ideology thesis in the 1950s see Daniel Bell, *The End of Ideology: On the Exhaustion of Political Ideas in the Fifties* (New York: Free Press, 1960). Bell's pronouncements were shattered by the civil rights movement, antiwar movement, and other social movements of the 1960s. For a more recent conservative version of the end of history thesis peddled in the 1990s see Francis Fukuyama, *The End of History and the Last Man* (New York: Harper Perennial, 1992).

105. Freire, *Pedagogy of the Heart,* 2007, p. 45.

106. Freire, *Cultural Action for Freedom,* 2000, p. 10.

107. Freire, *The Politics of Education,* 1985, p. 190.

108. See Gaye Tuchman, *Wannabe U: Inside the Corporate University* (Chicago, IL: University of Chicago Press, 2009). See also Henry Giroux, *Neoliberalism's War on Higher Education* (Chicago, IL: Haymarket Books, 2014).

109. See Obama's statement in U.S. Department of Education, "A Blueprint for Reform: The Reauthorization of the Elementary and Secondary Education Act," March 2010. In the section of the report subtitled "Homeless Children and Youths Education" the blueprint states that "systems and services" will be put in place to "meet the educational needs of homeless students" (p. 21). It is hard to understand the logic behind this formulation. How will "systems and services" that address the educational needs of homeless students and ignore homelessness meet the true needs of these students?

Conclusion

1. See Theodor W. Adorno and Max Horkheimer, *Dialectic of Englightenment,* trans. Cumming (New York: Continuum, 1993).

2. Wendy Brown, *Undoing the Demos,* 2015.

3. For a provocative analysis of the concept of rule that avoids these polarities, See Patchen Markell, "The Rule by the People: Arendt,

Archê, and Democracy," *American Political Science Review* 1 (2006): 1-14.

4. Double contradictory imperative is an expression that I borrow from Jacques Derrida. See *The Other Heading: Reflections on Today's Europe*, trans. Brault and Naas (Indianapolis, IN: University of Indiana Press, 1992), p. 79.

5. See Wendy Brown, *Undoing the Demos*, (New York: Zone Books, 2015). See Giorgio Agamben, *Homo Sacer: Sovereign Power and Bare Life*, trans. Heller-Roazen (Stanford, CA: Stanford University Press, 1998).

6. Mouffe states: "In an agonistic politics, the antagonistic dimension is always present, since what is at stake is the struggle between opposing hegemonic projects which can never be reconciled rationally, one of them needed to be defeated. It is real confrontation, but one that is played out under conditions regulated by a set of democratic procedures accepted by the adversaries." See Chantal Mouffe, *Agonistics: Thinking the World Politically* (New York: Verso, 2013), p. 9. But what if the procedures define certain people outside of the realm of struggle, as we saw in the case of the fugitive slave Frederick Douglass?

7. See Paul Magnette, *Citizenship: The History of an Idea* (Colchester, UK: ECPR Press, 2005).

8. See Michael Hardt and Antonio Negri, *Commonwealth* (Cambridge, MA: Harvard University Press, 2009).

9. Balibar states: "Any effective democratic constitution remains dependent on the idea of insurrection" in *Masses, Classes, Ideas: Studies on Politics and Philosophy before and after Marx*, trans, Swenson (New York: Routledge, 1994), xiii.

10. Balibar, *Equaliberty: Political Essays*, trans. Ingram (Durham, NC: Duke University Press, 2014), p. 175.

11. Balibar, *We, the People of Europe? Reflections on Transnational Citizenship*, trans. Swenson (Princeton, NJ: Princeton University Press, 2004), p. 195.

12. Balibar, *Politics and the Other Scene*, 2002, p. 6.

13. Balibar, *We the People of Europe? Reflections on Transnational Citizenship*, 2004, p. 115.

14. Balibar, *Equaliberty: Political Essays*, 2014, p. 190.

15. Rogers M. Smith, *Civic Ideals*, 1997, pp. 497-98. See Lee Camp "Anti-Protest Bill Passes Nearly Unanimously and Is Signed by

the President," March 14, 2012, *Huffington Post*. See also Tom Carter, "US Congress Expands Authoritarian Anti-Protest Law," *World Socialist Website*, March 3, 2012: "the laws expanded by H.R. 347 help create for the US president and other top officials a protest-free bubble or 'no-free-speech zone' that follows them wherever they go, making sure the discontented multitude is kept out of the picture."

Bibliography

Adarand Constructors, Inc. v. Peña. 515 U.S. 200 (1995).

Agamben, Giorgio. *Homo Sacer: Sovereign Power and Bare Life.* Trans. Daniel Heller-Roazen. Stanford, CA: Stanford University Press, 1998.

———. *State of Exception.* Trans. Kevin Attell. Chicago, IL: University of Chicago Press, 2005.

Ahmad, Muneer I. "A Rage Shared by Law: Post-September 11 Racial Violence as Crimes of Passion." *California Law Review* 92, no. 5 (2004): 1259–330.

Alexander, Leslie M. "The Black Republic: The Influence of the Haitian Revolution on Northern Black Political Consciousness, 1816–1862." *African Americans and the Haitian Revolution: Selected Essays and Historical Documents.* Eds. Maurice Jackson and Jacqueline Bacon. New York: Routledge, 2010.

Alexander, Michelle. *The New Jim Crow: Mass Incarceration in an Age of Colorblindness.* New York: The New Press, 2012.

Allen, James, Hilton Als, John Lewis, and Leon F. Litwack. *Without Sanctuary: Lynching Photography in America.* Santa Fe, NM: Twin Palms Publishers, 2000.

Althusser, Louis. *Machiavelli and Us.* Ed. François Matheron. Trans. Gregory Elliott. New York: Verso, 1999.

Anzaldúa, Gloria, ed. *Making Face Making Soul Haciendo Caras: Creative and Critical Perspectives by Feminists of Color.* San Francisco, CA: Aunt Lute Books, 1990.

———. *Borderlands/La Frontera: The New Mestiza.* San Francisco, CA: Aunt Lute Books, 2007.

Aptheker, Herbert. *American Negro Slave Revolts.* New York: International Publishers, 1993.

Arendt, Hannah. *On Revolution.* New York: Penguin, 1991.

———. *Lectures on Kant's Political Philosophy.* Ed. Ronald Beiner. Chicago, IL: University of Chicago Press, 1982.

———. *Between Past and Future: Eight Exercises in Political Thought*. New York: Penguin Books, 1968.

———. *The Human Condition*. Chicago, IL: University of Chicago Press, 1958.

———. "Socrates." *The Promise of Politics*. Ed. Jerome Kohn. New York: Schocken Books, 2005.

———. *Eichmann in Jerusalem: A Report on the Banality of Evil*. New York: Penguin, 1977.

———. *Crises of the Republic*. New York: Harcourt Press, 1972.

———. *The Origins of Totalitarianism*. New York: Harcourt Press, 1968.

———. *Men in Dark Times*. New York: Harcourt Press, 1968.

———. "Personal Responsibility under Dictatorship." *Responsibility and Judgment*. Ed. Jerome Kohn. New York: Schocken Books, 2003.

———. "The Moral of History." *The Jew as Pariah: Jewish Identity and Politics in the Modern Age*. Ed. Ron H. Feldman. New York: Grove Press, 1978.

———. "Europe and the Atom Bomb." *Essays in Understanding*. Ed. Jerome Kohn. New York: Harcourt, 1994.

———. *Origins of Totalitarianism*. New York: Harcourt, 1968.

Aristotle. *Nicomachean Ethics*. Trans. Roger Crisp. New York: Cambridge University Press, 2000.

Aristotle. *Politics*. Trans. C. D. C. Reeve. Indianapolis, IN: Hackett Press, 1998.

Arizona House Bill 2281, H.R. (2010). https://www.azleg.gov/legtext/49leg/2r/bills/hb2281s.pdf

Arnold, Kathleen. "Enemy Invaders! Mexican Immigrants and the U.S. Wars against Them." *Borderlands* (2007): 1-24.

Aronowitz, Stanley. *The Knowledge Factory*. Boston, MA: Beacon Press, 2001.

Aronowitz, Stanley. *Against Orthodoxy: Social Theory and Its Discontents*. New York: Palgrave Macmillan, 2015.

Arum, Richard, and Josipa Roksa. *Academically Adrift: Limited Learning on College Campuses*. Chicago, IL: University of Chicago Press, 2011.

Ashcraft, Richard. "Economic Metaphors, Behavioralism, and Political Theory: Some Observations on the Ideological Uses of Language." *Western Political Quarterly* 30, no. 3 (September 1997): 313-28.

———. "Political Theory and the Problem of Ideology." *Journal of Politics* 42, no. 3 (1980): 687-705.

Axinn, Sidney. "Kant, Authority, and the French Revolution." *Journal of the History of Ideas* 32 (July–September 1971): 423-32.

Baker, Houston A. "Scene . . . Not Heard." *Reading Rodney King, Reading Urban Uprising.* Ed. Robert Gooding-Williams. New York: Routledge, 1993.

Balfour, Lawrie. *Democracy's Reconstruction: Thinking Politically with W.E.B. Du Bois.* New York: Oxford University Press, 2011.

———. *The Evidence of Things Not Said: James Baldwin and the Promise of American Democracy.* Ithaca, NY: Cornell University Press, 2001.

Balibar, Étienne. *Citizenship.* Trans. Thomas Scott-Railton. Cambridge, UK: Polity Press, 2015.

———. *Equaliberty: Political Essays.* Trans. James Ingram. Durham, NC: Duke University Press, 2014.

———. *Masses, Classes, Ideas: Studies on Politics and Philosophy Before and After Marx.* Trans. James Swenson. New York: Routledge, 1994.

———. "Outlines of a Topography of Cruelty: Citizenship and Civility in the Era of Global Violence." *Constellations* 8 (2001): 15–29.

———. *Politics and the Other Scene.* Trans. Christine Jones, James Swenson, and Chris Turner. New York: Verso, 2002.

———. *We, the People of Europe? Reflections on Transnational Citizenship.* Trans. James Swenson. Princeton, NJ: Princeton University Press, 2004.

Balot, Ryan, and Stephen Trochimchuk. "The Many and the Few: On Machiavelli's 'Democratic Moment.'" *Review of Politics* 47, no. 4 (2012): 559–88.

Baldwin, James. "Notes of a Native Son." *Collected Essays.* New York: Library of America, 1998.

Barford, Vanessa. "Why Americans Are so Angry?" *BBC News.* February 4, 2016.

Barkin, Kenneth. "W.E.B. Du Bois' Love Affair with Imperial Germany." *German Studies Review* 28, no. 2 (May 2005): 285–302.

Barlow, Andrew L. *Between Fear and Hope: Globalization and Race in the United States.* New York: Rowman & Littlefield, 2003.

Barrow, Clyde W. "The Coming of the Corporate-Fascist University?" *New Political Science* 36, no. 4 (2014): 640–46.

———. "The Intellectual Origins of New Political Science." *New Political Science* 30, no. 2 (2008): 215–44.

———. *Universities and the Capitalist State: Corporate Liberalism and the Reconstruction of American Higher Education, 1894–1928.* Madison, WI: University of Wisconsin Press, 1990.

———, Sylvie Didou-Aupetit, and John Mallea. *Globalisation, Trade Liberalisation, and Higher Education in North America: The*

Emergence of a New Market Under NAFTA? Dordrecht, The Netherlands: Kluwer Academic Publishers, 2003.

Bay, Christian. "Politics and Pseudopolitics: A Critical Evaluation of Some Behavioral Literature." *American Political Science Review* 59 (1965): 39-51.

Beck, Hubert Park. *Men Who Control Our Universities.* New York: King's Crown Press, 1947.

Beck, Lewis W. "Kant and the Right of Revolution." *Journal of the History of Ideas* 32 (July–September 1971): 411-22.

Beckett, Katherine. *Making Crime Pay: Law and Order in Contemporary American Politics.* Oxford, UK: Oxford University Press, 1997.

Bell, Daniel. *The End of Ideology: On the Exhaustion of Political Ideas in the Fifties.* New York: Free Press, 1960.

Bell, Derick. *Face from the Botttom of the Well.* New York: Basic Books, 1992.

Beltrán, Cristina. "Patrolling Borders: Hybrids, Hierarchies and the Challenge of Mestizaje." *Political Research Quarterly* 57 (2004): 595-607.

Beltrán, Cristina. *The Trouble with Unity: Latino Politics and the Creation of Identity.* Oxford, UK: Oxford University Press, 2010.

Benhabib, Seyla. *The Reluctant Modernism of Hannah Arendt.* New York: Rowman & Littlefield, 2003.

Berlin, Isaiah. "The Originality of Machiavelli." *Against the Current: Essays in the History of Ideas.* Princeton, NJ: Princeton University Press, 2001.

Bernard, Stephen. "Bailed out Banks Gave Millions in Executive Bonuses, NY AG Report Shows," *ABC News* (accessed February 4, 2016).

Blakely, Edward J, and Mary Gail Snyder. *Fortress America: Gated Communities in the United States.* Washington, DC: Brookings, 1997.

Blum, Hester. "Douglass's and Melville's 'Alphabets of the Blind.'" *Frederick Douglass and Herman Melville: Essays in Relation.* Eds. Robert S. Levine and Samuel Otter. Chapel Hill, NC: University of North Carolina Press, 2008.

Boal, Augusto. *Theatre of the Oppressed.* Trans. Charles A. McBride and Maria-Odilia Leal McBride. New York: Theatre Communications Group, 1985.

Boggs, Carl. *Empire versus Democracy: The Triumph of Corporate and Military Power.* New York: Routledge, 2011.

———. *Imperial Delusions: American Militarism and Endless War.* Lanham, MD: Rowman & Littlefield, 2005.

Bohman, James, and William Rehg, eds. "Introduction." *Deliberative Democracy: Essays on Reason and Politics*. Cambridge, MA: MIT Press, 1997.

Bromell, Nick. "Democratic Indignation: Black American Thought and the Politics of Dignity." *Political Theory* 41, no. 2 (2013): 285-311.

———. "W.E.B. Du Bois and the Enlargement of Democratic Theory." *Raritan* 30, no. 4 (2014): 140-61.

Brown, Wendy. "American Nightmare: Neoliberalism, Neoconservatism, and De-Democratization." *Political Theory* 34, no. 6 (2006): 690-714.

———. "At the Edge." *Political Theory* 30 (1997): 556-76.

———. *Manhood and Politics: A Feminist Reading in Political Theory*. New York: Rowman and Littlefield, 2002.

———. *Politics Out of History*. Princeton, NJ: Princeton University Press, 2001.

———. *Regulating Aversion: Tolerance in the Age of Identity and Empire*. Princeton, NJ: Princeton University Press, 2006.

———. *States of Injury: Power and Freedom in Late Modernity*. Princeton, NJ: Princeton University Press, 1995.

———. *Undoing the Demos: Neoliberalism's Stealth Revolution*. New York: Zone Books, 2015.

———. *Walled States and Waning Sovereignty*. New York: Zone Books, 2010.

Buchan, Bruce. "Duo pezzi in su la piazza: The Death of the Body Politic in Western Political Theory." *South Atlantic Quarterly* 110, no. 4 (2011): 901-15.

Butler, Judith. *Giving an Account of Oneself*. New York: Fordham University Press, 2005.

Callender, Lenval A. *Kant and Revolution*. Bury St. Edmunds, UK: Arima Publishing, 2011.

Caputi, Mary. *Feminism and Power: The Need for Critical Theory*. Lanham, MD: Lexington Books, 2013.

Carmichael, Stokely [Kwame Ture]. *Stokely Speaks: From Black Power to Pan-Africanism*. Chicago, IL: Chicago Review Press, 2007.

Carrigan, William D., and Clive Webb. "The Lynching of Persons of Mexican Origin or Descent in the United States, 1848-1928." *Journal of Social History* 37 (2003): 411-38

Carter, Tom. "US Congress Expands Authoritarian Anti-Protest Law." *World Socialist Website*. March 3, 2012.

Chukwudi Eze, Emmanuel, ed. *Race and the Enlightenment: A Reader*. Malden, MA: Blackwell, 2001.

City of Richmond v. J.A. Croson, Co. 488 U.S. 469 (1989).

Cobb, Jr., Charles E. *This Nonviolent Stuff'll Get You Killed: How Guns Made the Civil Rights Movement Possible.* New York: Basic Books, 2014.

Cohen, Patricia. "Oxfam Study Finds Richest 1% Is Likely to Control Half of Global Wealth by 2016." *New York Times.* January 19, 2015.

Colaiaco, James A. *Frederick Douglass and the Fourth of July.* New York: Palgrave, 2006.

Coles, Romand. *Rethinking Generosity: Critical Theory and the Politics of Caritas.* Ithaca, NY: Cornell University Press, 1997.

Coles, Romand. "Traditio: Feminists of Color and the Torn Virtues of Democratic Engagement." *Political Theory* 29 (2001): 488-516.

Compact Edition of the Oxford English Dictionary. 2 Vols. New York: Oxford University Press, 1971.

Connolly, William E. *Capitalism and Christianity, American Style.* Durham, NC: Duke University Press, 2008.

———. *The Ethos of Pluralization.* Minneapolis, MN: University of Minnesota Press, 1995.

Cooper, John M., and J. F. Procopé eds. "On Anger." *Seneca: Moral and Political Essays.* Trans. John M. Cooper and J. F. Procopé. New York, NY: Cambridge University Press, 1995.

Critchley, Simon. *Infinitely Demanding: Ethics of Commitment, Politics of Resistance.* London, UK: Verso, 2007.

———. *On Humour.* New York: Routledge, 2002.

Crozier, Michael, Samuel P. Huntington, and Joji Watanuki. *The Crisis of Democracy: Report on the Governability of Democracies to the Trilateral Commission.* New York: New York University Press, 1975.

Dahl, Robert. *A Preface to Democratic Theory.* Chicago, IL: University of Chicago Press, 2006.

Darder, Antonia. *Freire and Education.* New York: Routledge, 2014.

Davis, Angela Y. "From the Prison of Slavery to the Slavery of the Prison: Frederick Douglass and the Convict Lease System." *Frederick Douglass: A Critical Reader.* Eds. Bill Lawson and Frank Kirkland. New York: Basil Blackwell, 1999.

———. *Are Prisons Obsolete?* New York: Seven Stories Press, 2003.

Deacon, Roger. "Michel Foucault on Education: A Preliminary Theoretical Overview." *South African Journal of Education* 26, no. 2 (2006): 177-87.

Dean, Jodi. *Democracy and Other Neoliberal Fantasies: Communicative Capitalism and Left Politics.* Durham, NC: Duke University Press, 2009.

Deleuze, Gilles. *Kant's Critical Philosophy: The Doctrine of the Faculties.* Trans. Hugh Tomlinson and Barbara Habberjam. Minneapolis, MN: University of Minnesota Press, 1993.

Derrida, Jacques. *Geneses, Genealogies, Genres, & Genius: The Secrets of the Archive.* Trans. Beverley Bie. Brahic. New York, NY: Columbia University Press, 2006.

———. *The Other Heading: Reflections on Today's Europe.* Trans. Pascale-Anne Brault and Michael B. Naas. Bloomington, IN: Indiana University Press, 1992.

Dewey, John. *Democracy and Education: An Introduction to the Philosophy of Education.* New York: The Free Press, 1916.

Dietz, Mary. "Trapping the Prince: Machiavelli and the Politics of Deception." *American Political Science Review* 80, no. 3 (1986): 777–99.

Donoghue, Frank. *The Last Professors: The Corporate University and the Fate of the Humanities.* New York: Fordham University Press, 2008.

Douglass, Frederick. *Life and Times of Frederick Douglass.* New York: Library of America, 1994.

———. *My Bondage and My Freedom.* New York: Library of America, 1994.

———. *Narrative of the Life of Frederick Douglass: An American Slave, Written by Himself.* New York: Signet, 2005.

Du Bois, W.E.B. *The Autobiography of W.E.B. Du Bois: A Soliloquy on Viewing My Life from the Last Decade of Its First Century.* New York: International Publishers, 1991.

———. *Black Reconstruction in America, 1860–1880.* New York: Free Press, 1992.

———. *Darkwater: Voices from Within the Veil.* Mineola, NY: Dover Publications, 1999.

———. *The Education of Black People: Ten Critiques, 1906–1960.* Ed. Herbert Aptheker. New York: Monthly Review Press, 2001.

———. *The Gift of Black Folk: Negroes in the Making of America.* Garden City Park, NY: Square One Publishers, 2009.

———. *John Brown.* New York: Modern Library, 2001.

———. *The Philadelphia Negro: A Social Study.* Philadelphia, PA: University of Pennsylvania Press, 1996.

——. *The Souls of Black Folk.* New York: Dover, 1994.

——. *Writings: The Suppression of the African Slave-Trade, The Souls of Black Folk, Dusk of Dawn, Essays and Articles.* New York: Library of America, 1986.

Duncan, Ian. "In Baltimore, Six Separate Trials Loom in Freddie Gray Death." *Los Angeles Times.* September 5, 2015.

Duncan, Roger. "Michel Foucault on Education: A Preliminary Theoretical Overview." *South African Journal of Education* 26, no. 2 (2006): 177-87.

Earhart, Amy E. "Representative Men, Slave Revolt, and Emerson's 'Conversion' to Abolitionism." *American Transcendental Quarterly: 19th Century American Literature and Culture* 13, no. 4 (1999): 287.

Easton, David. *The Political System: An Enquiry into the State of Political Science.* New York: Alfred A. Knopf, 1953.

Eastwood, Clint, dir. *American Sniper.* Hollywood, CA: Warner Brothers, 2014.

Edelman, Murray. *Constructing the Political Spectacle.* Chicago, IL: University of Chicago Press, 1988.

Ehrenreich, Barbara. *Nickel and Dimed: On (Not) Getting by in America.* New York: Holt, 2001.

Eulau, Heinz. "Skill Revolution and Consultative Commonwealth." *American Political Science Review* 67 (1973): 169-91.

——. "Wayside Challenger: Some Remarks on the Politics of Henry David Thoreau." *Antioch Review* 9 (1949): 509-22.

Fanon, Frantz. *The Wretched of the Earth.* Trans. Richard Philcox. New York: Grove Press, 2004.

Fenves, Peter. *Late Kant: Towards Another Law of the Earth.* New York: Routledge, 2003.

Foner, Philip S., ed. *Frederick Douglass: Selected Speeches and Writings.* Chicago, IL: Lawrence Hill Books, 1999.

Foucault, Michel. *Discipline and Punish: The Birth of the Prison.* Trans. Alan Sheridan. New York: Vintage Books, 1979.

——. *The History of Sexuality: An Introduction.* Vol. 1. Trans. Robert Hurley. New York: Vintage Books, 1990.

——. "On Popular Justice: A Discussion with Maoists." *Power/Knowledge: Selected Interviews & Other Writings, 1972-1977.* Ed. Colin Gordon. Trans. Colin Gordon, Leo Marshall, John Mepham, and Kate Soper. New York: Pantheon Books, 1980.

———. "Revolutionary Action 'Until Now.'" *Language, Counter-Memory, Practice: Selected Essays and Interviews by Michel Foucault.* Ed. Donald F. Bouchard. Trans. Donald F. Bouchard and Sherry Simon. Ithaca, NY: Cornell University Press, 1977.

———. "Technologies of the Self." *Technologies of the Self: A Seminar with Michel Foucault.* Eds. Luther H. Martin, Huck Gutman, and Partick H. Hutton. London, UK: Tavistock, 1988.

Frank, Jason. *Constituent Moments: Enacting the People in Post-revolutionary America.* Durham, NC: Duke University Press, 2010.

Friedman, Milton. *Capitalism and Freedom.* Chicago, IL: University of Chicago Press, 2002.

Freire, Paulo. *Cultural Action for Freedom.* Cambridge, MA: Harvard Educational Review, 2000.

———. *Education for Critical Consciousness.* New York: Bloomsbury Publishing, 2013.

———. *Pedagogy of Freedom: Ethics, Democracy, and Civic Courage.* Trans. Clarke. New York: Rowman & Littlefield, 1998.

———. *Pedagogy of Hope.* Trans. Robert R. Barr. New York: Continuum, 2009.

———. *Pedagogy of Indignation.* Boulder, CO: Paradigm Publishers, 2004.

———. *Pedagogy of the Heart.* Trans. Donaldo Macedo and Alexandre Oliveira. New York: Continuum Press, 2007.

———. *Pedagogy of the Oppressed.* Trans. Myra Bergman Ramos. New York: Continuum, 2000.

Freire, Paulo. *Politics of Education: Culture, Power, and Liberation.* Trans. Donaldo Macedo. Westport, CT: Bergin & Garvey, 1985.

———. *Teachers as Cultural Workers: Letters to Those Who Dare Teach.* Trans. Donaldo Macedo, Dale Koike, and Alexandre Oliveria. Boulder, CO: Westview Press, 2005.

Freire, Paulo and Antonio Faundez. *Learning to Question: A Pedagogy of Liberation.* Geneva, Switzwerland: WCC Publications, 1989.

Freud, Sigmund. *Group Psychology and the Analysis of the Ego.* Trans. James Strachey. New York, NY: W. W. Norton & Co, 1959.

Fromm, Erich. *The Anatomy of Human Destructiveness.* New York: Henry Holt, 1973.

Fukuyama, Francis. *The End of History and the Last Man.* New York: Harper Perrenial, 1992.

Galeano, Eduardo. *Open Veins of Latin America: Five Centuries of the Pillage of a Continent.* Trans. Cedric Belfrage. New York: Monthly Review Press, 1997.

Galston, William A. *The Practice of Liberal Pluralism*. New York: Cambridge University Press, 2004.

García Bedolla, Lisa. *Latino Politics*, 2nd ed. Cambridge, UK: Polity Press, 2014.

Garnet, Henry Highland. "An Address to the Slaves of the United States of America." *Great Speeches by African Americans: Frederick Douglass, Sojourner Truth, Dr. Martin Luther King, Jr., Barack Obama, and Others*. Ed. James Daley. Mineola, NY: Dover, 2006.

Gerard, Alexander. *An Essay on Genius*. London, UK: W. Strahan, 1774.

Gilens, Martin. "Political Ignorance and Collective Policy Preferences." *American Political Science Review* 95, no. 2 (2001): 379–96.

Ginsberg, Benjamin. *The Fall of the Faculty: The Rise of the All-Administrative University and Why It Matters*. New York: Oxford University Press, 2011.

Giroux, Henry. *Neoliberalism's War on Higher Education*. Chicago, IL: Haymarket Books, 2014.

———. *On Critical Pedagogy*. New York: Bloomsbury, 2011.

Gleaser, Edward L. "The Political Economy of Hatred." *Quarterly Journal of Economics* 120, no. 1 (2005): 45–86.

Gleason, William. "Volcanoes and Meteors: Douglass, Melville, and the Moral Economies of American Authorship." *Frederick Douglass & Herman Melville: Essays in Relation*. Eds. Robert S. Levine and Samuel Otter. Chapel Hill, NC: University of North Carolina Press, 2008.

Goldstein, Leslie Friedman. "Morality & Prudence in the Statesmanship of Frederick Douglass: Radical as Reformer," *Polity* 16, no. 4 (1984): 606–23.

Gonzales, Rodolfo. *I Am Joaquín/Yo Soy Joaquín*. New York: Bantam Press, 1967/1972.

Gooding-Williams, Robert. *In the Shadow of Du Bois: Afro-Modern Political Thought in America*. Cambridge, MA: Harvard University Press, 2009.

Grandin, Greg. "Interview with Noam Chomsky on the Crisis in Central America and Mexico." *The Nation*. October 31, 2014.

Grutter v. Bollinger. 539 U.S. 306 (2003).

Gunnell, John G. "Professing Political Theory." *Political Research Quarterly* 63 (2010): 674–79.

———. "The Reconstitution of Political Theory: David Easton, Behavioralism, and the Long Road to System." *Journal of the History of the Behavioral Sciences* 49, no. 2 (2013): 190–210.

Gurr, Ted Robert. *Why Men Rebel*. Princeton, NJ: Princeton University Press, 1970.

Gutiérrez, José Angel. *The Making of a Chicano Militant: Lessons from Cristal*. Madison, WI: University of Wisconsin Press, 1998.

Gutmann, Amy and Dennis Thompson. *Why Deliberative Democracy?* Princeton, NJ: Princeton University Press, 2004.

Guyer, Paul. "Feeling and Freedom: Kant on Aesthetics and Morality." *Journal of Aesthetics and Art Criticism* 48 (Spring 1990): 137-46.

———. "Kant's Conception of Fine Art." *Journal of Aesthetics and Art Criticism* 52 (Summer 1994): 275-85.

Gwynn, Stephen. "Hatred." *North American Review* (October 1923): 529-36.

Habermas, Jürgen. *Between Facts and Norms: Contributions to a Discourse Theory of Law and Democracy*. Trans. William Rehg. Cambridge, MA: Polity Press, 1996.

Hamilton, Alexander, James Madison, and John Jay. *The Federalist Papers*. New York: Bantam Books, 1982.

Hancock, Ange-Marie. *The Politics of Disgust: The Public Identity of the Welfare Queen*. New York: New York University Press, 2004.

Haney López, Ian F. *Racism on Trial: The Chicano Fight for Justice*. Cambridge, MA: Harvard University Press, 2003.

———. *White by Law: The Legal Construction of Race*. New York: New York University Press, 1996.

Hardt, Michael, and Antonio Negri. *Commonwealth*. Cambridge, MA: Harvard University Press, 2009.

———. *Multitude: War and Democracy in an Age of Empire*. New York: Penguin, 2004.

Harris, Cheryl. "Whiteness as Property." *Harvard Law Review* 106, no. 8 (1993): 1707-791.

Harris, Leonard. "Honor and Insurrection or A Short Story about why John Brown (with David Walker's Spirit) was Right and Frederick Douglass (with Benjamin Banneker's Spirit) was Wrong." *Frederick Douglass: A Critical Reader*. Eds. Bill Lawson and Frank Kirkland. New York: Basil Blackwell, 1999.

Harvey, David. *A Brief History of Neoliberalism*. Oxford, UK: Oxford University Press, 2005.

Hasseler, Terri A. "Socially Responsible Rage: Postcolonial Feminism, Writing, and the Classroom." *Feminist Teacher* 12, no. 3 (1999): 213-22.

Hawkesworth, Mary. "From Constitutive Outside to the Politics of Extinction: Critical Race Theory, Feminist Theory, and Political Theory." *Political Research Quarterly* 63 (2010): 686-96.

Heidegger, Martin. "The Question Concerning Technology." *Martin Heidegger: Basic Writings.* Ed. David Farrell Krell. Trans. William Lovitt. New York: Harper & Row, 1977.

Herrnstein, Richard, and Charles Murray. *The Bell Curve: Intelligence and Class Structure in American Life.* New York: Free Press, 1994.

Hill Collins, Patricia. *Fighting Words: Black Women and the Search for Justice.* Minneapolis, MN: University of Minnesota Press, 1998.

Hobbes, Thomas. *Leviathan.* Ed. Edwin Curley. Indianapolis, IN: Hackett Press, 1994.

Hoermann, Raphael. "Thinking the 'Unthinkable'? Representations of the Haitian Revolution in British Discourse, 1790 to 1805." *Human Bondage in the Cultural Contact Zone: Transdisciplinary Perspectives on Slavery and Its Discourses.* Eds. Raphael Hoermann and Gesa Mackenthun. New York: Waxman, 2010.

Holland, Catherine A. *The Body Politic: Foundings, Citizenship, and Difference in the American Political Imagination.* New York: Routledge, 2001.

Honig, Bonnie, ed. *Feminist Interpretations of Hannah Arendt.* University Park, PA: Pennsylvania University Press, 1995.

———. *Political Theory and the Displacement of Politics.* Ithaca, NY: Cornell University Press, 1993.

Hooker, Juliet. "Hybrid Subectivities, Latino American Mestizaje, and Latino Political Thought on Race." *Politics, Groups, and Identities* 2 (2014): 188-201.

hooks, bell. *Black Looks: Race and Representation.* Boston, MA: South End Press, 1992.

———. *Killing Rage: Ending Racism.* New York: Henry Holt & Co., 1995.

———. *Teaching to Transgress: Education as the Practice of Freedom.* New York: Routledge, 1994.

Howe, Irving. "Black Boys and Native Sons." *Dissent* (Autumn 1963).

Huntington, Samuel. "The Clash of Civilizations?" *Foreign Affairs* 72, no. 3 (1993): 22-49.

———. *The Clash of Civilizations and the Remaking of the World Order.* New York: Simon & Schuster, 2011.

———. *Who Are We? The Challenges of America's National Identity.* New York: Simon & Schuster, 2004.

Isaac, Jeffrey. *Arendt, Camus, and Modern Rebellion.* New Haven, CT: Yale University Press, 92.

Jacquette, Dale. "Kant on Unconditional Submission to the Suzerain." *History of Philosophy Quarterly* 13 (January 1996): 117-31.

James, C. L. R. *The Black Jacobins: Toussaint L'Ouverture and the San Domingo Revolution.* New York: Vintage, 1989.

——. *A History of Pan-African Revolt.* Chicago, IL: PM Press, 2012.

Jones, Jeffrey M. "In U.S., New Record 43% are Political Independents." *Gallup.* January 7, 2015.

Kant, Immanuel. "Answer to the Question: What Is Enlightenment?" *Kant, Political Writings.* Ed. Hans Reiss. Trans. H. B. Nisbet. New York: Cambridge University Press, 1991.

——. *Anthropology from a Pragmatic Point of View.* Trans. Victor Lyle Dowdell. Carbondale, IL: Southern Illinois University Press, 1978.

——. *Conflict of the Faculties.* Trans. Mary J. Gregor. Lincoln, NE: University of Nebraska Press, 1992.

——. *Critique of Judgment.* Trans. Werner S. Pluhar. Indianapolis, IN: Hackett Press, 1987.

——. *Critique of Practical Reason.* Trans. Mary J. Gregor. New York: Cambridge University Press, 1997.

——. *Critique of Pure Reason.* Trans. Norman Kemp Smith. New York: St. Martin's Press, 1965.

——. *Education.* Trans. Annette Churton. Ann Arbor, MI: University of Michigan Press, 1960.

——. *Groundwork of the Metaphysics of Morals.* Trans. Mary J. Gregor. New York: Cambridge University Press, 1998.

——. *Kritik der Urteilskraft.* Frankfurt am Main, Germany: Suhrkamp Verlag, 1974.

——. *Metaphysics of Morals.* Trans. Mary J. Gregor. New York: Cambridge University Press, 1991.

——. *Perpetual Peace and Other Essays.* Trans. Ted Humphrey. Indianapolis, IN: Hackett Press, 1988.

——. *Religion with the Boundaries of Mere Reason.* Eds. and Trans. Allen Wood and George di Giovanni. New York: Cambridge University Press, 1998.

——. "What Is Orientation in Thinking?" *Kant: Political Writings.* Ed. Hans Reiss. Trans. H. B. Nisbet. New York: Cambridge University Press, 1991.

Kateb, George. *Hannah Arendt: Politics, Conscience, Evil.* Totowa, NJ: Rowman & Allanheld, 1983.

——. "The Adequacy of the Canon." *Political Theory* 30 (2002): 482-505.

Kaufman Osborn, Timothy V. "Political Theory as Profession and as Subfield?" *Political Research Quarterly* 63 (2010): 655-73.

Keating, Ana Louise, ed. *The Gloria Anzaldúa Reader.* Durham, NC: Duke University Press, 2009.

Kemp, Simon and K. T. Strongman. "Anger Theory and Management: A Historical Analysis." *The American Journal of Psychology* 108, no. 3 (1995): 397-417.

King, Jr., Martin Luther. *Why We Can't Wait.* New York: Signet, 2000.

Klein, Naomi. *The Shock Doctrine: The Rise of Disaster Capitalism.* New York: Metropolitan Books, 2007.

Kohn, Margaret. "Frederick Douglass's Master-Slave Dialectic." *Journal of Politics* 67, no. 2 (2005): 497-514.

Kompridis, Nikolas. "Normativizing Hybridity/Neutralizing Culture." *Political Theory* 33, no. 3 (2005): 318-343.

Korsgaard, Christine. "Taking the Law into Our Own Hands: Kant on the Right to Revolution." *Reclaiming the History of Ethics. Essays for John Rawls.* Eds. Andews Reath, Barbara Herman, and Chrstine M. Korsgaard. Cambridge, UK: Cambridge University Press, 1997.

Korsgaard, Christine M. *The Constitution of Agency: Essays on Practical Reason and Moral Psychology.* New York: Oxford University Press, 2008.

Kristeva, Julia. *Revolt, She Said.* Trans. Brian O'Keeffe. Ed. Sylvère Lotringer. New York: Semiotext(e), 2002.

——. "Is There a Feminine Genius?" Trans. Ross Guberman. *Critical Inquiry* 3 (2004): 493-504.

Le Bon, Gustave. *The Crowd: A Study of the Popular Mind.* Mineola, NY: Dover, 2002.

Lehr, Valerie C. "Redefining and Building Community: The Importance of Anger." *Women & Politics* 15, no. 1 (1995): 37-63.

Levine, David P. "Hatred of Government." *Administrative Theory & Praxis* 20, no. 3 (1998): 345-62.

Li, Shan. "Bodyguard Business Is Booming." *Los Angeles Times.* December 18, 2010.

Liu, Yu. "Celebrating both Singularity and Commonality: The Exemplary Originality of the Kantian Genius." *International Philosophical Quarterly* 52, no. 1 (March 2012): 99-116.

Lorde, Audre. "The Uses of Anger." *Women's Studies Quarterly* 9, no. 3 (1981): 7.

——. *Sister Outsider: Essays and Speeches by Audre Lorde.* Berkeley, CA: Crossing Press, 2007.

Luanne, Clarence. *The Black History of the White House.* San Francisco, CA: City Lights Books, 2011.

Lugones, Maria. "On *Borderlands/La Frontera*: An Interpretive Essay." *Hypatia* 7 (1992): 31-37.

Lyotard, Jean-François. *Lessons on the Analytic of the Sublime.* Trans. Elizabeth Rottenberg. Stanford, CA: Stanford University Press, 1994.

Lytle Hernández, Kelly. *Migra! A History of the U.S. Border Patrol.* Berkeley, CA: University of California Press 2010.

Machiavelli, Niccolò. *Discourses.* Ed. Bernard Crick. Trans. Leslie J. Walker. New York: Penguin, 2003.

——. "History of Florence." *Machiavelli: The Chief Works and Others*, 3 Vol. Trans. Allan Gilbert. Durham, NC: Duke University Press, 1989.

——. *Prince.* Trans. George Bull. New York: Penguin, 2003.

——. "Tercets on Ambition." *Machiavelli: The Chief Works and Others*, 3 Vol. Trans. Allan Gilbert. Durham, NC: Duke University Press, 1989.

Macedo, Donald. *Literacies of Power: What Americans Are Not Allowed to Know.* Boulder, CO: Westview Press, 1994.

Magnette, Paul *Citizenship: The History of an Idea.* Trans. Long. Colchester, UK: ECPR Press, 2005.

Malcolm X. *By Any Means Necessary.* New York: Pathfinder, 1992.

Mansfield, Harvey. *Machiavelli's Virtue.* Chicago, IL: University of Chicago Press, 1966.

Marable, Manning. *W.E.B. Du Bois: Black Radical Democrat.* Boston, MA: Dwayne Publishers, 1986.

Marcuse, Herbert. *One-Dimensional Man: Studies in the Ideology of Advanced Industrial Society.* Boston, MA: Beacon Press, 1964.

Markell, Patchen. "The Rule by the People: Arendt, Archê, and Democracy." *American Political Science Review* 1 (2006): 1-14.

Mayer, Jane. *Dark Money: The Hidden History of the Billionaires behind the Rise of the Radical Right.* New York: Doubleday, 2016.

McCormick, John P. "Machiavellian Democracy: Controlling Elites with Ferocious Populism." *American Political Science Review* 95, no. 2 (2001): 297-313.

——. *Machiavellian Democracy.* Cambridge, UK: Cambridge University Press, 2011.

——. "Subdue the Senate: Machiavelli's 'Way of Freedom' or Path to Tyranny?" *Political Theory* 40, no. 6 (2012): 714-35.

McGrath, Earl J. "The Control of Higher Education in America." *Educational Record* 17 (April 1936): 259-72.

McKeen Cattell, James. *University Control.* New York: Science Press, 1913.

McLaren, Peter. *Che Guevara, Paulo Freire and the Pedagogy of Revolution.* New York: Rowman and Littlefield, 1999.

Medearis, John. *Why Democracy Is Oppositional.* Cambridge, MA: Harvard University Press, 2015.

Michels, Robert. *Political Parties: A Sociological Study of the Tendencies of Modern Democracy.* Trans. Eden Paul and Cedar Paul. New York: Free Press, 1962.

Mikkelsen, Jon M., ed. *Kant and the Concept of Race: Late Eighteenth Century Writings.* Trans. Jon M. Mikkelsen. Albany, NY: State University of New York, 2013.

Mill, John Stuart. "On Liberty." *On Liberty and Other Writings.* Ed. Stefan Collini. New York: Cambridge University Press, 2005.

Mills, Charles W. *Blackness Visible: Essays on Philosophy and Race.* Ithaca, NY: Cornell University Press, 1998.

——. *The Racial Contract.* Ithaca, NY: Cornell University Press, 1997.

Moraga, Cherríe, and Gloria Anzaldúa, eds. *This Bridge Called My Back: Writings by Radical Women of Color.* New York: Kitchen Table: Women of Color Press, 1983.

Morrell, Michael. *Empathy and Deliberation: Feeling, Thinking, and Deliberation.* University Park, PA: Pennsylvania State University Press, 2010.

Mouffe, Chantal. *The Democratic Paradox.* London, UK: Verso, 2000.

——. *The Return of the Political.* New York: Verso, 1993.

Murray, Charles. *Losing Ground: American Social Policy, 1950-1980.* New York: Basic Books, 1984.

——. *Coming Apart: The State of White America, 1960-2010.* New York: Crown Forum, 2012.

Nevins, Joseph. *Operation Gatekeeper: The Rise of the "Illegal Alien" and the Making of the U.S.-Mexico Boundary.* New York: Routledge, 2002.

Ngai, Mae M. *Impossible Subjects: Illegal Aliens and the Making of Modern America.* Princeton, NJ: Princeton University Press, 2004.

Nietzsche, Friedrich. "The Greek State." *On the Genealogy of Morality*. Ed. Keith Ansell-Pearson. Trans. Carol Diethe. New York: Cambridge University Press, 1994.

———. *On the Genealogy of Morals*. Trans. Walter Kaufmann and R. J. Hollingdale. New York: Vintage, 1989.

———. "On the Utility and Liability of History for Life." *Unfashionable Observations*. Ed. Ernst Behler. Trans. Richard T. Gray. Stanford, CA: Stanford University Press, 1995.

———. "On Truth and Lying in the Extra-Moral Sense." *Philosophy and Truth: Selections from Nietzsche's Notebooks of the Early 1870s*. Ed. and Trans. Daniel Breazeale. Atlantic Highlands, NJ: Humanities International Press, 1979.

———. "Schopenhauer as Educator." *Unfashionable Observations*. Ed. Ernst Behler. Trans. Richard T. Gray. Stanford, CA: Stanford University Press, 1995.

Nimtz, August H. *Lenin's Electoral Strategy from Marx and Engels through the Revolution of 1905: The Ballot, the Streets—or Both*. New York: Palgrave Macmillan, 2014.

———. *Lenin's Electoral Strategy from 1907 to the October Revolution of 1917: The Ballot, the Streets—or Both*. New York: Palgrave Macmillan, 2014.

Noble, Charles. *The Collapse of Liberalism: Why America Needs a New Left*. Lanham, MD: Rowman & Littlefield, 2004.

Nyhan, Brendan, and Jason Reifler, "When Corrections Fail: The Persistence of Political Misperceptions." *Political Behavior* 32 (2010): 303–30.

Ochieng, Omedi. "A Ruthless Critique of Everything Existing: Frederick Douglass and the Architectonic of African American Radicalism." *Western Journal of Communication* 75, no. 2 (2011): 168–84.

Ollman, Bertell. "What Is Political Science? What Should It Be?" *New Political Science* 22, no. 4 (2000): 553–62.

Olson, Joel. *The Abolition of White Democracy*. Minneapolis, MN: University of Minnesota Press, 2004.

———. "The Freshness of Fanaticism: The Abolitionist Defense of Zealotry." *Perspectives on Politics* 5, no. 4 (2007): 685–701.

Ost, David. "Politics as the Mobilization of Anger: Emotions in Movements and in Power." *European Journal of Social Theory* 7, no. 2 (2004): 229–44.

Petegorsky, David W. "The Strategy of Hatred." *The Antioch Review* 1, no. 3 (1941): 376–88.

Pistor, Nicholas J. C. "Obama Makes Statement on Ferguson Grand Jury Decision." *Huffington Post*. November 24, 2014.

Pitkin, Hanna Fenichel. *Fortune Is a Woman: Gender and Politics in the Thought of Machiavelli*. Berkeley, CA: University of California Press, 1987.

———. "Meditations on Machiavelli." *Feminist Interpretations of Niccolò Machiavelli*. Ed. Maria J. Falco. University Park, PA: Pennsylvania State University Press, 2004.

Pettit, Becky. *Invisible Men: Mass Incarceration and the Myth of Black Progress*. New York: Russell Sage Foundation, 2012.

Pettit, Philip. *Republicanism: A Theory of Freedom and Government*. New York: Oxford University Press, 1999.

———. *A Theory of Freedom: From the Psychology to the Politics of Agency*. New York: Oxford University Press, 2001.

Piven, Francis Fox. *Challenging Authority: How Ordinary People Change America*. New York: Rowman & Littlefield, 2006.

Piven, Frances Fox, and Richard A. Cloward. *Poor People's Movements: Why They Succeed, How They Fail*. New York: Vintage Books, 1977.

———. *Why Americans Still Don't Vote and Why Politicians Want It That Way*. Boston, MA: Beacon, 2000.

Pizarro, Marcos. *Chicanas and Chicanos in School: Racial Profiling, Identity Battles, and Empowerment*. Austin, TX: University of Texas Press, 2005.

Plato. *Republic*. Trans. G. M. A. Grube & C. D. C. Reeve. Indianapolis: Hackett Press, 1992.

Pocock, J. G. A. *The Machiavellian Moment: Florentine Political Thought and the Atlantic Republican Tradition*. Princeton, NJ: Princeton University Press, 1975.

Rampersad, Arnold. *The Art and Imagination of W.E.B. Du Bois*. New York: Schocken Books, 1990.

Rancière, Jacques. *Disagreement: Politics and Philosophy*. Trans. Julie Rose. Minneapolis, MN: University of Minnesota Press, 1999.

———. *Dissensus: On Politics and Aesthetics*. Ed. and Trans. Gabriel Rockhill. New York: Continuum, 2004.

———. *Hatred of Democracy*. Trans. Steve Corcoran. New York: Verso, 2006.

———. *The Ignorant Schoolmaster: Five Lessons in Intellectual Emancipation*. Trans. Kristin Ross. Stanford, CA: Stanford University Press, 1991.

Rasmussen, Paul J. *Excellence Unleashed: Machiavelli's Critique of Xenophon and the Moral Foundations of Politics.* Lanham, MD: Lexington Books, 2009.

Rawls, John. *A Theory of Justice.* Cambridge, MA: Harvard University Press, 1971.

———. *Political Liberalism.* New York: Columbia University Press, 1993.

———. "Justice as Fairness: Political not Metaphysical." *Philosophy and Public Affairs* 14 (1985): 223-51.

Reed, Jr., Adolph L. *W.E.B. Du Bois and American Political Thought: Fabianism and the Color Line.* New York: Oxford University Press, 1997.

Reich, Robert B. *Saving Capitalism: For the Many, Not the Few.* New York: Alfred A. Knopf, 2015.

Reiss, H. S. "Kant and the Right of Rebellion." *Journal of the History of Ideas* 17 (April 1956): 179-92.

Reiss, Hans. "Postcript." *Kant: Political Writings.* Ed. Hans Reiss. Trans. H. B. Nisbet. Cambridge, UK: Cambridge University Press, 1991.

Rhodes, Gary. *Managed Professionals: Unionized Faculty and Restructuring Academic Labor.* Albany, NY: State University of New York Press, 1998.

Ricci, David. *The Tragedy of Political Science: Politics, Scholarship, and Democracy.* New Haven, CT: Yale University Press, 1984.

Rios, Victor. *Punished: Policing the Lives of Black and Latino Boys.* New York: New York University Press, 2011.

Rogers, Melvin L. "The People, Rhetoric, and Affect: On the Political Force of Du Bois' *The Souls of Black Folk.*" *American Political Science Review* 106, no. 1 (February 2012): 188-203.

Romo, Ricardo. *East Los Angeles: History of a Barrio.* Austin, TX: University of Texas Press, 1983.

Ronell, Avital. *Stupidity.* Chicago, IL: University of Illinois Press, 2002.

Rosenblum, Nancy L. "Anything but Partisanship: Anti-Partyism, Bipartisanship, and the Luster of Independence." *Dissent.* October 15, 2009.

———. "Democratic Education at Home: Residential Community Associations and 'Our Localism.'" *The Good Society* 7 (1997).

———. "The Moral Uses of Civil Society: Three Views." *Newsletter of PEGS* 3 (1993): 3-4.

———. *On the Side of Angels: An Appreciation of Parties and Partisanship.* Princeton, NJ: Princeton University Press, 2008.

——. "Political Parties as Membership Groups." *Columbia Law Review* 100 (2000): 813-44.

——. "Religious Parties, Religious Political Identity, and the Cold Shoulder of Liberal Democratic Thought." *Ethical Theory and Moral Practice* 6 (2003): 23-53.

——. "Romantic Militarism." *Journal of the History of Ideas* 43 (1982): 249-68.

——. "Strange Attractors: How Individualists Connect to Form Democratic Unity." *Political Theory* 18 (1990): 576-86.

——. "Thoreau's Militant Conscience," *Political Theory* 9 (1981): 81-110.

Santa Ana, Otto. *Brown Tide Rising: Metaphors of Latinos in Contemporary American Public Discourse.* Austin, TX: University of Texas Press, 2002.

Sarlin, Benjy. "Nine Dead in Charleston Church Massacre," *MSNBC.* June 18, 2015.

Schaper, Eva. "Taste, Sublimity, and Genius: The Aesthetics of Nature." *The Cambridge Companion to Kant.* Ed. Paul Guyer. New York: Cambridge University Press, 1992.

Schmitt, Carl. *The Concept of the Political.* Trans. George Schwab. Chicago, IL: University of Chicago Press, 1996.

——. *Political Romanticism.* Trans. Guy Oakes. Cambridge, MA: MIT Press, 1986.

——. *Political Theology: Four Chapters on the Concept of Sovereignty.* Trans. George Schwab. Cambridge, MA: MIT Press, 1988.

Schott, Joan, ed. *Feminist Interpretations of Immanuel Kant.* University Park, PA: Pennsylvania University Press, 2007.

Schumpeter, Joseph. *Capitalism, Socialism, and Democracy.* New York: Harper & Row, 1976.

Scott, Barbara Ann. *Crisis Management in American Higher Education.* Westport, CT: Praeger Press, 1983.

Scott, Ridley, dir. *Black Hawk Down.* Santa Monica, CA: Revolution Studios, 2002.

Shapiro, Ian. *The State of Democratic Theory.* Princeton, NJ: Princeton University Press, 2003.

Shapiro, Michael J. "Samuel Huntington's Moral Geography." *Theory & Event* 2, no. 4 (1999).

Shelby County v. Holder. 570 U.S. (2013).

Shulman, George. *American Prophecy: Race and Redemption in American Political Culture.* Minneapolis, MN: University of Minnesota Press, 2008.

Shumar, Wesley. *College for Sale: A Critique of the Commodification of Higher Education*. Oxfordshire, UK: Routledge Falmer Press, 1997.

Sinclair, Upton. *The Goose-Step: A Study of American Education*, rev. ed. Pasadena, CA: Privately Printed, 1923.

Skinner, Quentin. *Machiavelli: A Very Short Introduction*. New York: Oxford University Press, 2000.

Slaughter, Sheila. *The Higher Learning and High Technology: Dynamics of Higher Education Policy Formation*. Albany, NY: State University of New York Press, 1990.

Slaughter, Sheila, and Larry L. Leslie. *Academic Capitalism: Politics, Policies and the Entrepreneurial University*. Baltimore, MD: Johns Hopkins University Press, 1997.

Slaughter, Sheila, and Gary Rhoades. *Academic Capitalism and the New Economy: Markets, State, and Higher Education*. Baltimore, MD: Johns Hopkins University Press, 2004.

Sloterdijk, Peter. *Rage and Time: A Psychopolitical Investigation*. Trans. Mario Wenning. New York: Columbia University Press, 2010.

Smidt, Sandra. *Introducing Freire: A Guide for Students, Teachers, and Practitioners*. New York: Routledge, 2014.

Smith, David N. *Who Rules the Universities? An Essay in Class Analysis*. New York: Monthly Review Press, 1974.

Smith, Kevin B. *The Ideology of Education: The Commonwealth, the Market, and America's Schools*. Albany, NY: State University of New York Press, 2003.

Smith, Rogers M. *Civic Ideals: Conflicting Visions of Citizenship in U.S. History*. New Haven, CT: Yale University Press, 1997.

Sokoloff, William W. "Between Justice and Legality: Derrida on Decision." *Political Research Quarterly* 58 (2005): 341-52.

———. "Frederick Douglass and the Politics of Rage." *New Political Science* 36 (2014): 330-45.

———. "In Defense of Hatred." *New Political Science* 37 (2015): 163-180.

———. "Jacobinism." *The Encyclopedia of Political Thought*. Ed. Gibbons. Hoboken, NJ: Wiley-Blackwell, 2014.

Sowell, Thomas. *Black Rednecks and White Liberals*. New York: Encounter Books, 2006.

Strauss, Leo. *Persecution and the Art of Writing*. Chicago, IL: University of Chicago Press, 1988.

———. *Thoughts on Machiavelli*. Chicago, IL: University of Chicago Press, 1958.

——. *What Is Political Philosophy?* Glencoe, IL: Free Press, 1959.

Strauss, Leo, and Joseph Cropsey. *History of Political Philosophy.* Chicago, IL: Rand McNally & Co., 1963.

Sullivan, Vickie B. "In Defense of the City: Machiavelli's Bludgeoning of the Classical and Christian Traditions." *Instilling Ethics.* Ed. Norma Thompson. Cumnor Hill, UK: Rowman & Littlefield, 2000.

Takaki, Ronald. *A Different Mirror: A History of Multicultural America.* New York: Little & Brown, 1993.

Tamdgidi, Mohammad H. "'I Change Myself, I Change the World': Gloria Anzaldúa's Sociological Imagination in *Borderlands/La Frontera: The New Mestiza.*" *Humanity & Society* 32 (November 2008): 311-35.

Taylor, Robert S. "Democratic Transitions and the Progress of Absolutism in Kant's Political Thought." *Journal of Politics* 68 (August 2006): 556-70.

Terry, Allie. "Donatello's Decapitations and the Rhetoric of Beheading in Medicean Florence." *Renaissance Studies* 23, no. 5 (2009): 609-38.

Tomlinson, Simon. "The World's First Hologram Protest: Thousands Join Virtual March against Law Banning Demonstrations Outside Government Buildings in Spain." *Daily Mail.com.* April, 14, 2015.

Tonelli, Gioragio. "Kant's Early Theory of Genius (1770-1779): Part II," *Journal of the History of Philosophy* 4 (July 1966): 209-24.

Trotsky, Leon. *The Permanent Revolution.* Ed. Will Jonson. New York: Create Space Independent Publishing Platform, 2014.

Truth, Sojourner. *Narrative of Sojourner Truth.* New York: Dover Press, 1997.

Tuchman, Gaye. *Wannabe U: Inside the Corporate University.* Chicago, IL: The University of Chicago Press, 2009.

U.S. Department of Education. Office of Planning, Evaluation and Policy Development. *ESEA Blueprint for Reform.* Washington, DC, 2010.

Vatter, Miguel. *Between Form and Event: Machiavelli's Theory of Political Freedom.* Dordrecht, Netherlands: Kluwer, 2000.

——. "The People Shall Be Judge: Reflective Judgment and Constituent Power in Kant's Philosophy of Law." *Political Theory* 39 (2011): 749-76.

——. "The Quarrel between Populism and Republicanism: Machiavelli and the Antinomies of Plebeian Politics." *Contemporary Political Theory* 11, no. 3 (2012): 242-63.

Vavreck, Lynn, and Stephen Friess. "An Interview with Lynn Vavreck." *PS: Political Science and Politics* 48. Supplement S1 (Sept. 2015): 43-46.

Vázquez-Arroyo, Antonio Y. "How Not to Learn from Catastrophe: Habermas, Critical Theory and the 'Catastrophization' of Political Life." *Political Theory* 41 (2013): 738–65.

Veblen, Thorstein. *The Higher Learning in America: A Memorandum on the Conduct of Universities by Businessmen.* New York: Sagamore Press, 1957.

Villa, Dana. *Arendt and Heidegger: The Fate of the Political.* Princeton, NJ: Princeton University Press, 1995.

———. *Socratic Citizenship.* Princeton, NJ: Princeton University Press, 2001.

Vonderhaar, David Mohammad Alavi, Glen Schofield, Steve Fukuda, Gavin Locke, Todd Alderman, Joe Cecot. *Call of Duty.* Los Angeles, CA: Infinity Ward, 2003.

Wahnich, Sophie. *In Defence of the Terror: Liberty or Death in the French Revolution.* Trans. David Fernbach. New York: Verso, 2012.

Washburn, Jennifer. *University Inc.: The Corporate Corruption of Higher Education.* New York: Basic Books, 2005.

Washington, Booker T. *Frederick Douglass.* Philadelphia, PA: George W. Jacobs & Co., 1906.

Washington, Harriet A. *Medical Apartheid: The Dark History of Medical Experimentation on Black Americans from Colonial Times to the Present.* New York: Doubleday, 2006.

Wells-Barnett, Ida B. *On Lynchings.* Amherst, NY: Humanity Books, 2002.

West, Cornel. *Black Prophetic Fire.* Ed. Christa Buschendorf. Boston, MA: Beacon Press, 2014.

———. *Democracy Matters: Winning the Fight against Imperialism.* New York: Penguin, 2004.

———. "Preface." *Paulo Freire: A Critical Encounter.* Eds. Peter McLaren and Peter Leonard. New York: Routledge, 1993

———. *Race Matters.* New York: Vintage, 1994.

White, Geoffrey, ed. *Campus, Inc.* Amherst, NY: Prometheus Books, 2000.

Williams, Eric. *Capitalism and Slavery.* Chapel Hill, NC: University of North Carolina Press, 1994.

Winter, Ives. "Plebeian Politics: Machiavelli and the Ciompi Uprising." *Political Theory* 40, no. 6 (2012): 736–66.

Wofford, Taylor. "After Grand Jury Decides Not to Charge Darren Wilson, What's Next for Ferguson?" *Newsweek.* November 14, 2014.

Wolfenstein, Eugene Victor. *A Gift of the Spirit: Reading The Souls of Black Folk.* Ithaca, NY: Cornell University Press, 2007.

Wolin, Sheldon. *Democracy Incorporated: Managed Democracy and the Specter of Inverted Totalitarianism*. Princeton, NJ: Princeton University Press, 2008.

———. "Fugitive Democracy." *Democracy and Difference: Contesting the Boundaries of the Political*. Ed. Benhabib. Princeton, NJ: Princeton University Press, 1996.

———. "Political Theory as a Vocation." *American Political Science Review* 63, no. 4 (1969): 1062–82.

———. *Politics and Vision: Continuity and Change in Western Political Thought*. Princeton, NJ: Princeton University Press, 2004.

———. *Presence of the Past: Essays on the State and the Constitution*. Baltimore, MD: Johns Hopkins University Press, 1989.

———. *Tocqueville between Two Worlds: The Making of a Political and Theoretical Life*. Princeton, NJ: Princeton University Press, 2001.

———. "What Is Revolutionary Action Today." *Dimensions of Radical Democracy: Pluralism, Citizenship, Community*. Ed. Chantal Mouffe. New York: Verso, 1992.

Wolin, Sheldon S. *Fugitive Democracy and Other Essays*. Ed. Nicholas Xenos. Princeton, NJ: Princeton University Press, 2016.

Yarbro-Bejarano, Yvonne. "Gloria Anzaldúa's *Borderlands/La Frontera*: Cultural Studies, 'Difference,' and the Non-Unitary Subject." *Culture Critique* 28 (1994): 5–28.

Zamir, Shamoon. *Dark Voices: W.E.B. Du Bois and American Thought, 1888–1903*. Chicago, IL: University of Chicago Press, 1995.

Zerilli, Linda. *Feminism and the Abyss of Freedom*. Chicago, IL: University of Chicago Press, 2005.

Zerilli, Linda M. G. "Machiavelli's Sisters: Women and 'The Conversation' of Political Theory." *Political Theory* 19, no. 2 (May 1991): 252–76.

Žižek, Slavoj. *Robespierre: Virtue and Terror*. Ed. Jean Ducange. Trans. John Howe. New York: Verso, 2007.

Index